MW00619401

Remember Me to All

Letters Home from Soldiers at Vicksburg

MOUNTAIN ARBOR
PRESS

MOUNTAIN ARBOR
PRESS

Copyright © 2017 by Brad Quinlin and Dick Ransom

All rights reserved. No part of this book may be reproduced or transmitted in any form or by any means, electronic or mechanical, including photocopying, recording, or any information storage and retrieval system, without permission in writing from the authors.

ISBN: 978-1-63183-213-0

Library of Congress Control Number: 2017958849

Printed in the United States of America

∞ This paper meets the requirements of ANSI/NISO Z39.48-1992 (Permanence of Paper)

Book Cover: Waterfront of Vicksburg   Library of Congress No restrictions on publishing

Disclaimer: Much of the material in this book falls into the public domain, otherwise, rights and permissions have been secured. All photos, unless otherwise noted, were taken by the authors.

Dedication

One of the thousands of Union soldiers who enlisted in 1861 was John J. James. He was born in Belgium in 1840 and migrated to the United States with his parents at the age of eight. John and his brother Francis both enlisted in the 93rd Indiana Volunteer Infantry. John was twenty-two and married at the time. He was a sickly man and returned home for a brief time to recover from his illness. Upon his recovery he returned to his regiment not knowing his wife was pregnant. John J. James is my Great, Great Grandfather. He died on August 16 1863 from a wound received during the fight around Vicksburg. He never got to return home to see his son, my Great Grandfather, Robert James. He died at the 93rd Indiana Infantry hospital at Markham's Plantation just north east of Vicksburg.

I looked for 23 years for the site of the Markham Plantation. No one could tell me where the site was. In the spring of 2016 I took a friend, Don Beckham, on a visit to the Vicksburg National Battlefield. Again I asked if anyone knew where the plantation was. This time was different and my efforts were finally rewarded.

A volunteer at the battlefield said she knew of the Markham Plantation and why I couldn't find it. The plantation's name was changed after the war. It was renamed the "No Mistake Plantation' by Mr. Markham's wife. It seems he had used his wife's money to buy the property and after the war she changed the name to "No Mistake" so he would make "no mistake" like that ever again. She then sold the plantation.

In the regimental books of the 93rd Indiana, the property is described as having a home (now gone) and an overseer's house. It had a pond and creek running through the property. I took these photos of the plantation grounds in the spring of 2016. Somewhere, here on these grounds, my great, great grandfather drew his final breath. Today it is an event site.

The Pond on the No Mistake Plantation

Above: Creek near 93rd Indiana Hospital. Below:
Overseer's House

Some 13,000 of the 17,000 Union soldiers buried in the Vicksburg National Cemetery are in graves marked as "unknown". I will never know the grave in which my Great, Great Grandfather rests. Not incidentally, John's brother, Francis, was captured and sent to Florence Prison in South Carolina where he, too, died and is buried in an unknown grave.

Having two ancestors whose resting places are in unknown graves has been a major motivator for my work to identify as many soldiers who lay in graves that bear no name, in order to return their identity to them. It is in that effort that I have found so many remembrances of their lives through the letters they wrote and those they left behind. Remember Me to All is dedicated to my ancestors and the thousands that sacrificed much, if not all, for the preservation of the Union, as well as to those who did the same for the Southern cause.

Brad Quinlin

Note: While this book contains no letters from Brad's ancestor there are three documents (one letter and two After Action Reports) included describing actions by the 93rd Indiana, his regiment.

Introduction

Brad and I want to tell the story of Vicksburg through the words of those who participated in the epic saga of that city's defense and conquest in the Civil War. The story is a complex one. Like the Mighty Mississippi on which it is situated, it took many turns and the current shifted along the way. We have used the letters, diaries and a few excerpts from memoirs to provide the reader with a compelling chronological story of those who lived the events as they were happening. The date of the first letter included in this book is March 13, 1862. The last letter was written on April 16, 1865.

Included are the transcripts taken from primary source documents written by 35 different soldiers and 2 civilian accounts, totaling over 110 documents. There are as few as one letter from specific soldiers and as many as fifteen from one soldier. As such, some letters are a snapshot of a specific moment in the continuum. Others left us feeling as if we truly began to know the writer as a person. One profound letter by a Confederate Chaplain was over 52 hand-written pages long when first penned to his wife.

As can be expected, the education and writing skills of each soldier represented here vary greatly. They range from the illiterate who need to have a fellow soldier write their letters as they dictated them, to extremely talented word smiths, who paint amazing word pictures with their pens. Each of the soldiers letters presented here was transcribed using the original spelling and, for the most part, grammar. A number of these letters were comprised of one, continuous, run-on sentence. In such cases they were edited simply by placing a period where each thought was determined to be completed, in order to make the reading less difficult. Occasionally a missing word or letter was added (in parenthesis) to complete a sentence as we assume the author intended.

While the intent is to let these soldiers own words put you in the specific place and moment when the soldier wrote the letters, we felt it helpful to provide a narrative which helps put context behind their words. This general narrative also provides the reader with limited but valuable details regarding the events along the timeline of this period related to Vicksburg.

Every soldier's primary thoughts, regardless of army affiliation, focused on the wellbeing of his family and the longing for news from home. He also wanted his loved ones to know that he was well and, if not completely well, not to worry for him. Almost every letter begins with the sharing of comments regarding his wellbeing and the fervent hope that his loved ones were healthy. Today we ask people how they are as a pleasantry when we meet. Back then, it was a very serious matter and the risk of death due to sometimes simple illnesses was profound. These were not rhetorical questions or assurances.

Many of the letters convey the individual soldier's experience during specific battles and actions executed by their units. In cases where there are several letters written by a specific soldier it is interesting to see how his thoughts and feelings evolve as the fate of his side changes over the course of the campaigns. Due to the final outcome of the campaigns and siege, this is particularly noticeable in the Confederate soldiers' communications.

Another common theme is the soldier's keen awareness of the sacrifices their families endured on the home front. One can only imagine the heartache suffered by a soldier whose family is struggling in his absence. Most particularly because there is nothing he can do about it.

Occasionally, dates recorded on some of the letters can be somewhat confusing. In some cases, the day of the week doesn't correspond correctly with the date for that year. The soldiers' recorded dates of certain events do not always match exactly with the historical date of an event or battle. In a few cases errors may have been made during the time of transcription due to legibility issues, but more often it is the soldier's recounting of the date that is incorrect. In all cases, the letters were placed in the book in approximate chronologic order as to tell the story from varying perspectives as events unfolded.

For me, personally, this has been a labor of love. Transcribing previously unpublished letters from images of the original letters and giving voice to these amazing stories is a thrill beyond description. My role in the project would not have been possible without the incredible skill and diligence provided by Brad in acquiring the documents through years of research. He has worked with government agencies, National Parks Service archives, public libraries, Universities, personal collections, and descendants of these soldiers, who graciously provided copies of letters and permission for them to be published.

Brad's years of expertise and experience in this area have resulted in a number of previous books, the identification of dozens of previously unnamed grave stones in more than one national cemetery and the telling of many, many previously unknown stories of the war.

It is an honor and privilege to call him my friend and to have been given the opportunity to contribute my efforts to this project. More than that, it is an honor to once more give voice to those who gave, or were willing to give, their last full measure of devotion to their respective causes on both sides of the bloodiest conflict in American history.

Dick Ransom

Acknowledgements

I want to thank my family for all their support and love. So much thanks to my friend and comrade, Dick Ransom, for all his work in putting all this research together to tell the story of the men who fought and died in the Vicksburg Campaign. We also want to thank the staff at the Historic City Hall and Museum at Vicksburg for opening up their archives and letting us get the soldiers letters that they have on hand. Thanks and gratitude go out to the Staff at Vicksburg National Battlefield Park for letting us hide in their archives building and get the letters housed there. Many of the letters used are from mother's pensions at the National Archives at 700 Pennsylvania Ave. Washington D.C. For years, this staff has been an incredible asset to my research. - **Brad**

In addition to those Brad has mentioned above, I want to also thank my loving wife and father-in-law for many hours of reviewing my work, offering their thoughts and gently correcting my punctuation and grammatical errors. They were instrumental in helping me establish the flow for the narrative and placement of letters.

Logistical help was provided by Hal Jespersen who allowed us to use his wonderful maps and Lee Newton for minor editing and final formatting of those maps. A big thank you goes to Jason Rusk who helped me finalize the formatting and layout for publication. - **Dick**

Contents

Illustrations

Maps

Images

The Campaigns for Vicksburg

The Navy and Farragut's Attempts

Why Vicksburg?

By the spring of 1862 Vicksburg, Mississippi had become the key stronghold for the Confederacy in the west. After the Federal Navy captured New Orleans on April 26, 1862 and its subsequent occupation by Union troops, Vicksburg's importance in the survival of the Confederacy became absolutely critical. The city was Located on the Mississippi River and midway between the northern and southern boundaries of the state. As such, it was the primary conduit for supplies from the western Confederate States (Arkansas, Louisiana, Missouri and Texas) to those states east of the river. The rail lines from the western states terminated on the Louisiana (western) bank of the River opposite Vicksburg. Supplies of every imaginable type, both military and civilian, were ferried across the river then continued their journey to the balance of the eastern Confederacy via the rail lines again.

Another role that Vicksburg played was equally important. Located on high bluffs above the Mississippi River, the "Gibraltar" of the Confederacy controlled all transport on the Mississippi River. This blocked all use by Union interests. This included both military and commercial use of the river. At the time of the Civil War the Midwestern states of the Union were producing great quantities of agricultural goods that far exceeded regional needs. While the economic opportunity to export this produce to the world was significant, without the use of the Mississippi River as a conduit, those exports were land locked in the Midwest. The inability to get this produce in an economic fashion to ports for foreign trade was a hardship that Lincoln was determined to alleviate.

So, the strategic value of Vicksburg was tremendous for both sides in the conflict. The Confederacy needed to maintain the flow of goods

14

from the western states while blocking northern commerce and military use of the river. The Union needed to open this much needed channel of commerce to the Midwestern states while literally cutting the Confederacy in half, depriving the eastern half of the states in rebellion from much needed materials. Union General in Chief Winfield Scott's original 1861 grand strategy for strangling the Confederacy via his "Anaconda" plan not only called for the blockade of all Atlantic and Gulf Coast ports, but the seizing of the Mississippi as well. Thus, from the beginning of the war it was inevitable that Vicksburg would become a site of great conflict.

The Union Capture of New Orleans

Admiral David Farragut's fleet stormed past Fort Jackson, at the mouth of the Mississippi River and the Gulf of Mexico, and received the quick surrender of New Orleans on April 26, 1862. Passing Fort Jackson had been surprisingly easier than anticipated by both Farragut and the Confederates. The ill prepared Mayor of New Orleans surrendered the city without out a fight. Infantry troops were quickly landed to occupy and garrison the city before the enemy could move reinforcements to thwart the Union success.

George Davis was a soldier in the 30th Massachusetts, one of the regiments involved in the capture and occupation of New Orleans. It was to be his first potential experience with combat and he wrote home in anticipation of the coming action.

March 13 1862

Dear father I write a few lines to you to let you no that I am well hopeing to fined the same from you. I hate to write the few lines I have to rite to you. Dear father and mother I have got to go in to battle farely soon. 4 of the regiments have got to go on the mane land to fite the rebels. Regiments has got to take the lead. On forth day we march the place where we ar going. First is the missing city. We ar going to Burn the city and then camp ther till the other regiments git redy and the hole 30 thousand march 25 miles to git there. There is a larg blocked (blockade?) and a morter fleet just com in. They will shell new Orleans and then the troops will march in and take the place.   One of the companies of the 26(th) regiment went over to the man land and had a fite. The rebels Brout (brought) canon (out) front of them loded with grape and fired on to them but they did not do as much as they thought. They had as to much as they fired on to them. The men al layed down and the grape shot flew all over ther heads and only killed one man and then they all jumped up agin and retreated in good order. They was about eight hundred rebels aginst them as much as our men got on board the steamer. They fired to shells in to them and made them all retrete in a hurry. I have not much more to rite now fore I have got to go on Brigade drill. You must excuse my bad writing.

From your son George L Davis

I hope that God will spare my life through the war and all the fites I go in. If I go in eny I spose they will be some hard fiteing. But I will try and do my Best for my contry & flag and the union. I spose we will have to take some Barity (batteries) at the front of the _____ (line?) and storm them. I wished I had a small flag to pute on some rebel bone so that I could git up in the ranks. Do not be afrade nor feel Bad Dear father and mother fore I may see home agin by the next forth of July. So good by

To Joseph Davis

On May 25th, George wrote to his brother describing their current circumstances outside of New Orleans as well as their landing and securing the city. As is often the case, estimates of enemy numbers are exaggerated in his report based on rumors that spread throughout the army.

New Orleans May 25 1862

Dear Brother John I write a few lines to you to let you no that I am well. I received your letter and mothers and fathers with great 16leasure. It *is Sunday now and all is well except the tread of the sentry that is on picket gard. I have just been picking black berries. Ther is a plenty of them hear. I am camped about 8 miles from the city of New Orleans. I am camped behind a rebble _____. Ther is about one hundred thousand rebbles about 40 miles from where I am and our army is about 10 miles from the rebbles. Burgrard (Beauregard) is there If he don't settle it in 30 days there will be a larg fite. My company is camped alone in a house and I have good times now but I don't now how long they will last. They ar discharging men from the service now. All the men that want to go home now can by loosing ther Bounty and _____ ade. I can get my discharge if I want it by loosing my Bounty. Ther was a trane of cars coming down the track and they was stoped by our pickets. The firemen was shot and our pickets up the track and put something on the track and stopped them. I would to have you send me your picter and send me something to eat in a box if you want to for I should like to have something. Now tell mother that I'm glad that she sent me such a good letter for I felt very happy when I read it. The best fun that I have had was coming up the Mississippi river. I was fireing at alegatores all the time The same time that I got thes letters. The news came that Burgard had shot him self but I don't now if it is true or not. Tell father that I saw my couson that is in the West Conn regiment. I see him and spoke to him. His regiment was last going of(f) and last time enough to see him he was glad to see me. The people in New Orleans had no idea that we could git apast fort Jackson. They was a lot of reb solders in New Orleans City and when they heard that we had got a past the fourts they left in double quick time. My company had most of the work to doo. They had all the gard to do. We went on the warf and marched in to line and halted and had the orders to lode at will. We all loaded and marched up through the city. As we was marching though the city our captain gave the orders to fire if we wer troubled. The custom hous in New Orleans is a very larg Bilding. If we had not got in New Orleans first as we had we could not never took it fore they was building boats like the Mery Mack. I cannot think of every thing now. You must excuse my Bad writing. From you brother*

George Davis

Farragut Heads North to Vicksburg

As quickly as New Orleans was captured, Farragut was ordered to immediately steam up river and capture Vicksburg in the same manner. He was to run the batteries at Vicksburg and join forces with Admiral Charles Davis who was steaming down river from Cairo, Illinois with his gun boats. Together, they were to subdue the city. Farragut would take 1,400 infantry troops with him to serve as the garrison of Vicksburg once the expected surrender occurred.

Upon receiving his orders, Farragut delayed his movement for two weeks while he repaired and refitted his ships. This delay would prove costly. His advance was further slowed by the fact that his ocean going fleet was ill suited for river duty due to their deep draughts. Periodically, deep draught ships ran aground and time was lost in dislodging them along the route.

In spite of these setbacks, optimism remained high as the Louisiana capital of Baton Rouge as well as Natchez, Mississippi surrendered along the way without contest.

As Farragut ascended the river on May 1st, significant Confederate forces began arriving in Vicksburg. By the time Farragut arrived before the city the batteries and available troops were too strong for him to coerce into surrendering. When the rebels refused the surrender demand Farragut realized that he had no chance of reducing the fortifications. His ships couldn't elevate their guns high enough to reach the enemy batteries positioned on bluffs 300 feet above the river. Equally important, the troops he had accompanying him were far fewer than would be necessary to dislodge the Confederate garrison now in place.

Foiled in this attempt, Farragut returned to New Orleans. Admiral Davis continued to move down river, destroying a Confederate fleet of rams that had attempted to thwart his progress. On June 6, 1862

Admiral Davis captured Memphis, Tennessee opening the river north of Vicksburg to the Union.

Admiral Farragut returned to Vicksburg on June 25th. He was better prepared this time with an accompaniment of 3,500 infantry and a squadron of mortar boats that could fire huge shells in a high arc capable of reaching the enemy batteries and beyond. After bombarding the city he ran the batteries in order to join Davis. Upon gathering further intelligence he realized that it would require an army of considerable size to take the city, for the rebel defenders had grown to over 10,000 men by then.

Consequently, Farragut disembarked his accompanying 3,500 infantry, under command of General Thomas Williams, on the Louisiana side of the river across from Vicksburg. Williams determined to put his men to work digging a canal from the northern end of a horseshoe bend in the Mississippi to the southern end of that bend. If this worked Vicksburg could be bypassed altogether, as it was situated on the far side of the Mississippi midway between the end points of the proposed canal. This would eliminate its strategic value as the Union would control the western side of the river and both military and commercial vessels could bypass Vicksburg with impunity. This experiment, as Ulysses Grant would call it later, had some merit and significant effort was put into the canal both at that point and later in the saga of taking the city.

As all of this was transpiring, the Confederates were hurriedly completing construction of an iron clad named the C.S.S. Arkansas on the Yazoo River. The Yazoo's confluence with the Mississippi was just north of Vicksburg on the eastern side of the river. With the Yankee armada just above the city, the Confederates needed to act fast to try to disrupt Farragut and Davis' plans. The Arkansas was sent down the Yazoo toward the Mississippi to do as much damage to the Federal fleet as possible then proceed to dock under the protective batteries of Vicksburg.

Aware of the Arkansas' existence and eminent completion, three Union gunboats were sent up the Yazoo River to find and destroy it. On July 15th the Arkansas, coming down the river, ran headlong into this squadron of gunboats sending them scurrying back to their fleet. There was not even time to sound an alarm before the Arkansas ran through the entire fleet of Yankee vessels, inflicting embarrassing damage to many of its ships, and arriving safely in Vicksburg.

Before the end of July, Farragut made 2 separate runs past the batteries while attempting to destroy the Arkansas. Neither run succeeded in destroying the iron clad. With the river dropping in depth, which threatened his deep drought ships, he determined to return to New Orleans. By this time Williams' infantry that had been digging the canal on the Louisiana side of the river was suffering dysentery and malaria and their project was not making much progress. They embarked with Farragut for the journey down river ending the first phase in the attempts to take Vicksburg. Things were definitely going the Confederates' way.

A Growing Storm

While Farragut and Davis operated on the Mississippi against Vicksburg, Union forces were building strength on the ground north of the fortress city. Recruiting in the north continued to bring new enlistees into the ranks. They were moved as quickly as possible to reinforce the armies in the field.

Union Soldier William Carpenter, whose regiment was unspecified, wrote home to his friends in late April from New Madrid, Missouri as his unit was preparing to move south. He describes the hardships they faced and the high price of foodstuffs which his stomach could tolerate:

New Madrid April 18, 1862

Dear friends at home I take my pen in hand to let you know how I am getting a long. I am well at this time and a doing well. We have not heard any news for a few days. The river is very high at this time and a rain it has raind for the last to nights. Swain is coming home and I will send some money with him. I will send 30 dols. and the rest I will keep for myself. James Millken paid me for them boots that I left him have. It was 4.00 dols. And I ode the sutlers some and I paid them up and I have spent some for butter and eggs and other things. Them we haven't had for a good while to eat. Butter is 40 cts. Eggs 20 cts and other things a corden (according). So I will send home 30 dols. I exp (expect) that it will come in handy. You may think that I spend a good deal of money for nothing that dose me any good but I don't (know) when we come to a place where we can get anything good to eat. We like to get it but that is not very often and a soldiers life is a hard life. Let him do the best he can. Well I wont write much, Swain can tell beter than I can so good by

Wm. Carpenter

I took 5.00 out of this to by a pair of boots at Caro (Cairo) that leaves 25.00 for you to have.

The 34th Indiana Infantry was encamped at Memphis when Dallas Chapman wrote home with another rumor. Vicksburg had been taken! This was obviously quite wrong but shows the extent to which unfounded rumors circulated in armies, both north and south. In closing, Chapman points out that his name on the company roster is incorrect, should anything happen to him.

Camped Memphis
June the 24th /62

Dear Friend,

I received a letter from you last week and also one from Lib and wrote one to Nan the same day   I believe directing it to Macedon thinking she would get it quicker there than if I would direct home. I believe I have written one home since some came here and one a few days before it. Am pretty well to day although I have been sick some since we came here. My ears are not well yet. There is very little sickings in the regiment now. This is a pretty healthy place I guess.

The news came up yesterday that Vicksburg was taken. The prisoners were brought up yesterday by the river. There was a good many taken I guess – all that mass there – There was a sodier (soldier) here that came up from New Orleans. He belongs to the 21st Ind. The regiment is camped at New Orleans. There is a good many troops here now. They are coming in all the time and nearly every day the cars are running from here to Corinth now.

After having a drink of cider I will procede with my letter but I expect I will soon have to quit for the want of something to write about but I will try to write a little more. It (is) very hot in our tents but there is a cool breeze outside today but it is not so every day for some days it is very hot with but little air and the heat is very severe at such times but the men seem to stand it pretty well. I have (not) heard of many cases of sun stroke yet there was a fellow in Company G died very suddenly the other night. I don't know what killed him. He was buried last night with the honors of war. I believe I have nothing more to write at present. No more Yours Truly

A D Chapman

P S If anything should happen (to) me remember my name on the pay role is Dallas D. Chapman by mistake. A.D.C.

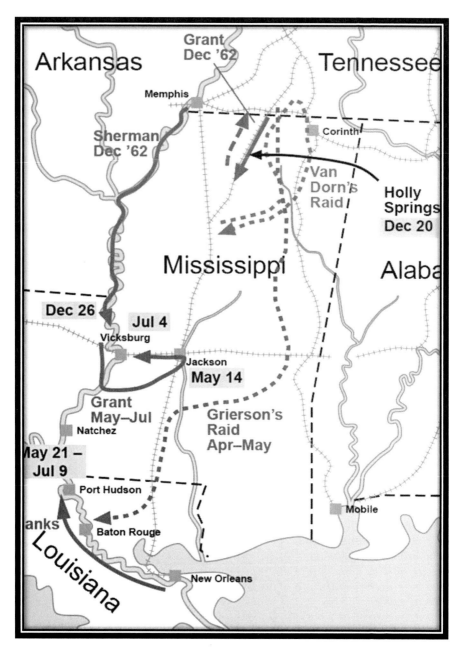

Western theatre Campaigns in Mississippi from Dec, 1862 – July 1863

(Hal Jespersen www.cwmaps.com)

Grant Takes Command

Corinth and Iuka , Mississippi

In July of 1862 Major General Ulysses S. Grant found himself in command of the Department of the West following the departure of his immediate commander, Henry W. Halleck, to Washington. Halleck had been ordered to the capital to become general in chief of the entire Union Army. This left Grant, almost by default, in command of the department. There had been much criticism of Grant following the battle of Shiloh back in April. Many claimed he would have lost the battle had it not been for timely reinforcements. Some talked of his drunkenness. All were looking to elevate themselves above him in the political arena and feared the success Grant had generated during the last 6 months might subordinate them to him. He was a fighter and Lincoln liked that, so his rivals couldn't simply make him go away. When Halleck asked for a suitable replacement for himself other than Grant, Lincoln gave no suggestions. Halleck immediately reduced the size of the department by almost half, leaving Grant with only 100,000 men to garrison Memphis, Tennessee, Corinth, Mississippi and the railroad between that city and Iuka, Mississippi. It was no wonder Grant felt a lack of commitment and confidence in his ability from his superiors.

In addition to garrison troops, Grant had two forces in the northeastern region of Mississippi. The Army of the Mississippi, under the command of Major General William S. Rosecrans, was strung out protecting the railroad between Corinth and Iuka, Mississippi, over 20 miles to the east. Major General Edward O. C. Ord's division of the Army of the Tennessee was defending Corinth, Mississippi which the Union army had occupied after a successful siege on May 30th. Corinth had now become a major Union depot in the department.

The rebels had two considerable forces of their own in northern Mississippi. One was at Holly Springs, Mississippi under Major General Earl Van Dorn and the other at Tupelo, Mississippi under Major General Sterling Price. Both forces were about 50 miles from Corinth; Holly Springs being located west of Corinth and Tupelo being to the south. The Confederate plan was for these two elements to combine in order to retake Corinth but their first movement was towards Iuka in order to obscure their intent.

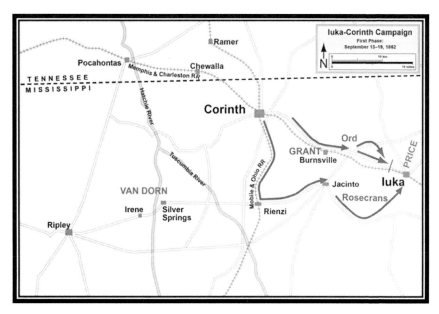

Iuka campaign- September 13-19, 1862. (Hal Jespersen www.cwmaps.com)

Made aware of this movement, Grant ordered Generals Ord and Rosecrans to combine their forces and dispatch Confederate general Sterling Price's 17,000 men before he could link up with General Earl Van Dorn's 10,000 troops. Price had occupied Iuka on September 14th after the aforementioned movement from Tupelo. The Union plan called for Rosecrans to attack from the south and hold Price's men in place. Then when Rosecrans was engaged and the fight could be heard, Ord would hit Price from the north. On the 19th Rosecrans hit Price as instructed but due to an atmospheric anomaly neither Grant nor Ord heard the sound of guns. Ultimately, Price escaped after a spirited fight with Rosecrans.

Price quickly moved to rendezvous with Van Dorn and head toward what had been their true objective all along, Corinth. Regaining this vital rail junction would mean much more efficient transportation of much needed supplies from the west to the eastern Confederacy while depriving the Union of a key communications point for operations in Mississippi. It quickly became obvious to Grant and his subordinates that Corinth was the real objective of the rebels.

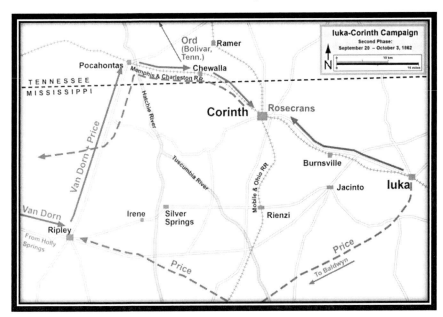

Corinth Campaign – Sept 20 – Oct 3, 1863 (Hal Jespersen
www.cwmaps.com)

Grant placed Rosecrans in overall command of the four divisions that would be responsible for holding Corinth against Van Dorn's now expanded force. Here a bit of good fortune befell the Northern defenders. Rosecrans had intercepted a letter written by a sympathetic civilian to Van Dorn, informing the latter that the defenses to the northwest of Corinth were weak. This presented him with the best opportunity to breach the Union defenses. Rosecrans quickly strengthened and reinforced these works then forwarded the letter on to Van Dorn. Van Dorn took the bait and did indeed make his primary assault on this sector on October 3rd. After a brutal fight for control of the rail hub city, Van Dorn was forced to retreat thus permanently securing Corinth for the Union.

James Carlisle, a private in Co. D of the 37th Mississippi Volunteer Infantry, wrote of his experiences during the period of May 1862 through May 1863 in a diary he penned while in a parole camp following his surrender at Vicksburg. The surviving pages of the diary are incomplete, particularly regarding the siege and surrender itself. His obvious passion for prose in describing the movement and actions of his unit are quite enlightening, showing his emotions regarding many aspects of soldiering. Keep in mind that Carlisle wrote this after the fall of Vicksburg and the subsequent demoralization of the rebel troops.

This excerpt covers the period from May of 1862 through the failed attempt of the Confederates to capture Corinth in October. As part of General Price's command he describes the action at Iuka, from his perspective, as well as the battle of Corinth where Price and Van Dorn were combined in the assault. The first paragraph is his opening of the diary while in the parole camp. The towns named in the many marches mentioned are all located in north eastern and north central Mississippi.

"At Enterprise, Miss and here I am. As how did it happen that you are here near the center of the Confederacy and you who went forth to the borders to meet the vandal foe and protect our homes and firesides? Have you thrown down your arms and quit battling for the sweetest, dearest boon

that mortals possess for the gratitude of Angelic women and the liberties of Freemen. Ah be patient and I will tell you as well as I can how it so happened.

The 5th of May, 1862. I did start for the frontier with as exhuberant thoughts and manly promptings of patriotism as the Kind Dispenser of human events had given to mortals trusting in His own right arm for my shield and in his benign mercy for my success in upholding the right. My arms are pinioned but I hope for a season only. Just so long as to give me moments of reflection and make me return to the Father of Mercies whom I in my hour of trouble and sore distress had thrown aside from my heart and raised my puny arm without the wings of his loving kindness to protect me.

I feel that I will yet battle manfully these dearest rights. That I could die in no holier a cause.

With dear loved friends – some of whom alas are now away on the field of their glory of happy spirits chanting the praise of the Eternal in the city of our God. I encamped at Columbus, Miss. Here 3 months were spent in the dull preparation for the battle's carnage. Many noble ones sunk down by disease in this unusual toil and change of diet. Over them we drop the tear of affection knowing that God took them early from the scenes of honor which would soon efface their innocence and blot out the sweet impress of Paternal Love and training.

Thence away to Saltillo (6 Aug) where August suns and thirsting hills made more gaps in our silently preparing host. My thoughts are still fixed firmly on the first practical lessons of well digging which I there fathomed and learned well. This was a pleasant change from the odious guarding of prisons at Columbus. But our wells proved useless and the ponds alive with innacles – alone checked the burning thirst which clouds of dust and hot suns generated. How sweet then were the limped streams and gushing springs of home? How feutal the groaning tables of former abidings where I dyspeptic had turned away with nausea.

5th of Sept. Sept 6th on We start for Baldwin. Oh horrid reality. Do we have to take it afoot to a fighting? Yes see those plethonic knapsacks; two or three holding as much as a company now possesses. On we wearily tread, before having flown forward with boistlery courage by steam. The romance of war oozed quickly out. The hopeful sight in future of heaps of slain foes grows dimly distant. But the gleam of patriotism burns still brightly. Night comes. Can't do without our tents. Whoever heard men raised in halls of luxury sleeping without a covering? foolishness. All trash! Can't be done. But Genl. Bragg Order No. --- says nine men to a fly. Well, Well, his jolly soul to joke us in that way. Have we find millions of flies to the man. So down we fall under our spread and think Bragg's demon in human shape and out lots as cast in evil times.

On the morrow the weary march is continued with sore feet and leaden knapsacks.

To Iuka! Our cavalry as usual – the scapegoat of the footmen – spoil a "nice trick" by their lack of courageous action. Three score or more of the enemy killed or captured. But won't we feast on fat things? See those well filled store houses of Abe's catering to the taste of the most fastidious? Those are ours. We did the work and took them. Let's in to them boys? Get us paper as well as eatables. Write to our sweethearts on beautiful sheets of embossed stationery whilst we laugh, drink and be merry. Halt there sir! No one but the officers allowed to have those things. But will not our loved leaders whom we elected give us these things. Why we have read of officers treating their men to the good things captured and we know our officers will give us their share. Ah, but come sir: No Talking with guards. Well, well here the unwholesome truth buds which soon blooms with all its unwholesome aroma that officers are superior animals to privates. And right daily too, they pop the hilarious champagne bottles and feast on the delicacies of sutlers whilst our dirty itching hands and watering mouths are gyrating at a respectable distance.

But soon the welkin rings with hellish artillery. All is confusion hurrying to and fro. Officers away from post. Can't find commands. With a few bottles of stuff which screws the courage up to the sticking point. Get it. But alas their legs stick badly on terra firma and their heads set less firmly in the direction of the field of glory. Soon the battle's lost and won. After some running on both sides the enemy beat us running and leave us on a hardly contested and bloody field. We wrest to be better able to run on the morrow. And run we do. Leaving all our officers stores behind except a sufficiency of liquors and nice things to keep them in oblivious reverie of the glory they didn't get and the honor brace privates won. Tramp, tramp in huddled, hurried run. The mighty war chief urges us back to Baldwin in the borders of Dixie. The enemy get tired or conclude that men who have relinquished such heavy burdens are now doubly mixed so leave us alone in our glory, thirsting, hurrying and dirty with drunken officers and with braggadocio wagon masters regaling us with their feats of heroism whilst --- - boil.

True, you will say this all looks very pleasant on paper and gives a nice dish of irony at the expense of the officials who are able to bear it judging from well filled stores of that article drained by them. But look with me at the worthy, weary hero with gun, accoutrements and all his earthly treasures on back as he plods lengthened miles away subsisting on raw potatoes if he fortunately passes the patch of some unfortunate farmer. Hours of burning thirst (in this lime country) making all lurid and hot with unearthly glow, his eyes glazed, tongue protruding, swollen, blackened between his cracked parched lips. The trees his shelter at night with no covering but exhausted nature which soon wraps her enchanted shroud around him, transporting him to regions of blissful plenty and ease. Sleep oh blessed harbinger of peace to the vexed angered soldier. The Queen of Fairies sweetly hovers over his careworn brow with downy wings, transporting to the airy folds of dreamland revisiting with him lovely ones who with bewitching smiles beguile his soul of its weariness. Ah this happy spell would that it ever continued. But soon the full painful consciousness breaks upon him, waffling away the "winged rosy hours", that he is still a soldier sore, restless and with mountains of difficulty to climb, as befits a soldier. Two days of rest. Wash, scrub, cook. Talk of the brave fortunate ones who have poured out freely their life blood, whose places vacant now, awe us into sadness. Oh will this dire distress never end. Are we brought into this world, reared, educated, refined for no other purposes than to fight the vile scum of creation. To skim away this filthy mass which threatens to cover up in whirling ruin the bright hopes of civilized centuries. God of Heaven raise up friends to fight our battles for us. Forbid that the excellency that thou hast planted in us should be blasted by contact with this loathesome, festering, sore of civilization, the Yankees.

25 Sept. Off for Ripley – A night spent under the weeping heavens with the chilling blast of a northwest wind, a wet couch of mud and leaves for our reveries and realities. Two days of camping in the mournful wilderness of Tippah County. At Ripley. Beautiful Villa. Lovely ladies. Little did we think then that your quiet little gathering would be changed to sadness and that your god-speeds would wing us forward to defeat and bring us back with broken ranks. Little did we think that your rural peace would soon be blackened ruins. Through the driest section in the Cotton States we endured the worst of distresses, thirst. What is comparable to this burning, parching fever? Lack of bread is sweet in comparison. Soon reports from front to rear of exaggerated skirmishes quicken our pulse, Slacken our thirst and hunger as onward we press to Corinth.

That name, would that it were stripped of all its sad association or blotted from the page of warfare in the West. The 4th of Oct masses of the enemy are met entrenched. Then commences the transcendent star of our hitherto rising glory to wane and hasten up its setting. Line after line of works are taken. Heaps of slain, painful protruding of broken limbs, crushed bodies, shrieks of wounded, dying mortals sicken the soul. But the hot blood of battle is up. Our brave leader has fallen cheering, leading us onward. His dying lips bequeath to the legacy of creet "That he who falls for his country is blessed in the sight of a just God who protects the right." We pant for blood. The iron heel of war is not tired with its blood stained tread. The wide field is swept with death-boaring, hell-aiding artillery. Roaring, harsh thunder grates upon the nerves, ceaseless rising and falling of miles on miles of awful musketry tells the harrowing tale that the rider of the pale horse is riding in high glee with flashing bloody sword. Night calms the scene. What a blessed respite from carnage. Moment for missions of mercy. Lamentations, groans, curses, shrieks of those who have poured out their lives and alas lost their souls. A beautiful moon looks down in weeping sadness. Hushed stillness awes the living as he proceeds on his mission of mercy or with preparation for tomorrow's sacrifice on the altar of freedom. The mock bird sings a sweet requiem for the silent gory dead. All is calm. Sleep holds her peaceful sway, broken anew by dreams of bloodiest anticipation. We lay us down with hearts of gratitude to God and bitter thoughts of tomorrow.

5th Oct. Reddened with furious portendings, the sun blazes above the Orient, frowning upon the battle, product of busy preparation of past night. Never did man fight more gallantly, more recklessly. The myriad host is driven by the furious onslaught: works taken, battle won, enemy fleeing. Where? Where is Sovell? Oh thou bastard blotch on our country's fair escutcheons. Thy disobedience has driven from the field of glory, moistened by the best blood of Southern honor. On the field the fond anticipation of thousands sunk to rise no more, these the fondest ties of dear ones were sundered around that wide altar of liberty the mourning, bleeding hearts of thousands still cluster and yearn toward it feeling that the last trumpet on earth sounding us to the Judgement will yet clothe it with a hale of glory as the freed spirits will enter the portals of Heaven through its gateway....

....The forest. Sore, wearied, we collect our shattered band to consider the prospects of escape and probability of falling into the hands of blood-thirsty jayhawkers. Our blood runs cold as we remember the many exhausted ones who must fall victims to these villain bands. Our hearts sink within us. Our knees knock with fear and horror for a moment when we think all is lost. A moment and the cool, calm determination to die ere surrender restores our nerves of steel and order soon comes out of chaos. A noble man, Genl. Price dubbed wagon master Genl. – takes the head of retreating columns. *Unpacks wagons destined to be burned. The wild shout it returned to the persuing host. The shrieking shell ceases its ghoul-like summonings. We take the dark wood and winding country path and are soon out of the grasp of the foe whose neglect in closing their Iron prandials was our safety. This is the darkest gloom that has ever been mine in struggling for freedom. As I turned wagon after wagon up from the dust, rolled them up hills and ceaselessly walked the hilly road my country, my bleeding country, seemed wrapped in robes of bloody hue; all was honor and faintness. Fasting and thirst brought about recklessness. The deeds witnessed and performed that night of retreat are past pennings. Lo pass them in review they seem miraculous, when attended with safety to body and limb. Plunging into deep abysses in search of water, falling over broken trees, brush, in pandemonium, confusion, with muskets and accoutrements as but glimpses of the hazardous retreat successfully conducted by Sterling Price. No nobler man ever ask men to follow him. No truer patriot and hero ever shed tears over his suffering more than did this magnanimous man…."*

A cavalry trooper with the 4th Illinois Cavalry and a part of the Union's Army of the Cumberland, Henry A. Ellsworth wrote home to his mother in mid-November from his post in Lagrange, TN. Lagrange is not far north of the Mississippi state line and Corinth, where Carlisle and his comrades had been defeated. Ellsworth had been an adversary.

Lagrange Tenn Nov 14 / 62

Dear Mother,

I Take the opportunity of writing to you to let you know that I am well at present and hope this letter will find you all the same. The weather is very fine now and the troops will move to Holy Springs soon. Price has retreated back from there. The army is in good spirits. There will be a big fight some where near the springs soon. If I should see the fight it will be the fifth battle that I have been in. I hope that I may never see another but I expect that there wont be a great many more before this war is closed. There is about fifty thousand fighting men in the army. There is several new regiments come hear. The old soldiers call them forty dollar men. Come or I will fetch you when the enemy marched from Jackson to Lagrange. They destroyed a great deal of property in the way of rail fences and old buildings. They would set fire to the end of a fence and then it would burn it all up. It looks very bad to see every thing destroyed but it can not bee helpt very well unless they stop the war. The soldiers take every thing they want. Our boys went out in the country and killed 8 sheep and got 20 bushels of sweet potatoes. We have plenty to eat just now but when we shall go into Miss. Soon and then there will not bee so plenty for they do not rais much to eat there this year. Soldiering is very nice when you are at home but when you get down in Tenn. Or Miss. It is played out. We live on hard bread now and the rest of the winter for I expect the enemy will not lay still much this winter. I received your letter last night and won from Charley West the same time. He was in Memphis then. he was well and all the rest of the boys. he says Albert will wish himself home a great many times and father should enlist. He will wish the same thing. I would rather husk corn than bee a soldier. John Whiting is hear. He is the same as ever. There is not any won else hear that you know. The 50 is hear but I have not been to see them for a long time. I do not know wether Gatehouse is there or not. John Jimbo was in Corinth the same time that I was but I did not know it until he had left. That is (the) trouble. If I knew what regiment I should look in. …All the children how does that pretty baby get along. I suppose that by the time I get home it will get so hansom that know won will bee allowed to see it because (it) will fade but I (think) that the baby will not. If it is not hansom when I get home to see it I shall think it never was. A picture loks (looks) hansom but the reel does not look so well. But with out Jokeing I expect that she is hansom. How is Herman? Tell him Hub is all right and that he weighs a bout 185 pounds. That is not very large. We have not ben paid of not for about 7 months but I have got money. Yet every thing is very high. I had sent my last stamps away & on that letter that I wrote with the led pencil. If you had not of sent that stamp I could not of wrote. I can get anything hear but stamps. I wrote to Ada three times but have not had an answer yet. I expect she did not get them. I can not think of *any more to write. All the news you can think of as it is late. I bid you all god bye (goodbye). To W. H. Ellsworth*

H. A. Ellsworth

Success at Corinth Boosts Grant's Status

While Grant had been in overall command during both of the actions at Iuka and Corinth, he was now formally given command of the Department of Tennessee by his superiors in Washington in recognition of his success in securing Corinth. With this boost of confidence he had but one objective in mind and that was to go after Vicksburg in earnest.

In preparing his strategy, Grant had decided that the best approach to Vicksburg would be from the east and rear of the river defenses. This provided the best ground for approaching the citadel as well as avoiding the strength of its defenses along the river. In order to gain this position it seemed the most direct route was overland from Northeastern Mississippi. He proposed moving south to the capital of Jackson, then moving due west to the river fortress. By early December he had advanced to Oxford, Mississippi, 40 miles south of the Tennessee line.

During the early fall of 1862 a would be rival of Grant, Major General John McClernand, had gone directly to Lincoln proposing that he make an amphibious assault on Vicksburg independent of Grant's plan. As an important political general from the state of Illinois, McClernand had been given tacit approval for his plan and had begun raising Illinois troops for that purpose. Now he was preparing to move them to Memphis in order to execute his plan, hopeful of usurping Grant's authority in the department through a brilliant victory.

Grant was aware of the political maneuvering and the risk it posed. It became necessary to alter his original plan in order to neutralize McClernand and maintain his sole control over the department.

He now determined to make a two pronged attack on Vicksburg. Splitting his troops between himself and Major General William T. Sherman, Grant would remain in command of the initial force moving south from Oxford while sending Sherman down river before McClernand could arrive. This would not only deprive McClernand of independent command but would distract the Vicksburg defenders with two forces moving against them.

Meanwhile, the Confederates had been working diligently at turning the defenses at Vicksburg into the true "Gibraltar of the Confederacy". President Jefferson Davis placed Lieutenant General John Pemberton in command of all Mississippi defenses with overall command of the larger department under General Joseph E. Johnston. Both were highly respected in the south and capable leaders.

On December 19th, as Sherman was beginning his movement down the Mississippi towards Vicksburg, Davis and Johnston met in Vicksburg to inspect those defenses and offer suggestions for further improvement. Then they moved to Grenada, Mississippi, south of Oxford where Grant's force was currently positioned, to ascertain the latter's intentions and plan accordingly. Johnston wanted to use all of his troops to smash any Federal forces in the area but Davis and Pemberton were determined to defend the Vicksburg fortress. The debate was never resolved before Davis and Johnston moved on to other sectors leaving Pemberton in charge.

Ultimately, Pemberton determined to cut Grant's supply lines so as to make further advances impracticable. He would send Van Dorn to destroy the Union depot at Holy Springs in Grant's rear and just below the Mississippi / Tennessee state line. This mission was accomplished on December 20th.

James Carlisle, of the 37th Mississippi, included descriptions of the brutal marches and terrible conditions suffered by the Confederate soldiers in northern Mississippi. This excerpt focuses on the retreat, repositioning and movement back to the Oxford area in December preceding Pemberton's orders to Van Dorn to attack Grant's supply lines at Holy Springs.

"…To Waterford we wearily march. Our banners torn and tattered by the briars and thick brush to be some day boasted over by some vainglorious cowardly official who never saw it amid the battle's smoke. To be some day, the sacredly kept memento of the battle's carnage with bullet perforations, shown to posterity as the banner of freedom when alas, no shot, no shell ever careened wildly over it to sing freedom's doom. I take it that many are the relics which are stored away too pure and holy for the gaze except on public and occasions of state are like our Flaps, in true history the reminders of our shame. Yet human nature like we ever boast in our shame. Weary months, shoeless, blanketless and clothless are driveled away at Waterford. The fond recollections of this place are massed with the memory of the Loathesome jaundice, suffocating dust and short rations made shorter. Many pleasant thoughts were mine at this place. I have heard from home after six months silence from that yearned over, distant, longed for, sweet place.

Latter part of November 62 we move to Abbeville on the Tallahatchie ten miles below Waterford. Here dullness rules the hours.

1st Dec. order in excited haste to prepare for marching. Soon the heavens are darkened and the first rain in two months pours down in torrents the whole night. I rarely ever knew it to fall raining when we commenced moving in the winter months. A night's marching and daybreak found us at Oxford, ten miles from the starting point. An hour's rest and the front column moves on. Pitiful scenes of lovely women in sadness preparing to follow in our wake. Mud in everything. Underfoot mud and raining mud. Travel all day on road, at night sleep on same. Camp out of the rear guard's lines, wake by the cry of the enemy. Worn to recklessness, coolly take time, and advance at leisure. Soon drop down guilty in mud, sleep sweetly until the patterning drops of rain cause change of base so often that hat falls off face. Then try vertical position. Then right angles and then oblique to the fire. The drop of cold icy water runs slowly down any back, stamp around, get wood, fall into running water, wet thoroughly, now satisfied that it can't be worse, so lie down in the sloppy mud, sleep, and wake about to float...."

(At this point several pages of Carlisle's diary are missing...)

Grant's Initial Strategy is Foiled Completely

Simultaneous to Van Dorn's attack on Holy Springs, General Braxton Bragg had sent General Nathan B. Forrest's cavalry to destroy a second of Grant's supply depots at Jackson, Tennessee. With both these crucial lines of communication severed Grant found his position untenable and abandoned the land route, retreating to Memphis. As quickly as he had made this decision he sent word to Sherman informing him that his own part of the plan had been thwarted. Unfortunately, Sherman never received the message as telegraph lines had been cut. Thus, Sherman continued with his plan to attack Vicksburg from north of the city using the Yazoo River as an approach.

In order to succeed, Sherman had depended on two crucial components of the plan. The first being Grant's, now failed, overland approach keeping the enemy divided and guessing where the primary assault would materialize. The second was surprise. This aspect was also lost. Unknown to the Federal command, there was a private telegraph line on the Western bank of the Mississippi established by local planters. Southern lookouts, posted along the river, were able to use this communication vehicle to quickly warn the Vicksburg defenders of Sherman's approaching armada of transports and gunboats. Utilizing this advance warning, the

Confederates were able to reposition their forces and deploy a formidable defense at Chickasaw Bluffs. This was the area north of the city, on the Yazoo, where Sherman had planned his landing and assault. On December 29th Sherman's 30,000 troops were stopped cold with heavy losses after three days of fighting.

At this point heavy rain and the rising river threatened any further immediate action so Sherman withdrew his force and established a base at Milliken's Bend, on the western bank of the Mississippi, about 20 miles north of Vicksburg. Grant's first attempt on Vicksburg was far from auspicious or successful.

Jared Sanders served in the 26th Louisiana Volunteer Infantry. Excerpts from his diary recorded these remembrances of Sherman's defeat at Chickasaw Bluffs. He also accurately relays word that Union General Burnside was defeated at Fredericksburg with heavy losses.

Jan 1863

...President Davis and Joseph Johnson (sic) are in Vicksburg. General Johnson will review our brigade this morning. I will write you about this appearance in my next. We have won a great victory over Burnside at Fredericksburg – 20,000 Yankees said to be killed...

The second attempt of the Federals to sieze Vicksburg came late in December. "According to Union plans the Confederate force under Pemberton near Grenada was to be kept occupied by Grant while Sherman and Porter surprised Vicksburg." Sherman attacking from the north from the Yazoo; but a Confederate drive to the Yankee rear under Van Dorn destroyed Grant's depot at Holly Springs, Mississippi, and threw the schedule off the timetable.

On December 24 the Twenty-sixth Louisiana Infantry was ordered, along with other regiments, eight miles north of Vicksburg near Chickasaw Bayou to meet the anticipated enemy attack on the Yazoo River. Union forces at the battle of Chickasaw Bluffs, as the resulting engagement was called, were commanded by Major General William T. Sherman, who had some 33,000 troops; Confederate forces were commanded by Lieutenant General John C. Pemberton, who had about 25,000 troops.

Movement of Federal gunboats on the Yazoo River not only rendered surprise impossible, but gave notice of impending attack. The orders to the Twenty-sixth Louisiana Infantry in this action were to annoy the gunboats, repel any attempt to land, and dispute the enemy's advance inland. Captain Bateman was ordered to take Company B and another company to the Yazoo and annoy gunboats there. He remained on the river bank until dark, when he left a strong picket there while the remainder of the regiment slept on their arms on a site afterward occupied by the enemy, and called by the Federals "Fort Morgan."

The next morning, Christmas Day, 1862, although heavily shelled, Captain Bateman continued to annoy the enemy until relieved about noon. The next day the whole command was reunited. On Saturday, the 27th, Captain Bateman was sent with his and another company to deploy in the woods to the Confederate right, and skirmish with the left flank of the enemy. The original order was countermanded and Bateman was sent to flank the enemy but soon found himself confronted by artillery and three regiments of infantry and was compelled to retire. A prisoner reported later that this detachment killed six and wounded two of the enemy before retiring.

On the 29th, the day of the main assault, Company B was on special detail when an unusual occurrence took place. The command reached a point where a body of the enemy was in full view only a hundred yards away. "The temptation was too great for the naughty boys," reported Colonel Hall. They stopped without orders and peppered the blue coats. Orders to cease firing and to march were issued in a little while, and were readily obeyed, perhaps in view of the fact that none of their opponents was visible from that point. A moment later, a blue coat being spied, a sergeant of Company A sent a "minnie" after him although the cease fire order had been given. Colonel Hall ran to the sergeant and gave him a smart rap on the back with the flat side of his sword, then went to the front of the command, ordered the column into line, cocked his revolver and said he would shoot the first man that fired. In order to quiet them, he put them through the manual of arms, in plain view of and entirely exposed to the enemy. The line went through the exercise, as if on parade. General Lee (Stephen D. Lee) rode up while the men were going through the drill, and the detachment presented arms to him, after which he ordered them to fall back to the rear and to a certain degree of safety.

While the company was at Chickasaw Bayou, an order came for a detachment of fifty men to aid in planting torpedoes (mines) in the Yazoo River – an enterprise full of hazard. Colonel Hall called for volunteers. "Representatives from every company stood out at once and the number of the detachment was made up. Company B (the dear old dirty shirts) then volunteered to a man, and requested that they alone be detached for the purpose Hall subsequently reported. The undertaking was, however, called off."

Sanders started a letter to "Dear Friend" on January 4th and finishing it the 6th. This letter provides further details of his experience during the battle of Chickasaw Bluffs and his prognosis for the end of the conflict.

January 4th 1863

Dear Friend,

…Since I wrote to you last I have seen the roughest side of a poor soldier's life. I have marched through rain & mud, passed sleepless nights in the hardest of weather, with nothing above me but the drenching clouds & beneath me – a wet blanket spread int eh mud, upon a few sticks or bushes, perhaps to keep me out of a mud-&-water bed. I have met the enemy; fought them, & seen the wounded, the bleeding & the dying upon two bloody fields. But, to give a more circumstantial account I will refer to my "Diary" & transcribe the particulars of our meeting the Yankee vandals. You know, for some time past, the 26th has been encamped about two miles behind

Vicksburg. On the 24th of December our regiment received marching orders to a point eight miles above town.

Having arrived at Captain Wofford's Battery our regiment was halted, & Co. "B" was detailed to proceed three miles further to prevent gunboats & transports from passing so freely up and down the Yazoo river. We were ordered to fire upon every boat as it passed when-ever any one appeared on deck. This was very hazardous fighting, but we continued it for three days. Christmas day was spent in that way and at one time I was nearly taken by some of the enemy who landed & came on shore. I hid in some vines & thus escaped them. I had nothing but a few potatoes to eat on Christmas day, but I was proud to know the cause of this deprivation of the delicacies that one usually has on that day. We were fired upon by gunboats, but being very near the banks and laying flat on the ground their shot could not hit us.   Very frequently though we were covered with dirt by their cannon balls. Our company was ordered back to the regiment which was in some rifle-pits thrown up in the Yazoo bottom where we thought the Yankees would land and attack our line of works on the hill-sides. To give you an idea of the position of our troops during the battle, I will draw an imperfect diagram of the surrounding line of works….

…shot flew around as fast. We commenced fire at 11 oclock & beat them back until night; and, I declare, I was glad to hear the enemy's bugle sound the "recall" for the return of their troops for the night – for our men were very tired, & our wounded needed attention. I took eight deliberate shots, and not being excited I think I killed at least three times – if I did, I am contented.

That night our regiment was ordered back to the rifle-pits on the hill-sides, and it was well, for the next day came off the battle when the enemy charged over the pits we had evacuated and came forward to charge the works on the hills – so we would have been taken prisoners had we remained there.

About 10 oclock on the 29th the blue lines of the Yankees were seen coming over the fallen timber toward our works on the hill-sides –

immediately our artillery opened upon them. They came forward in daring style, with banners flying. Many an old U. S> was floating to the breeze, & far stretched their heavy columns. Very soon our infantry opened fire upon them & our cannon belched forth a perfect stream of lead and iron. Then could be seen the grandest and most magnificent aspect of war, an angry collision of hostile forces. Peal after peal from our batteries and the continued rattle of our rifles, mingled with shouts of men created a most "indescribable confusion.." It was magnificent to lock upon, and I enjoyed it greatly. I could see the hostile forces pressing forward at a "double-quick" – their men shouting, & their officers cheering them onward. When they came closer to our lines I could see men falling by crowds – officers tumbling from their horses & horses dashing over the field; and then our brave men began to fire in such volleys upon them that they could advance no further but turned about & made off "at a run." Shout after shout rose from our lines that told – "Victory was ours." The repulse was about one oclock; the rest of the day was spent sharpshooting & in artillery dueling. The enemy lost about 200 killed & wounded in this battle and 400 prisoners. The Yankees attacked our lines closer to town and were repulsed there also. This attempt to pass our lines so General Lee (Stephen D.) sent us back to our tents. We marched back on the 2nd to camp, eight miles distant, it pouring down rain on us every step of the way. The night of the 29th after the fight I slept in the rifle-pits at the edge of the field, & as it rained all night & I was laying on a few rails & not being well, I could not sleep. I could hear the groans & piteous monad of the wounded & dying arising from the field. You cannot imagine how pitiful their cries did sound. They would cry out "Oh boys! Come & help me," "O God, I am dying," & all such exclamations that would make one's blood "run-cold." We got many from the field, but a great many remained upon the field until the 31st when the enemy sent in a flag of truce to bury their dead.

Our men have a many large overcoats & other Yankee equipments. Some of them got over 100$ in "green-backs." For 10$ in Yankee green-backs one can get 15$ in Confederate notes in Vicksburg. Smugglers buy them to trade off to the enemy for contraband goods. There is a great deal inspiring excitement on the battle field…..

I saw, and talked to, many prisoners. They don't want to fight us any more. They say the army of Yankees does not expect to take Vicksburg. They are mostly conscribed (conscripted) men who do not wish to fight. I send you a Yankee government skin-plaster gotten on the battle-field. I saw many letters, and other foreign curiosities gotten on the field…

<u>Jan. 6th</u>. I intended to send this letter on the <u>4th</u>, but as I did not find an opportunity to do so, I will answer some parts in your last which I overlooked in… my last to you. I will write you a long letter for the enemy is now near Vicksburg and I may not have time to write but short notes hereafter. Before you get this, perhaps the great battle for Vicksburg will have been fought, and my next weill bear you tidings of another victory in which I was engaged. I have heard that the Yankees have gone back to <u>Memphis</u>. If this is so, I think the war is beginning to close; and that <u>sic months</u> will find us – "home again" – that we will feel the warm July sun in our own sunny homes. Lee has lately beaten Burnsides; on the 28th Bragg whipped Rosecrans; on the 29th; on the 29th we drove back Morgan here – three defeats, I think, will demoralize them, and one or two more will make peace… This letter will go by mail and it may be long on the rout, but I trust it won't go <u>astray</u> – and never reach you….

A view of Vicksburg, looking north toward the bluffs. The Yazoo River meets the Mississippi River a number of miles off the frame to the upper left. Chickasaw bluffs proceeds north east from that point. (Library of Congress)

Another Confederate, John Douthit, serving with the 52nd Georgia, also participated in blunting Sherman's assault at Chickasaw Bayou. He described the experience like this.

January the 1th 1863

Vicksburg Mississippi

Dear Companion

I write you again to inform you that I am well at the present time hoping these lines will come to hand and find you all well. There have been fighting here five or six days. Our boys have been to hard for them. So far we arrived at Vicksburg the 28th December at 11 OC. We moved up the river two or three miles and struck up camps We stayed here until 8 OC at night when we moved a mile further and stoped in the road within less than half a mile of the enemy We lay here until the brake of day when we moved one or two hundred yards behind the top of a hill here We lay until two hours by sun when we were ordered to relieve a regiment that had been in our rifle pits for two or three days thugh the cannon had been roaring and the small armes firing the whole day. there were two men wounded close to me. This was while we were behind the top of the hill. There were nothing to be heard the whole day but the sound of gunes and the whizzing of balls that passed over our heads When we left this place to go to the breast works we went down a deep ravine or branch, the banks of which was high enough to shelter us from the balls though they would come pretty close some times though we gotten to our trenches with out the loss of any men. There was but one man killed in our Regiment and one wounded. The Enemy was fireing at us all the time. We fired three or four rounds at them. done execution for the next evening they come with a flag to bury there dead and there were nine within twenty five steps of our entrenchments. Yesterday the 31th Dec They sent in for permission to bury there dead which was granted so there was not much fighting done yesterday. We left the entrenchments this morning at daylight and are tolerably pleasantly situated on the top of a high hill within sight of their batteries. There is no fighting going on this morning as I can hear. They have a large number of boats lying of two or three miles in Yawsue (Yazoo) River though Vicksburg is on the Mississippi. I will stop writing about the fight for I might not right the truth as I know but little about what was done outside of my own regiment.

Yesterday morning after the flag of truce had been sent out they came and hollowed to our boys and asked them if they didn't want a dram so there was a good many questions and finealy one of them agree to meet Captain Woodard half way and take drink. They met and taken a dram swaped coat buttons.

I sent you my likeness from Atlanta which I hope you have received before now. I received a letter and a pair of socks from you by the hand of Lieutenant Underwood when he com to camps and also tell S. M. Douthit I received his letter and have not had the chance to answer it. Give my compliments to all inquiring friends and write yourself. Direct your letters to Vicksburg, Miss. So nothing more at this time but remains your husband until death.

John M. Douthit

Likeness of 2nd Sargent John M. Douthit.

52nd Georgia Volunteer Infantry. (Vicksburg National Military Park)

After their impressive victory, the optimistic Louisianan, Jared Sanders, expressed high confidence in the Confederacy's ability to hold off any Union attempt to take the city in this letter written later in the month.

Vicksburg
Jan 23rd, 1863

Dear Friend,

…. Our old friend Lieutenant D. C. Daniels, is here in our camp – just from St. Mary's parish and hence a more than welcome visitor to Company "B". I am sure if our "home folks" could see how eagerly the boys gather around one just from our parts to catch every word he speaks, they would spare no trouble in order to send us news. Our only pleasure is hearing very often from those we love; and if these be denied us, what follows but low spirits! I hear quite frequently from Eva, & my brothers – but only very seldom from those at my old home. As we have very few candles, I sit by the light of our fire, when nights come on, and recall the names of those who are far away. It is then my memory flows full upon me bringing up visions of other & happier times _ may those times be not gone for-ever! We are comfortable here in our tent – the men being in their winter quarters. It is only when we go above the city to fight that we suffer much.

I wrote you a long letter after the fight giving particulars. We suffered greatly during that time.

We are now amidst the jury & confusion of a second preparation, for the enemy have come again, & are up the Yazoo river.

We are ordered to Vicksburg yesterday morning – as an attack was expected – but we soon returned to camp. The Gen. thinks the Yankees will try to "storm" the place some night, hence he has troops in town most of the time. I do not think this city can be taken by an <u>hundred</u> thousand northerners – so very strong is it. We can now hear the <u>booming</u> of cannon here – those dreadful notes of death! I think it will long be a question of old Abe's – "Who will bring me into the <u>strong city</u>"! You may expect to hear of our victory here again <u>soon</u> – perhaps before this reaches you "angry conflict" will gain bothe these hills with the noble blood of our soldiers. I *hope all will be well with us – if not, then "Peace to those that perish, may the warrior's mud and tears of triumph their reward prolong," as your* <u>*Byron*</u> *says.*

I send you some papers. I must close – Mr. Daniels is about to start for town….

McClernand Arrives

As Sherman was establishing his camps, McClernand was arriving in Memphis with the force he had raised in Illinois. Upon that arrival, the war department ordered Grant to place McClernand in command of the XIII Corps which was to include the troops McClernand had brought with him as well as Sherman's men at Milliken's Bend. Grant grudgingly issued the order. Sherman, likewise, turned over his command to McClernand.

During the period immediately following the repulse at Chickasaw Bayou, Sherman had been busy assessing the situation and any opportunities for offensive action. When McClernand arrived Sherman suggested they take a strong force a few hundred miles up the Mississippi River, taking the Arkansas River to the west from there, and capture Fort Hindman, a Confederate stronghold. McClernand was ready to claim glory and agreed to move immediately. On January 11th, 1863 Fort Hindman, also referred to as Arkansas Post, was assaulted by the XIII Corps. Outnumbered 30,000 to 5,000 the Confederates were quickly subdued and the Union troops captured the entire garrison, as well as 17 canons and all of their small arms.

Back in Memphis, Grant was department commander, but not in physical command in the field. Grant knew he had to move to the front and take direct command of the army. McClernand's success at Arkansas Post, along with his higher ranking of Grant's other Corps commanders, meant that Grant had to either move to direct command himself or turns the army in the field over to McClernand. In Grant's opinion the latter was unimaginable. McClernand had relocated the corps headquarters to Young's Bend at the mouth of the Yazoo River on the Louisiana side of the river. On January 29th Grant traveled to that headquarters at Young's Point and took direct command.

During the early months of 1863, Confederate forces continued to be reinforced in order to strengthen the defenses of Vicksburg and Pemberton's army. David Spigener was a member of an unspecified Alabama Regiment. Upon arriving in Vicksburg he wrote his sister, Liza

Vicksburg, Miss
Jany 5th, 1863
> *Dear Sister:*

> *I will embrace the present moment to respond to your (letter) bearing the date of 1862, 17th of Dec. I am very well at present and hope this may find you all in good health. I got your letter when we was at Meridian. We lay over there five days. I answered it was ready to mail it in which time we received orders to this place. Then I had not time and concluded I would wait until we stopped again. We landed here on the 1st about dark. It rained hard all night. We faired pretty bad that night. As soon as we got here our company and _____ was detailed and sent over the Miss. River to stand picket. Yesterday we got back and our regiment was in the court house a pretty fine building, but we had orders to another place about 4 miles from town for the purpose of guarding some bridges I think. The battlefield is about 8 miles from here (Chickasaw Bluffs). They have been fighting _____ here, but not since we have been here. There was nine prisoners brought in day before yesterday morning. The gun boats are not in sight but the smoke is very plain from them. This place is about the size of Montgomery. Jackson is about the same size, we came through Jackson but did not stop. They say the smallpox is at every*

little town between Mobile and Meridian. It was at Meridian short time before we got there. Tell Maw I received the package of clothing she sent me, it was alright. I also got a letter from Sammy but I don't know how to ____it to him. Christmas Day I was on the cars between Chattanooga and Atlanta. I came close by home but the stay was short. I wish you could have met me in Montgomery. I would like to have seen you very well, Liza. I will write again soon. Excuse this short letter. Give my love to all. Tell little Annie howday and kiss her for me. _____ _____, I remain your affectionate brother.

David Spigener

Send your letters to Vicksburg, Miss.

G H Burns and his 34th Georgia and essentially followed the same route to Mississippi as part of the growing force in the Vicksburg area. He describes in detail the route by rail and steamer from Murfreesboro, Tennessee to Meridian.

Maredian Mississippit Jan 3rd 1863

Dear wife I can inform you That I am well and hope this will find you well. This is the tenth day since we left Murfreesboro. We have been 8 days of that time on the car and steam boat. We came The first to Chattanooga a distance of one hundred & thirty miles arriving at 800 at night. We left that point next morning at 3 oclock arrived at Atlanta late in the evening. Distance from Chattanooga one hundred & thirty eight miles. We lay over that night. Atlanta Is a large and beautiful City. Its useless for me to try to name all the towns on the Road. We left Atlanta at 8 in the morning took the Atlanta and West Point Railroad arrived at West Point at 5 in the evening. 86 miles. This town is on the Chattahoochia River & is near the line between Georgia and Alabama. We lay over that night & left next morning on the Westpoint & Montgomery Railroad. This was a dangerous Road it being laid with string timber & iron. We got to Montgomery at 11 oclock in the night. 82 miles. This is the capital of Alabama State. It is situated on the Alabama River. It's a large city but I cant describe it to you for we passed Right on through the City down to the boat landing. We left before daylight on the steam boat. We went one hundred and ten miles down the River to Selma. This is a large City and as pretty a place as I ever saw. They are building 4 gun boats at this place. We lay over one night left next morning on the Alabama and Mississippit Road for Demopolis a distance of 52 miles. We got hear in the evening. The citizens give us a dinner hear. This place is on the Tombigby River. We crossed Black warrior that day. Names familiar to father. We got on a steam boat went 4 miles down the River to the end of the Jackson Road. Here we lay over two days and nights. Whilst hear one of Colonel Watkin's men came into our Regiment & stold a pair of boots (and) some blankets. They striped him gave him one hundred lashes shaved one side of his head drove him out of camp. I saw this done. We left there at night & came to this place. Distance 64 miles. We got hear yesterday morning & are waiting hear for transportation. It is one hundred miles yet to Jackson. Some say we will go to Mobile from hear. The Mobile & Ohio Railroad connects hear. Its one hundred & forty miles to Mobile from hear.

You will see we have come 669 miles from Murfreesboro & about 500 from home. You can look on the map and see our rout. This place is a new place. Its not on the map. I have not been waid lately but it is my opinion I am heavier now Than I ever was in my life. We are now drawing corn meal bacon beef salt sugar rice and rye to make coffee.

I don't know where for you to write till we get to our journeys end. We are looking to be carried on to day or tomorrow. I will write as soon as we get there. I find my shirt to be a great friend Though its warm hear to what it was. Herd all our boys that stoped off at home that has not got up with us now is reported as deserters. I don't know what will be done with Them. Tell John I still see him in my imagination as the brain carries me off from him weeping after me. I thought will we ever meet again in peace. I must close this letter. We are to draw money to day. When I write a gain I will tell you where to wright to me. We have got news hear that Bragg is whipping the yanks in Tennessee. We have whipped them three times at Vicksburg in This State. I remain your ever loving husband

G H Burns to Nancy Burns

Five days later, Burns was in Jackson, Mississippi continuing on to Vicksburg.

Jackson Miss   Jan the 8th 1863

Dear wife I embrace This opportunity of addressing you a few lines to let you know that I am well. I had two or three days of sickness since I wrote last but nothing serious. I hope this will find you all well. We left Maridian last Monday night & arrived here Thursday night. The country so far I have seen in Miss is low wet & swampy with bad watter. I fear if we stay hear until summer we will have a heap of sickness. The yankys have all left Vicksburg but it is thought they will Return with larger forces. We expect to be ordered on to Vicksburg though I hope we will be sent back to Tennessee shortly. We just herd of the great Murfreesboro fight a few days (ago). We left to soon for that fight and got hear two late for the Vicksburg fight. We have been vary lucky. Gen Vaughns Brigade was in the Vicksburg fight. I fear from the last dispatches we got that Brag was defeated at Murfreesboro though the Yanks acknowledge we …

…miss you at times it has its effects upon me but I drive it away as quick as possible. I wish you a hapy New Year. May God spare you through this eventful year is the prayer of your husband,

GH Burns

By February 10th, Burns, the 34th Georgia and their entire brigade (Taylor's) were in the works of Vicksburg facing shelling from the Union fleet of gunboats. A common theme with soldiers on both sides was disappointment and sadness at not receiving regular mail from home and loved ones as he expresses here.

Vicksburg Mississippi

Feb the 10th 1863

Dear wife & family with a heavy heart I seat myself to inform that I am in common health The reason I have a heavy heart I have never heard a word from home since I saw John at _____ . It came with him. I have written letter after letter and has got no answer. why is this So(?) have you thus far forgotten me(?) No never have you quit writing me. I cant believe this. then it must be the fault of the mail we are hear looking for a big fight every hour. the Yankees gun boats are in site up the River. we can see their camps from hear on the opposite side of the river. one of their gunboats leaped our batteries and went down the River. it sliped by in the night but did not get out of reach of our batteries before daylight. our big guns opened on it but it had got to far by to do it any injury. you might ought to have heard The lumbering of our guns. We have to go 8 miles down the river on picket every five or six days. 4 Regiments at a time. This is picketing on a large scale The first time we went it commensed a cold rain on us just after we started The rain fell in torrents The Road was a slosh of mud shoe mouth deep. we had nothing but one blanket a peace with us. we had a ruff time of it sure. our Regiment is not in good health at this time. we draw coars corn meal beef some Bacon melasses sugar rice salt and peas. I don't like this place at all. it is the ruffest country I ever saw. There ar cold winds hear on the River all the time & the worst water I ever drank. I long to be back in Georgia or Tennessee It is thought by our officers that we will not stay hear long but I think it uncertain. I hope we will not stay hear long. I think it impossible for the yanks ever to take this place. The cannon are booming away up the River. we are near the City inside the line of fortifications and breastworks. The roar of cannon has become an old thing. To us we hear them all times in the day. That gunboat leaped down in the half mile of us where we were on picket. Ther was a little town on the River called Warrenton. Our batteries opened on it. They struck her 4 times. she returned the fire. one ball went through the house where general Tracy was and broke his negroes leg. This was all the damage that was done. it is the opinion of all hear that if the enemy lands hear we will badly defeat them.

James Redwine & the other boys from that settlement are all well. write one to me. maby a letter will get through to me some time. I am so uneasy I dream of home every night. I would give any price just to hear from home one time more

Write to me how you are all making out these hard times and how the last conscript is taking with some of our neighbors and all the news you know and how my little Tennessee Jane is getting along. I can see her just as plain yet as my hand. I want you all to write to me. I must close this letter by hopeing it will find you all well. I remain your affectionate husband G. H. Burns

To my ever loving wife Nancy Burns
Back your next letter this way
To G. H. Burns in care of Capt Jackson 34th Regt Ga Vols
Taylors brigade

On the 24th of February Burns writes home about his regiment's severe duty marching back and forth between the city and picket posts south of their encampments. While miserable from the strain and weather he remains confident that Vicksburg can never be taken.

Vicksburg Miss

Feb the 24th 1863

Dear wife I can inform you that I am well at this time. I hope this will find you all well. I rec'd your letters by the hand of Mr Boner. that is the only letter I have got from you since I left Tennessee. Why it is I can't tell. The other boys gets letters regularly but I get none. we are still hear. no more prospect for a fight than when we came hear. our duty is vary heavy hear. we have to go in to town every three or four nights and down to warenton every ten or twelve days. I must tell you about our last trip down there though its no pleasure for me to tell of such expeditions. we left camp soon in the morning with our blankets. it rained the day before till we could get us no bread baked to take with us. I got a little meat boiled. I left camp with my meat in one haversack my 3 days rations of meal in an other haversack my canteen 2 blankets all drawn on my back. it rained all the way on us. it fell in torrents until the whole earth was almost covered. we trudged on until we came to a creak with a bridge over it. it had overflowed and was from the foot of one hill to the other a distance of a quarter of a mile. we walked in. I led the way. we waided over. The water was up to our bodies. we got to our place of picket cold and wet it still raining. I built me a fire put one blanket up for a shed and put up for the night but not to sleep. Next day it cleared away. I baked me some bread. we staid over 3 days got back to camp all strate. I am well fixed up now to what I have been. I have dug me a hole in a bank. dug me a fine place in the bank then a hole up out at the top like we used to make Little play houses. I set my tent in the hole so I have a snug little fireplace in one end of my tent. I sleep as warm as a rat in a hay stack my bed is a little plank scaffold with some broom straw I pulled and carried in. The Yankees bombarded Vicksburg two days last week from across the River. we could stand at our camp and see them burst in the air. one man got his arm torn off with a shell was all that got hurt. Our forces have captured both the Yankee gun boats that's went down the river. I don't hardly think we will have much fighting hear. my opinion is they are just keeping up a big show hear to keep us drawed off from some other point. There is a great deal said hear about peace but I can't tell how it will work out. to day is warm and spring like. every thing scarce and high hear. pies not larger than a butt plate is 59 cents milk 50 cents a quart eggs 1.50 cents a dozen. Tobacco 1.00 a plug flour one hundred & twenty dollars a barrel. Soap 1.50 cents a bar I paid 15 cents for a nough to wash shirts and 2 pair of drawers. how soldiers are to live at this & only get 11 dollars per month I can't tell. God knows these are trying times. James Redwine, Bomans Jones, Peppers Masters and all they boys in the 39th well but Faith he is vary sick. I saw them start of(f) with him to the hospital the other day. tell John to Breed Kit this spring if he thinks best. There is a chance for him to get to sign on for this Regiment. our preacher has quit but I dare not persuade my best friends in to this war. I would try to fix some way to have a little corn made this summer but I have no chance to get there. now I must close. Your ever loving Husband G H Burns -To Nancy Burns

Meanwhile, on the Federal side of the river, Henry Elsworth and the 4th Ill had been previously posted in Lagrange, Tennessee. By this time they were repositioned to Sherman and McClernand's headquarters camp at Young's Point as part of the growing Federal forces on the Louisiana side of the river.

Youngs Point La Near Vicksburg
Feb the 18 – 1863

Dear Mother

I received your letter and was glad to hear that you were all well. The weather has been very stormy for the last week but it is very plesant to day . I have been as well as usual but it is very unhealthy. I saw Charley West a few days ago. He has been sick but he is well now. Things is very quiet. They have commenced shelling Vicksburg today but not much. We expect to get paid off soon but I do not know how soon. The soldiers are very much dissatisfied with this war and I think that they have reason to be so. I am glad that I came to war when I did for I should of come in the last call and then I should have been worse off than I be now and I think that I am bad off now. I have got postage stamps. I got them in Memphis before I left. I have not been out of money but have not been paid off for over eight months.

I shall make this letter short. Please write soon.

H Ellsworth

The Period of "Experiments"

The Peninsula Canal and A Water Way to the Red River

Looking for ways to circumvent or get in the rear of the Vicksburg defenses, Grant attempted four "experiments" over the next two and a half months. Two of these were attempts to bypass Vicksburg on the Louisiana side of the river. The other two were attempts to gain a foothold north of the city in order to attack from its rear by potential exploiting waterways on the Mississippi side.

The first bypass experiment was to restart the work begun by Williams and his infantry the previous year by widening and deepening the canal across the peninsula on the western bank opposing Vicksburg. If this succeeded Vicksburg would indeed be bypassed completely and made irrelevant. The first deterrent to this project was the weather. January saw more rain than it had in years. It was nearly impossible to work in these conditions. Further examination of the canal's proposed route also indicated that this approach would not succeed. The northern end of the canal was situated on an eddy in the river and water wouldn't naturally flow into the canal. Where the southern end of the canal met the Mississippi, it would still be within range of Vicksburg's batteries. Grant stopped work on the project.

The Confederates were aware of this attempt to bypass their fortifications. John Douthit of the 52nd Georgia reported the following. He also comments on the weather and miserable conditions in seas of mud.

Feb 2 1863

Camped near Vicksburg, Miss.
    Dear Companion

    I now take my pen in hand to write you a few lines which will inform you I am well at this time. Hoping these lines will come to hand and find you all enjoying the same like blessing. I do not know that I have any thing to write which will interest you. We have moved from where we were camped when I last wrote. We are camped now about two miles below Vicksburg. Our former camps being above. The enemy is still in sight. that is their boats. They are trying to cut or open the canal below this place so they can get below without having to pass our heavyest guns. They may pass with there gun boats and there hole fleet if they get the canal open . They passed our batteries with one gun boat this morning. Our guns firing at her all the while. How often they struck her I do not know. Those that saw her says she went through in a hurry. If they get possession of the river below here Vicksburg will be of little importance to us but before they injurs us very bad they will have to take Port Hudson. some two hundred miles below here stand them and Port Hudson. The weather is very warm and wet here and mud there is no end to it. You need not send any clothes now unless it is some socks as we have drawed clothing. I do not know how long we will stay here. I hope we will not have to stay here through the summer. I hope the war will end so I can get to come home and stay next summer.

I would be glad to see you all and think I will get to come home and see you all this spring. I want you to be shure and write for I have received but one letter from you since I have been here and it was dated in December. Give my best respects to your father and family. So nothing more but remains your husband until death.

John M. Douthit

Six days later, Douthit writes home again. He repeats that he needs little in terms of clothing at this juncture but he misses home and family and hopes to live long enough to see them again.

Camped Near Vicksburg
Feb 8th 1863

Dear Wife,

Your kind favor of the 28th of Jan. was received today and gave me great joys for nothing pleases me better than to hear that all are well at home.

You need not send me any clothing for I do not need anything unless it is one pair of socks and if Mr. John Hicks wants pay for bringing them you need not send them by him. I do not need socks very bad – I draw plenty of clothing and have now as much as I can toat on a march. I received the braids of hair you sent and would be a great deal better pleased to see the heads they come off of but that can not be yet awhile. But I hope the time will speedily pass off when the way worn the best you can and not get out of heart for I hope I will live to see the close of this cruel war and enjoy many pleasant days afterwards with my friends and family. If you see Harriet you can tell her that Davis is in common health. Tell Mother Douthit that Uncle Jack McClure Harrison McClure Thomas Bly and Chickman Gallaway are here and was well the last time I saw them. Give my best respects to all inquiring friends. So I will close hoping to hear from you soon. So nothing more at present only remains your affectionate husband until death.

John M. Douthit

By the first of March, John Douthit wanted to leave Vicksburg as soon as possible. Conditions and weather were not to his liking and while possible he didn't think the Yankees would ever really attack the place.

March the 1th 1863

Camped Near Vicksburg, Miss

My Dear Companion:

As it has been three weeks since I have written you a letter I take my pen in hand to drop you a few lines this morning which will inform you that I am well at the present time. Hoping these few lines will come to hand and find you all well, I have nothing strange to write you at this time. The enemy's fleet is still in sight. They throw boomes occasionaly in to the city but do little or no damage. They may attact us here again, but I hardly think they will. I want them to do what they are going to do for I want to get away from this place.

Spring has come and the farmers are planting here and when it is not raining it is very warm here.

I want you to write to me for I have received an answer to the first letter that I wrote home. I come to this place. you either don't write or your letters don't come to hand....

Two weeks later, John Douthit despairs even more at not receiving letters from home. This is an oft repeated concern from the soldiers on both sides.

March the 17th 1863
Near Vicksburg Miss.

Dear Companion

  I write you again to let you know that I am still at __ though not well but I am mending and think if I get no back set I will be well in a few days. Hoping these lines will come to hand and find you well. I have nothing new to write you at this time. I have written so much and get no letters back. I am almost out of heart of writing but I will write as long as there is any hopes of your getting the letters that I send you. You can not imagine how I want to be at home so that I can get something that I could eat. The most I have eaten for several days has been milk for which I gave fifty cents per quart and butter at two dollars per pound.

Davis Douthit is in moderate health though I don't think he will stand ____ life. So I will close by signing my name. Your husband until death.
  John M. Douthit

The second bypass experiment was an attempt to cut a path from Lake Providence, approximately 50 miles north of Milliken's Bend on the Louisiana side of the river all the way south to the Red River, some 150 miles. This would certainly bypass Vicksburg altogether but would require swamps and bayous to have channels cut through them in order to permit the passage of steamers. Two months of effort made little progress and this experiment was also abandoned.

George Deal was a soldier in the 20th Ohio Volunteer Infantry. By the third week in February, the 20th OVI was positioned on the banks of Lake Providence, 60 miles above Vicksburg. Lake Providence was the northern point of the second experiment to find a channel through the bayous to Red River. Deal describes the area of encampment and the condition of the fields left by the planters who had fled the area earlier.

Lake Providence, Lousiana
Feb the 24th 1863

Dear Wife

I take this opportunity to let you know that I am well at this time and sincerely hope that these few lines will find you all well. We are now in the state of Louisiana. We are camped in about a mile of the Mississippi river on the bank of Lake Providence. We are in sixty miles of Vicksburg. I don't think that our forces will attack Vicksburg. I think the effect is to surround the place and cut-off there supplies and thus take the place without the shedding of much blood. We are camped in a cotton field. I think there is over five hundred acres of cotton in this field. It has not been picked. Everything is going to waste here. Our men is tearing down and burning all the houses. The crops that was raised here last season was all left on the ground and the owners run away.

This looks like the sunny south. The woods is beginning to look green and the peach trees is in full bloom. This may not appear true to you but to prove the thing I will send you some blossoms. The boys is running about in there shirt sleeves and are too warm. At that, if you don't get letters regular, you must not think strange for the letters has a good ways to go. I suppose about 14 or 15 hundred miles. I expect to get further off yet before I start for home but it is no use to talk about home. For my part, I have no time set but would be glad if this would come to a close.

Direct you letters to the
20 Ohio regt Co K
In care of Capt. Kaga
Give my respects to……

In his letter dated March 19th, 1863, Deal provides his opinion on housing options for his family at home. War or not, family struggles at home were ever present in the mind of the soldier. He also describes the breaking of the Lake Providence levy which was a part of the experiment's design to flood the lower bayous and passages to the Red River.

Camp near Lake Providence, Louisiana
About 5 miles….
March the 19 of 1863

My Deary Affectionate Wife,

I once more take my pen to answer your kind affectionate letter that I received from you. It was wrote on the 1 (or 7) of March and it was received on the 11th of March and was glad to hear from you once more. I am well and enjoying good health as can be expected out in the service. I hope these few lines will find you and all the rest of my folks well and enjoying good health. You wrote something about Baker wanting you to go out of his house. I don't want you to out with out you get paid for it and if he pays you or builds you a house on the old…place or if anybody else builds it, it will be alright but not go out with out you. get one or the other done for yourself. I don't want you to trouble yourself about it, just let them do as they want about it, pay you or build you a house. You spoke about your hope for a better time a coming. I hope for to see the time I can get home to see you again and live with you as I used to do. If I should not get home to see you anymore, I hope I will meet you in a better lane above where parting is no more where sickness and sorrow is no more. Oh won't it be a happy time then. I long for the time to come when we will live together on earth but I hain't discouraged yet. I am as lively as I used to be.

You spoke about me a coming home. I would like to come home but I can't. It is impossible for me to come home but I hain"t discouraged yet. I think the war can't last any longer than fall to the furthest but I don't now want you to content yourself and don't fret about me. I would like to see my little children. Tell them be good to their mother and I will be home to see them before long when the war is over. We hain't got paid off yet and I don't know when we will be paid off for wee are so far off, but I hope we will be paid soon but no sign (as) of yet of pay. All though I can get along with out any money here for everything Uncle Sam furnishes us so I can get along.

I seen Cicero Cole and stayed with him one day. I was glad to see him enjoying good health and in good spirits. They camped in one mile of this place or one mile from camp at that time before we moved from camp Lake Providence. We got over the board of the boat on the 1rst of March and then we stayed there on board of the boat waiting for orders to go up or down the river but we at last went up the river about 5 miles and camped on an old planters farm. He has a mill and a saw mill and a cotton gin and niggers and everything that man wants to get along with but I tell you we made the boarders fly and corn meal and fences and sweet potatoes. They have cut the levee at Lake Providence and I was there to see the water come in. I tell you it came in fast. It is drowning out the rebels in Lake Providence.

Oh my paper is all gone so no more.
Your husband George Deal, to his wife.

Deal's response to his wife's letter, dated March 31st 1863, displays more of the stress placed on soldiers by the circumstances their families face at home. Deal's wife Sarah has obviously begged him to come home, putting great pressure on him. Deal has a fellow messmate who writes his letters for him. His messmate adds an aside to her in the letter suggesting she gets the neighbors to help with some of her chores.

Lake Providence, Louisiana
Or near lake Providence
March the 31st, 1863

Well my dear affectionate wife, I take this opportunity to answer your kind letter that I received from you on the 29th of March. I was glad to here from you and I was glad to hear you was all well and enjoying good health for health is a blessing for anybody to have but I was sorry to hear you was carrying your own wood and chopping your own wood. I think the neighbors ought to do something for my family while I am in the service and fighting for them as well as for myself. They are at home enjoying their fireside and their good beds and I am here laying on the ground and fighting for them as well as for myself and I think as little as they could do is to helping my family chop wood and so on and not let them suffer.

For me to come home is out of the question for I can't do it, for to take a French it is not safe and is called a deserter. I will stay my time out but I think I would like to see my family as well as anybody else would like to see their family. Yes, there is other men here married and has a family at home and I know they want to go home as bad as I do and they can't get home neither, but I hope the time will come soon when we will all come home to see our families. I have a family that is as good as anyone else. I know I would like to see them as well as anyone but it is out of the question to go home now. If he does take a French, he better not show himself here in this regiment anymore.

My name is Henry Souder. I am a cooking for a mess and George hes in the mess and he is a good fellow to help me when I get in a pinch and lots to do. I pity any man that has a family at home. Now I do think the neighbor is good to my family. I get all my wood falled and chopped for nothing. There is good union men there left to take care of my family. I don't say there is none there where you live but it is something is the matter.

I hope they will do better for you and try and help you. Now my good woman don't fret so about me. I do pity you and I do think as much of you as I always did but I am in a place I can't get home now. Just as soon as I can get home I will come home but I can't tell when. Now don't write to me to desert or to take a French for the boys will talk where is so many together and I don't want no one know it here.

We got on a boat on the 19th of March and started to Vicksburg and we stopped at Eagles Bend and got off the boat to burn the railroad bridge between Jackson and Vicksburg in Mississippi but the water was so high we couldn't get through. We got to…(within) one mile from the river and couldn't go any further so we stayed there over night and marched back again to the boat and now we are in our old camp about lake Providence, Louisiana, 20th Ohio Reg't in the care of Capt. Kaga, Co K, via Memphis and then they will come all right. Cicero was here today and took dinner with me. He was…for what is out.

So no more. I am in good health and glad of that so no more at present but I remain your husband till death and lover. From George Deal to Sarah Deal. So good by at this time.

On April 8, 1863 Deal defends his number of letters home due to the fact that he can't write and must rely on others to pen his words for him. Clearly Sarah is distraught back home in Ohio.

Camp Logan & Briskel Landing
Louisiana, near lake Providence
April 8th, 1863

My Dear affectionate wife I take my pen in hand to write to you to answer you letters that you wrote to me. I received two letters on the 6th of April. They was wrote on the 28th of March and one on the XX of March. So you can see just how long they was a coming to me. You wrote so about a not a writing to you. If I could write myself, I would write oftener to you but I have to get others to write to you and so I have to wait for others to write for me. You musn't think you can get letters so often but I am well and I hope these few lines will find you enjoying the same blessing the rest of the boys is. Well as far as I know camping… is all bulley for cooks or any other man or woman.

You said you had wrote me four letters and hadn't received any. Now I have wrote to you and answered every letter I got from you yet so far and I wrote you. I expect you have got them before now. I hope so anyhow. You asked me if I thought anything of my family. I do as well as ever I did nor I never forgot to write nor I never forgot my family. That you know. You stated something about my wheat. I would like help to cut it but it is out of the question. You said old mam would bake a big pot… and you said she would have it ready for my dinner. I guess I will come George and help him to eat his free for hot…. I am fond of and other things to. I am sorry there is so many rebels in the north and around home but I wish the old Co K regiment would come home and clean out the butternuts in the north but I expect we will go to Vicksburg soon but I don't know how soon we will go. You spoke about the mud a been so deep to a ….. You don't know how nice it is here to me. Sun is warm here and the….(weather) Is getting warm.

I am glad you are going to stay where you are. Permelia Jane is a going to get married. I wish I was there to put them to bed or get in bed with them or eat dinner with them. The next time any one writes for you, you state who he is and him name. I have drawed all my money and I will send it the first chance I get. It may be two weeks or three before I can send it and I expect to send it by Fry the old sutler that is for the Co G. regiment. He is a going to Sidney and when I do send it, I will write a few lines to let you know where to go to get it. I expect to send it to Sidney. When I do send it, I am a going to send you twenty five dollars of my money. I don't know too much to write this time. I was down (to) see Cicero today. He was well.

So no more to write but you remain my wife. So good by for this time Sarah Deal.
This from George Deal. Henry J Souder wrote this

Direct your letters as before and they will come alright to me. The Sothern men I do say I do hate and despise to see and I wouldn't be too good to shoot any such man. They deserve killing. So they do and that is to good for them or hanging is to good for them. I think hell will be full of such kind of men. So good by for awhile. George Deal. H. J. Souder, his writing to democrats.

Attempts to Gain Northern Approaches to the City

By the end of March the two attempts to bypass Vicksburg via water routes on the Louisiana side of the river were being abandoned. Grant was still willing to look at other opportunities to get behind the Vicksburg defenses from the northern approaches to the stronghold.

The first of the experiments to gain a foothold north of the city began on February 2nd. A levee at the northern mouth of the Yazoo and Mississippi Rivers, hundreds of miles above Vicksburg, was blown in order to reestablish a waterway known as Yazoo Pass. At one time it had been used to enable passage to the interior of the state while returning to the Mississippi River just north of Vicksburg. The levee had been built to prevent flooding that frequented this waterway. If this 350 mile waterway could be used, Federal troops could land at Haynes Bluff just above the city and avoid attacking the strength of the defenders.

An expedition was sent through the blown breech and down the waterway. Rebels had felled trees and created barriers along the entire route, slowing the advance to a crawl. Less than half way through the journey the expedition encountered its final barricade. On a tight bend in the pass the Confederates had constructed a strong fortification which they named Fort Pemberton. The pass was too narrow to allow more than one or two gunboats to come into range of the fort and the rebel cannon were too much for them. This ended the attempt to leverage the Yazoo Pass waterway.

Samuel Hawkins Byers was a member of the 5th Iowa Infantry, Company B. His unit was part of the forces moving down the passageway being attempted through Yazoo Pass. The following is an excerpt from his book "Fire and Sword" describing the effort.

" March 23 1863"

"Now for days and days our little fleet cruised its way toward Vicksburg among the plantations, swamp, woods, bayous, cane brakes creeks, and rivers, of that inland sea, where ever the water seemed deepest that was our course, but almost every hour projecting stumps and trees had to be sawn off under the water to allow our craft to get through, sometimes we advanced only four or five miles a day. At night the boat would be tied to some tall sycamore, here and there we landed at some plantations that seemed like an Island in the flood. The negroes on the plantation, amazed at our coming, wondered if it was the day of jubilee or if it was another Noah's flood and that these iron gunboats arks of safety."

Grant's final experiment and second attempt to find a water route that would enable a foothold north of the city also involved the Yazoo Passage and River. An unintended consequence of blowing the levee 300 miles north of Vicksburg was realized by millions of gallons of water rushing down the Yazoo pass and flooding Steeles Bayou to a depth of 15 feet. Admiral Porter had reconnoitered the flooded region and determined that his gunboats could navigate five different waterways through the forests to get beyond the defenses at Chickasaw and Haynes Bluffs north of Vicksburg and establish a landing. Grant approved the expedition but it too failed just short of reaching its objective due partly to the Confederate defense at Deer Creek as well as natural barriers that were not uncovered initially.

Jared Sanders described the role of the 26th Louisiana in the Deer Creek episode of the campaign as well as rumors that the Yankees were moving away due to their failures to date.

In Vicksburg
April 11th '63

Dear Friend,
……Considering the present unreliable condition of the Confederate States mail facilities, perhaps I should not be so much vexed when letters from my friends fail to come regularly. Getting letters has become quite a provoking game of hazard here of late; and we know how (when we are writing) the idea worries us that it is <u>problematic</u> whether our friend will ever see the sheet. From you the last letter received was dated in <u>January</u> – yours of the 14 March was received yesterday however – about two months intervening….. Well – since I wrote to you last which, I think, was numbered 10, our regiment has been on a very fatiguing trip up Deer Creek, a small bayou entering the Yazoo river above Snyder's Bluff. We left here on the 22 of March & returned on the 29th. From here we walked to Haynes' Bluff on the Yazoo – <u>fourteen</u> miles, spent a night there on the steamer <u>Paytona</u> waiting for the "Dew Drop" to take us up Deer Creek which enters Yazoo four miles higher up. After each soldier had sought his hard couch I walked up to the hurricane deck & spent a most delightful hour thinking of what had transpired upon that same deck in <u>better</u> times <u>not "lang syne"</u> and enjoying the picturesque appearance of all around me – the sullen frown of our great guns on the bank, the warlike preparation, the low murmur of the swift waters beneath, the bright lights from thousands of camp-fires on the hills, the beautiful starlight above added to the stillness of the night encouraged a pleasant reverie. The next day found us up Deer Creek making <u>breast</u> works. In a couple of days we intended to move upon the enemy but he heard of it and left. The night of the 28 I shall long remember. I lay down by a log to sleep early – about 8 o'clock it began to rain in torrents, and you can imagine how I spent the rest of that night. The land is all inundated

except a strip on the bank, and rain stands upon the ground without entering for the soil is full of water. So our fires went out, and no shelter being near, I stood up through the night in rain as cold as I have ever felt, wind as piercing, in fact it was a storm, and water over shoe top. The trees fell so fast that it sounded like a bombardment to me – all kinds of trees were uprooted. We were in an old field of dead timber, and five men in "Company A" became alarmed and ran leaving their blankets where they lay; in the morning a tree 3 feet in diameter was laying (on) them – how providential their escape. Some 14 men were killed around Vicksburg by timber. I shall long remember that night. Were it not that I <u>suffered</u> for my country I should ever animadvert <u>harshly</u> upon the long hours of the night spent standing in water, rain & cold. Every soldier has his own strange experience, his own odyssey of adventure – but I hope the Deer Creek <u>chapter</u> will never repeat itself in the <u>part</u> that I will have to act in this tragic war. The hardships incident to "soldiering" are well brought out in our <u>late</u> experience. While we were gone we spent several nights in cotton gins; very comfortable quarters compared to some I have seen. On one occasion we walked or waded knee-deep back into the field to reach a gin' some of the lint is now on my flannel shirt. I suppose you know it is <u>fashionable</u> to wear colored shirts all the time. I have white shirts but never wear them, owing to this "army-fashion"! we all were glad to get back to quarters in this place. The Yankees had gone through a chain of bayous from the Mississippi into Deer Creek, hoping thus to get into the Yazoo River above our works. But General Featherston gave them a good drubbing just before they arrived at Sunflower, a large river running into the Yazooo. I am much afraid they will sometime get into the Yazoo through to some of those little creeks. They have little "Skedaddle boats", as they call them, which go ahead with <u>axes</u> & <u>saws</u> running by steam for the purpose of cutting down trees & sawing up logs which obstruct their way. It is astonishing how soon they render creeks, in which a boat never floated before, navigable to their iron clad gunboats.

Over the river the indications are that we will have no fight here; they are removing their men, it is thought to Kentucky, where they fear

"Stonewall" Jackson is. They are afraid to even try to run by their gunboats now since we sunk one, the "Lancaster," in front of the city.

There will be another change among our field officers soon I expect, owing to an improper promotion which took place some time ago. Captain Legarde, it has been decided, cannot refuse promotion, & hence he becomes lieutenant colonel. vice Crow, who will become "major," and Major Whit Martin will return to his company as captain. Lieutenant Lewis Guion, who resigned a few weeks ago, has been ordered again to the regiment, his resignation having been revoked by the war department. Our colonel is very unpopular in the regiment unfortunately. This is all the regimental news; except perhaps a grand anniversary celebration given by the colonel on the 3d of April in honor of the organization of the 26th. We had egg-nog, music, wine & cake – with other things that make the heart <u>merry</u>. General Lee (Stephen D.) and members of his staff were present. Our brigadier is a young West Pointer, of the old family of Lees of Virginia. He is considered the best general in the department, though there are many who rank him. On his staff is a young <u>"Scott"</u> who lately ran the blockade (a month or so ago) to take up arms for the South – he is a lieutenant in the English army.

Prices in this city are enormous; almost as high as they can safely be. Not so bad as in "Revolutionary" times when it required one hundred dollars continental money to secure a chicken!....

Your sincere friend,

J. Y. Sanders

Preparing the Final Strategy for Taking Vicksburg

Confederate Confidence is High

This last setback occurred in early April. Grant had been willing to attempt these "experiments" hoping one might succeed. He had also wanted to keep his troops engaged and active over the winter months. Throughout this entire time he continued to work on an alternative plan. By now it was clear to him that the overland path he originally planned to the rear of Vicksburg was the only way to take the city. He also realized that politically he could not withdraw the army to Memphis in order to restart the campaign. That left him one alternative.

While the Confederate defenders of Vicksburg had been successful at beating back the early Federal challenges and were very confident in holding the city. Within the next several weeks this would all change. Unaware of what lay ahead, Confederate morale was already being tested by fatigue duty and conditions brought on by weather. G H Burns (34th Georgia) wrote home regarding the misery of his condition while describing the execution of a deserter during this period.

Vicksburg Miss

March The 12th 1863

My Dear wife I can inform you that my health is not good at present. though I am about yet I have a vary bad cough. I can hardly sleep of a night. it is caused I recon by cold and exposure. I am takeing medicen for it. I hope with care I will soon get over it. I hope this will find you well with all the rest of my folks. I recd' a letter from Anderson & one from Jane the other day. I have wrote both them and to William since I wrote to you last. I wrote Milly a letter the other day. I have nothing new to write. Times are awful hard hear but I recon this is the case every where now. I have got no letter from you since I wrote last. The last one I got was wrote the 22nd of last month. The one I got from Jane was wrote the 1st day of this month. There has been so much wet weather. The rail Roads are out of fix so much the mails are vary irregular but it gives me great pleasure to hear from you though it be seldom. Mr. Vandiver got a letter yesterday from his wife who wrote that too of my sisters were at her house the night before and that you were all well and that you had wrote me 7 letters. I have never got but too besides the one Mr. Jones brought me. Our division consisting of 17 regiments were all marched out the other evening to see a man shot. he belonged to a Louisonnia Regiment. he Deserted last summer and joined the Yankees. our forces took him since that in a fight and condemned him to Death. He was brought out in a wagon seated on his coffin with his fine white shroud on. The Drum & fife playing a religious tune in presents of his grave his coffin sitting by him. he was tied to the post Then in the presence of all our Division 12 men steped forward and at the command fire he was completely Riddled with balls. Thus he paid the debt of a Deserter & Traiter to his country Two others were shot the same evening. A man sees many strange things in the army. Oh how I want to see old home and all of you. you have no idea how bad I want to come home. If I only knew I would live till peace is made and get home I could bear these hardships but to think that I must bear them all then maby never see home any more its almost two intolerable but I still have some hope that I will see you all again. I hear that captain Jackson is coming to us shortly. If he would bring it I would like to have a small box of a little butter & a few eggs etc. I get me some milk every few days which helps one smartly. I give 25 cents a quart for buttermilk 50 cents for sweet milk. I bought several custards at 50 cents. I found it took my money two fast. I have quit buying them. try to make you a good garden and maby the good Lord will fix some plan that I can get home a few days This Summer. I could eat onions now show (sure) and lettice to but show (sure) no use to talk about these things hear. might as well hunt for a kneedle in a hay stack as these things hear. I will close for The present

Your husband   G.H. Burns

To Nancy Burns

Five days later, Burns' spirits were high. His health was improving somewhat and the rumor was that 34th would be transferred to Savannah!

Vicksburg Miss

March The 17th 1863

Dear wife & family I have the chance to send a few lines home to morrow by Mrs. Beford Jones. I am not well yet but some better Than I was when I wrote last. I have not been on duty for a few days. it is cold that ails me. my cough is getting better. I got some milk and onions which helps my weak stomach. we drew some good fresh bacon to day . I have to me a canteen of sweet milk seting by me for supper. I paid 50 cents for it. we are all much lifted up now. it is reported hear to day that we are ordered to Savannah. we hope it is so. if it is I will write whenever I ascertain the fact. The Yankees are all leaveing. we don't know where they are going to. They got off up the River in there Boats. our forces whipped them down at Port Hudson the other day. I have not yet Read any other letter from you. I can't tell why. Oh that I could get your letters regular. I hope you get mine and hear from me. If you got my other letter and goes to send me any thing by the captain don't send much or it will spoil. if you send any butter put it in some small vessel and box it up. if we get to go to Savannah which I hope we will I can then get little things from home. don't be uneasy about me for I am not in a critical state of health. I am up and knocking around but Spring as usual in The Spring of the year. I am spending my money pretty fast but I must have some little luxuries for I don't know that I will kneed them long. I hope this is all agreeable with your feelings. I must close as it is late and Jones is going to start soon in the morning do the best you all can and may God bless you all is the prayer of your kind husband

G.H. Burns

To Nancy Burns & family

On the 25th of March, Burns writes with more good news regarding his health and the progress of the war on the Vicksburg front.

March 25th 1863

My Dear wife – I can inform you that I am again about well. I hope this will find you all well. I read your kind letter of the 15th inst. The 3rd one I have ever got from any of you since I left home. I am just of your notion about our letters. Don't send any more letters to the office now. Send for letters by him for he thinks soldiers will send money in the letters and breaks them open for that purpose and thus destroy them. I know there is something of the kind up for the Tilton boys gets their letters regular. We are having fun hear with the yanks. A few days ago our forces up on The Yazoo River took 16 transport boats 3 gun boats and whipped there land forces down at Port Hudson below hear. We destroyed 2 or 3 boats that fast. We have them pinned up between hear and there. This morning I dreampt The yanks were Throwing Corns at us. When I awoke our batteries were fireing so fast you could not count them. We fell in lines. I got a sick mans gun and away we went to the scene of action. Just as we got in town we heard a hapy shout go up from our batteries. The fire then ceased. We went ahead to see what was done. The Result was two gun boats had started down past our batteries. Just as one large Boat got opposite Vicksburg our big (canon) sunk her with all her crew. The other one went floating down badly injured. We heard our lower batteries fireing on her but have not heard the result but I guess our boys will take her in out of the wet. I Think a few more such cases and they will leave hear and let us go some where else. This is what they call a glorious day in Vicksburg. 3 or four more Boats started down and saw what was done. They made quick time back again. Our prospects are bright now. All over The confederacy we are getting plenty of new Bacon and pork now to eat so be of good cheer. Maby a better day is comin. I saw the letter James Redwine got. He is well now. Nancy you wanted my advice about going home. I dont like to give it but you have ast me for it. I will give it. I have no objections to you going to see your people and staying a while with them but Rather you would not go to stay. My Reasons you well know. I am undergoing hardships that home folks can form no idea of for what for one of the nobelest women & little innocent babes in the world. God knows I wish them not insulted in my absence and forever (not using This as an oath but polititcally) Damned be he who dare to do it. I write this in good feelings so go and see your folks but don't move back up in amongst Those Devlish people who tried to ruin me so hard. I cant tell how long we will stay hear. It is summer hear now. The woods are green plenty of Rose blossoms and such things. Write often. I will do the same. I will close.

your affectionate husband.

G H Burns

To Nancy Burns

To Lydia Its to far a trip for you to Vicksburg. Console yourself by offering up some of those good old prayers. To Caroline I hope to eat some of that bread you are making. While you work pray for me. To father and mother Dry up your tears and be composed. Await Gods will to be done. To John & Elizabeth My love and best wishes for your welfare. Still Remember me with your prayers. To Caroline & children My love to you. May the widows & orphans God preside over you to feed and cloth you is a prayer I often say for you. I hope one day to see you all face to face. So fare you well for the present.

Give my respects to Mr. George & family
GHB

In two letters dated April 2nd, one to his wife and one to his sisters, Burns expressed how homesick he is and how difficult and expensive it is to maintain his digestive health. He asks his sisters to keep him in their prayers.

Vicksburg Miss

April The 2nd /63

Dear wife I am hapy to inform you that my health is still improving. I am almost well. I hope this will find you all well. I recd Lydia's letter of the

77

25th which gave me much pleasure to hear from you all one time more as I get in my tent on my rude scaffold bed and Read how you all wanted to see me and the interest you all felt in my behalf. The tears comed down my weather beaten cheeks and fell on the plank beneath.

O how I long to see you all again. You know nothing about it. you are all there together. You can meet and talk about it but I am hear by myself seven hundred miles from home. No one but strangers to talk to. No kind hand to administer to my wants when sick but Thank God I have one friend who is always present in time (of) need. I am as cheerful as could be expected. I don't suffer myself to get down in heart but have adopted a smile to keep up my spirits in all cases. I have been so week stomached that I could not eat the diet we get. I have bought little pies milk skillets and some eggs. Pies for 50 cents to one dollar. Milk 50 cents a quart. Eggs two dollars a dozen. Potatoes seven dollars per bushel. Butter two dollars per pound. Tobacoo one dollar a plug. Paper 3 dollars a quire with what little debts I owed I have spent upwards of thirty dollars since draw day. This is pretty heavy but I could not help it. We are getting fine meal and plenty of Bacon & pork now. My stomache is pretty good now to what it was when we got beef that you might cook half the day and it would not grease the water you cooked it in and corn meal coarser Than you ever had choped up to fed a cow on and about half anough at that. I hope such times are over now. Still write often. I will get one letter occasionaly. I must close. We will move two mile up the River tomorrow.

G.H. Burns

To Nancy Burns

Vicksburg Miss

April the 2nd 1863

Dear sisters I hope this will find you well. It leaves me in common health. I read your kind letter the 30th which was written the 25th. I read it with much joy whilst I read of your wanting to see me so bad. The Thoughts of former days glided before me and I could but shed tears of sorrow. You

spoke of fast day and how you would meet at the cove and pray (for) me and
_____ Burns got a pass and went to town and heard Those sermons. One
large house was crowded mostly with soldiers (a few women) while the aged
man of God spoke of the dear ones at home. How they were praying for us
and longing for our return but few eyes were dry in that large assembly of
very worn soldiers. We then knealt and sent up a long and furvent prayer
for peace and our return home. I feel that all those prayers will not be lost. I
mind was with you at the cove meeting house that day though my body was
far away. The Boys are all well. I was (with) them all to day. James Faith is
at Jackson. The last They heard from him he was mending. Caroline, Jim is
as stout as a bull. I haven't seen Zack Johnson nor unkle Johns boys in 2 or
three weeks. They were well then. Write often. I will get some of your
letters. We are going (to) move 2 miles up the River above town tomorrow.
Our Regiment is in the Reserve Corps. If there is a fight we will be held
back as a reserve. Our company is on an detail.   Has been for 8 days. I am
hear with the rest of the Regiment and a few sick boys of our company. My
(rank) keeps me confined right hear all the time. I am going to quit it. Its to
much trouble and only one more dollar a month which is nothing. Tell Jeffs
little children I hope to see them some day and talk to them. Tell father and
mother I hope to see them one Time more this side of the grave. Tell John to
cheer up and not let trouble take such hold on him as to injure his health. I
will close this hasty written letter by subscribing myself your loving brother.
G.H. Burns

To Lydia & Caroline Burns.

Packages from home have a magical impact on the soldier at the
front. Burns writes to his wife on the 6th of April that he received his
"little trunk" and the joy it has brought to him and his messmates.

Camp 4 Miles above Vicksburg

April The 6th 1863

Dear wife with much satisfaction I can inform you that I am well at present.
I hope this will find you all well. I am hapy to say to you that I got my little

trunk yesterday evening. James Redwine came down and told me it had come. I went up & got it. Every thing in it was as nice and good as it was when it was first put in it. The boys all said it was nice. My butter was nice and firm. You can just imagine my delight over it by supposing you had lived nearly Twelve months on meat and bread and Then got holt of it. But I could not eat half as much as I thought I could. I gave Three of my mess some cake last night and some butter this morning for breakfast. They did not want to take it but I could not feel right to eat it and not give Them a taste. I will eat the rest myself. It will do me several days. There is 5 in my mess besides myself. Four of them are such hogs I wont give them anything. They wont cook and we have to divide our meat when we draw it to keep them from eating it all up. My two cronies are James Belk and Keister brother to Doctor Keister of Spring Place in my mess. Keister said whoever made that Butter knew how to make it. They talk much about Lydia and you all.

Now Nancy if you could know how I feel when I am eating Those delicious presents it brings feeling of mingled Joy & sorrow. I handel it. I know your hands have fixed it up. You there. me hear. You miles away and still eating your cooking. Oh noble woman who can excel you. Women are The glory of this world. If it was not for woman I would go home and fight no more. My heart overflows with Thanks and gratitude for The little Trunk. I imagine I can see your Mother and Caroline all busteling about fixing it up. Father steps in stands with his hand on his hip a while then utters a deep sigh such as only a father can utter for a son far away. After it is fixed up and some tears shed John takes the little Trunk off to start it on its long journey. This is just imagination you know. The Tobacco came safe to hand and in good Time. It has just got up to 1.50 cents a plug hear. I had 3 plugs I bought when we drew money last. Your Three letter(s) came safe. They were like Angels visits. Sweet and refreshing.

Tell father and Mother I am trying to be a good boy so as to do nothing I would be ashamed for them to know. Bear all your troubles the best you can trusting in an alwise God for protection. Write to Jane & Bob to. call their boy Henderson with any other name they wish you said I wrote *like. I Thought I would never get home. Don't understand me that way. I have strong hopes of getting home again but Think it doubtful some times. I don't fear the yank as much as sickness. My fears are that I have been so exposed that my health will entirely fail me. I must close. Write often. I will send this by Mayfield. Your husband   G H Burns*

To Nancy Burns

That same day, Burns writes to his brother sharing his disregard for speculation and rumors at home as well as the front.

Brother J L   your letter came to hand and was gladly read. You tell much truth in it. The speculation don't stop at home. I hear in the army soldier speculating off of soldier and stealing from each other and every other wickedness conceivable. I fear the war will last a long time yet. there is to much wickedness and meanness in the country yet for peace. I think God will humble the people before he lets them go.

I think as you do that the peace excitement was gotten up for a censation to encourage The weary soldier in the hardship. Write often. Don't let trouble impair your health but pass it off as light as possible. The weather is warm hear. every thing green like harvest. I hope we wont stay hear much longer but don't (know) where we will go to. I must close. We have moved up hear. I suppose on the account of water. G.H. Burns

J.L Burns

Miss Caroline you will hear from me some of these Days.

Building the Federal Ranks for the Campaign

During these early months of 1863, Union troops continued to be moved along the Mississippi to Grant's army. James Ritter's 29th Illinois proceeded through Memphis as part of this troop buildup. The opening of the letter had several holes from insects making it difficult to completely comprehend but he speaks of the loss of his wife and loneliness.

Memphis _____ **March 22nd, 1863**

    Dear Father and mother I take this kind pleasure of wrighting you a few lines to let you know that I am still living yet and thank God that _____ I hope when this _____ it may find you _____ am still living _____ yet and standing guard every day. I have been reduced to ranks since I hand my rate to _____ I can't tell when I will get to come home. We have not got our money yet but as soon as I get my money I will come. I think I will come between know and the last of May. That time certain if I live. I am getting well fast. I want you to save me some of them peaches that my aunt Mollie dried last _____ to eate. Some _____ bed clothes _____had Mollie's left here on the warff boat at metropolis where she started down the river its first time. I don't expect you can get them at all. I want you to get my Red trunk at Mrs. Amidans at Camp Massag where I and Mollie staid. I have got a pare of shasey (?) there and several other things. Call for Mr. Riters things and she will let you have them. if you have not got them tell the old Man that I am glad to think that he is willing to take up Mollie but tell him she is too much trouble. I am satisfied where she is. Just let her stay. She is as well of(f) there as she would (be) any where. ___ tell old Jess Simpson that I will remember him for his kindness towards helping bury my wife. I believe I have said about all I have to say at present. Rite soon and let me hear from you all soon. I want all the children to rite to me. It does me a great deal of good to hear from you all for I feel lonsom by myself. Nothing more at present. I remain your affectionate son until death.

    James A. Riter

    To father and Mother

    Wm A Johnson and Elizabeth Johnson

Lieutenant Seth Hall, 8th Iowa Infantry, wrote a detailed letter to his wife describing their descent of the Mississippi from Iowa to Millikens Bend. On the 10th of April he described their passage as well as a "man overboard" incident and their stops along the way including his thoughts on the City of Memphis.

Adrift aboard the boat John H. Dickey some 60 miles South of Memphis Aprile 10th /63

Dear Wife

    I am well & the entire 8th Regt. Is enjoying excellent health. Our Union Brigade left Davenport Sunday noon March the 29th. our Co. was quartered on the hurican deck. the boat being large we were not crowded. we at that time was about 800. we had a good crowd present on that morning to see us quit the shores of Old Iowa. Some time near 4 Oclock one of our men got rocked overboard he fell off at the fore end of the boat & passed between the boat & a barge which was lashed to its side until he came to the wheel house wher he knew he would be dashed to peases if he did not dive under it so he made the atemped & by raising a little too soon one of the wheel paddles struck him on the back of the head giving him a 3rd blows, he however kept the presence of mind & raised again in the 3rd heaveing of the waves in the rear of the wheel. he then got his head out of water for the first time to do him aney good & he keped it out. The boat was going at such spead that he was near ½ mile back when the men reached him with a sciff which was don with as much rapidity as men could under the screams & the excitement which prevailed. he was rescued & being a good swimmer was all that saved him. we then passed along quiet & were all enjoying ourselves very well until 12 O'clock Monday night. (At that) time their was quite a storm arose blowing hats, caps & every thing that was loose at one end over-board Some of the boys declair the wind blew the filled out of their shirts I found my cap at the oposet end of the boat & lodged down on the 2nd deck on gard. we arrived at St. Louis about sun up. it was 12 a m before we got to Benton Barracks. we were marched to Geddis's head Quarters wher he separated us from the Union Brigade. Lieut. Lewis was sent immediately to take Comd. of us. Our prisoner boys wer sent to join us April the 1st. Col Geddes ordered an election of officers in our Co. which resulted as follows 1st Lieut. Irwin was elected Captain myself 1st Lieut & J.F. Sturdivent 2nd Lieut the 2nd 3, 4, & 5 of the month we wer busey drawing armes cooking utensals & c for traveling. At 3 Oclock on the 6th our Regt. Was formed & we marched to the boat named <u>Nebraska.</u> we wer all aboard & ready at 5 Oclock & started. we arrived & stoped a short time at Cape <u>Gereadau</u> at 3 Oclock P.M. of the 7th and arrived at Cairo at 6 Oclock same evening remained their for 2 hours & then started on passed Island no <u>10</u> some time in the night ariveing at New Madrid next morning at sun up on the morning of the 8th. our run was then continued & we arrived at Ft Pillow 3 Oclock P.M. same day and arrived at Memphis at 10 Oclock that night in front of the building Aprile 8th. prisoners wer put in when first run their from Shiloh & just 12 months from the time the Rebbels wer housing them their. We then lay their all night all next day & night again Leaveing Memphis at 9 Oclock on the morning of the 10th . during this time we got to go out in the city & see it. we went & seen Jackson's monument which was worth seeing. besides the City is large. a butiful location & is a place of the very largest & best of buildings. every thing seamed to be alive to the interest of the sucksess of our forces & the rumble of business never seaseed its <u>echo.</u> the square wher Jackson's monument is is as large as our Court House square in Sigourney & fensed with Iron. the ground is all a thick bluegrass sod except the walks. the square is full of large trees & evergreens of the most admirable kind & pet squireles playing on the branches of the

—————————

(remainder of the letter missing)

In his continuing movement towards the Vicksburg front, Henry Ellsworth reported home upon arriving at Millikens Bend, a now growing base on the Louisiana side of the river north of Vicksburg. The encampment was on the land of a beautiful plantation and the Union troops were enjoying their springtime stay there.

April 11th 1863

     Dear Mother, I have taken the pleasure of writing to you to inform you that I have received the papers and letters that you sent to me. We have been running about from this place to another for the last three months. We are in camp now. It is a very nice place to camp. The weather is very warm. The trees have been leaved out for a long time. I never had better health in my life. I should like to come home very much and see the folks. It will be a long time before I can.

     Charles West is but very short distance from hear. He is well and the rest of the boys that went with him. There was five gunboats went down by Vicksburg. There was 500 shots fired at them but did not hurt them. There was but one man killed. I think that they will have a fight soon. I saw Morgan Jenkins the other day. He is well. He is first Lieut. I have been paid off. I have got plenty of money but there is no way to send it home. We will get paid off again in to or three days. The express office is expected hear in a few days. I don't know how soon.

     I have got plenty off postage stamps. I bought them in Memphis. I have plenty off every things now. If I can get a chance to send my over coat home I shall do it. It is a great deal of trouble in the hot weather. I cannot think off much more to write. I will bring my letter to a close. Please give my love to all and write soon.

     H. A. Ellsworth

On April 18th, 1863 Robert Hamilton, a true romantic, and his 33rd Illiinois Infantry were also encamped at Millikens Bend. His highly descriptive letter to his wife is as follows. Note that the actual battle of Raymond did not occur until later in May, so his report here is most likely based on rumor.

Camp in the Field
Millikens Bend, So A.
Saturday April 18th 1863

My Dearest and
 Ever Loved Kate:

 We embarked on the Steamer "City Belle" the same that conveyed me from Paducah to Pittsburg Landing last year – Yesterday a little after noon, and a few minutes afterward she was gracefully steaming down the river. The weather was clear and beautiful and from the deck of the noble Steamer has had a fine view of the scenery of the lower Mississippi, and is remarkable for nothing save its monotony and romanticness. The banks are lined by a continuation of dense cottonwood thickets except where it is interrupted by large and numerous plantations, which are nice. Either completely submerged in the water or overgrown with rank weeds. They are all with hardly an exception deserted by the planters and their retinues of colored servants, save a few aged and infirm slaves. I have not seen an acre of cultivated land this year – no appearances of any produce from the soil in this region, the present season. On our way here we met from 15 to 20 transports upward bound – many had been used in the Yazoo Pass Expedition and were very near "used up". The Chimnies scape pipes, balustrades, funel work etc. was torn completely off. They presented a most forlorn and dilapidated appearance from their contact with the overhanging trees while navigating the narrow bayous creeks and other inlets to the Yazoo. That entire expedition has arrived here. The firing we heard night before last – 16th – was caused by our gunboats running the blockade at Vicksburg, as we had surmised. Seven or eight gunboats with two transports succeeded in running past without any material injury. One transport the "Henry Clay" being disabled was set on fire by her crew and abandoned. The gunboats ran on the side of the river next to the batteries, while the transports kept on the opposite side. Thus the gunboats attacked the attention of the batteries while the steamers passed unmolested. All the troops have left here, except Logan's, Burnby's & Ross's Division and gone to Richmond, a small village twelve miles from here, and thence they are going to Carthage opposite to Warrenton. It is the intention to cross the river there and go to the rear of Vicksburg. The transports that run the blockade are to be used as ferry boats.

It is rumored that a heavy skirmish occurred between a small force of our troops & the Secesh at or near Richmond a few days ago (not the Reb Capital) 7 that our force captured near 2000 of the enemy. The 47th Ohio had their Col. Killed, so reported. That is the Regt. Isreal Brown is in. We can learn nothing definite about the skirmish – perhaps it is a groundless rumor. (Our men are hopeful as to the result here. It is believed to be Grant's object to cut the rebels supplies compel them to come out of their fortifications & give us battle. By the Grace of God we hope to capture the entire force of rebels in tow. It may be months before a battle is fought. It may be but a few days. We can tell nothing about it.

Now for a brief description of our encampment. Millikens Bend is eight miles above Young's Point and from twelve to sixteen above Vicksburg by the river. The direction of the river is east there. We are encamped in a large plantation ¼ of a mile south of the river. The grounds are flat and level, but dry at present. The scenery as from us viewed from camp although possessed of nothing remarkable is interesting. To our north flows the Majestic Mississippi in sluggish and silent grandness. Beyond is a heavy verdant slightly undulating fringe of cottonwood which being reflected in the bright mirror like surface is really an object of beauty. The levee is lined with steamers for two or three miles. To our East south and west a continual line of tents far as the eye can reach. To our south is the broad level plantation relieved in the distance by a dense, dark green forest of cypresses and other timber & princely residence surrounded by a grove of rare and beautiful shade trees lies to our N.W. The stately China tree now covered with gorgeous clusters of modest purple lilac like blossoms. The magnificent magnolia with its brilliant glistening green leaves, the long slender drooping branches of the weeping willow, and hundreds of other varieties of ornamental trees contribute their part toward adorning as well as refreshing and rendering the place comfortable. The yard is completely overshadowed by the trees & is beautifully laid out in refreshing frescades, which are skirted of a large variety of beautiful and fragrant flowers. Oh *what delightful walks for lovers! The scene is <u>filled</u> with poetry. The flowers, the trees, the carpet of verdure, the beautiful birds of sweetest song and even the <u>very air</u> perfumed by the thousand flowers <u>all</u> conspire to make the lover enthusiastic. In imagination I walk with you, hand in hand, repeating how well I love you, sport with you, breathe out my soul in love to you. Enjoy your tender caresses, and endearing smiles, in the midst of the rapturous scenes. Would to God it were <u>reality.</u> I can not admire any thing of beauty or sublimity without <u>you are in the foreground.</u> Like an angel you stand prominent in my imagination when any elevating or transporting scene passes in review before me. You even accompany me. I sigh to have you <u>in reality</u> accompany me. The poetry of the objects which may surround me would be augmented ten fold, were they viewed in concert with you. Dearest Kate: I love you passionately and <u>truly.</u> "<u>God bless</u> you Dearest. I remain in all truth Your Ever Loving, Faithful & Devoted Husband. Robert*

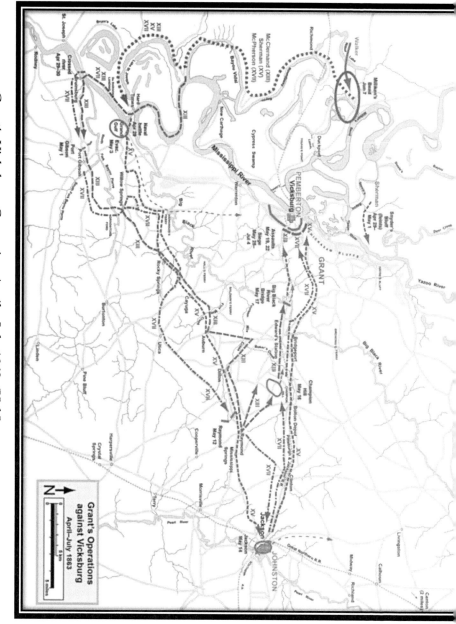

Grant's Vicksburg Campaign April – July 1863 (Hal Jespersen www.cwmaps.com)

The Great Campaign for the Capture of Vicksburg

A Winning Strategy

Grant intended to move three Corps of infantry down the West Bank of the Mississippi and cross the river well below the city and attack from the south. Once he left the river landing, Grant would be leaving his lines of communications behind and his army would subsist off the land as he approached the fortress city. He also knew that he would have to lead this advance personally.

The plan was full of risk. Grant's initial force of 33,000 would potentially face Pemberton's entire force of nearly 60,000 at the river crossing and the available transports could carry no more than 10,000 per crossing. If Pemberton was there waiting for him it would spell disaster.

The first step was to move his army and its supplies 40 miles south of their Millikens Bend base to New Carthage, Louisiana, on the western bank of the Mississippi. Spring rains had left the roads wet with deep mud making it nearly impossible to move supplies, so Grant concluded to move supplies via Porter's fleet by running the batteries at Vicksburg under cover of darkness.

Robert Hamilton's 33 Illinois was part of the troops ordered to corduroy roads along the path southward on the Louisiana side of the river through the bayous. Again he describes the countryside in great detail as well as one of Porter's preparations to run the batteries at Vicksburg.

Camp in the Woods
Canal Bayou, Loa.
Tuesday April 21st 1863

My Dearest,
My own Sweetest Wife:

I embrace the first leisure moment since last Sabbath of writing you to let you know _where_ & _how_ we are. Last _Sabbath_ we received orders at Millikens Bend to get ready with two days rations for a march. We were ordered to leave all our tents & take mothing with us except what was absolutely necessary. A little after noon our Regt. & the 20th Ohio started for _Somewhere._ After going about six miles in a southerly direction we were ordered to hault & stack arms. Soon as we had rested a little we were ordered to carry rails from some fences near us to a road a few hundred yards off for the purpose of making "corduroy". Since then we have been corduroying a military road running from Millikens Bend to Richmond. The country is a vast plain & extremely level. With the exception of large plantations it is densely wooded. A thick growth of large trees & nearly every tree covered with a perfect mat of vines, almost excludes the sunlight. It is emphatically a "_deep tangled wildwood._"

Canal Bayou is a deep narrow sluggish stream, about midway between Millikens Bend and Richmond. I do not know from what its name is derived unless it is from its slow, sluggish current and from a slight level on one side resembling the tow path of a canal. The water in it is very highly colored. It looks just like water that runs from a barnyard or a manure hill. It abounds in mammoth bull frogs, water moccasins, mud turtles and alligators.

Immense plantations of unsurpassed fertility are around us, but they are now numbered with the waste places of the Earth. The Scriptural order of things reversed. "Instead of the fir tree shall come up the thorn, instead of the myrtle tree shall come up the brier." We have seen some hedges of _rose bushes._ They were so dense that a bird could not go through them. They are now out on full blooms & of course present a most beautiful appearance.

Numerous Mounds are scattered over the surface of the country, embracing about 1/8 of an acre and from ten to fifteen feet high.   All concur in saying they are artificial, but no one conjectures or seems to know for what purpose they were built. It is my opinion they were thrown up many centuries ago by the aborigines, and was a place of resort and safety at seasons when the Mississippi overflowed the whole region. They were built centuries before an era was discovered for some are covered with large forest & trees.

Oh, Kate, you ought to see the <u>agricultural implements</u> that are used in Dixie. It is questionable whether it would be a violation of the second commandment to worship them or not. They are not the likeness of <u>anything.</u> Such plows, harrows, hoes you never saw. The only worries to me is that the soil can be cultivated <u>at all</u> by such utensils. It is an utter impossibility for me to give you anything like a lucid description of them. They are "nondescripts" in the full sense of the word.

James Moore has been assigned 1st Lieut. Of Co "G" 9th Lu Regt. (African) and J. A. Forsythe is orderly of the same Co. Shaw of Co "F" is Capt and Luclese of Co. "I" is 2nd Lieut. of the same Co. They are out to day recruiting. They will soon fill up their Co. and go to Island No. 10 where they are to be stationed, rendezvous soon as the Regt. is organized.

<u>Several transports</u> are preparing to run the blockade at Vicksburg soon. They are putting two rows of cotton bales around the boilers and machinery of the steamers and each one (boat) is to be protected by barges laden with hay bales. Com Davis called for volunteers from McPhersons Corps to go on the boats as firemen & He only recruited about seventy five men, but neads all of McPhersons Corps <u>Volunteered</u> to undertake the hazardous enterprise. It is thought they will undertake to pass tonight.

<u>Heavy Cannonading</u> was heard south east of us yesterday. Do not know the cause of it. It was <u>rumored</u> that about 8000 troops from Texas & Arkansas marched across the country to reinforce the Enemy at Vicksburg but Gen. McClernand had surrounded them & was to open on them yesterday. <u>Perhaps</u> it was so, But I think it doubtful.

The advance of our army is at Carthage – a few miles below Vicksburg. A sufficient number will be there in a day or two, to cross over and march to the rear of the "Gibraltar of the West." We hear today that our fleet
…balance of letter missing.

Porter actually made his first passage the night of April 16th. Despite a furious barrage he succeeded with minimal loss. This and the success of subsequent passages assured initial supplies for the campaign could now be counted upon.

Vicksburg waterfront as it would have appeared in daylight when Porter ran the gauntlet. (Library of Congress)

Two days after his initial letter from this period, Hamilton writes another highly descriptive letter to his "own Sweetest Wife" Kate. His regiment is still occupied with corduroying roads. While the work is hard, remaining in this location those additional days affords him the opportunity to see General Grant, the Governor of Illinois and General McClernand's wife all pass through on their way to Carthage.

Camped in the Woods
Canal Bayou Lou.
Thursday, April 23rd 1863

My Dearly Loved

     My own Sweetest Kate:

          You little know how rejoiced I was yesterday on receiving your kind and loving missive of the 12th Inst. I was pained to learn that your jaw had swollen & caused you so much suffering, in consequence of your unfortunate and unsuccessful attempt to have your teeth extracted. My solicitude has somewhat diminished since the recipt of yours of the 12th informing me of that the pain had in a great measure subsided and that you expected soon to muster up courage enough to have the dentist make another trial. Hope you may be more successful the next time. You seem to think my presence would inspire you with greater courage. Perhaps so But I would rather endure the infliction myself then see you suffering from the painful operation. Indeed I would have been glad to eat of the cherries you spoke of. The Sutlers have little pint cans of fresh cherries, peaches and other fruits which they sell for one dollar apiece. They are rather too expensive a luxury for me. Don't you think so? I hope you may have plenty of "vegetable oysters" when I return home, but I would like extremely well to get home long before they will have time to Mature. Yes, I wish I had some of the nice apples you have. The sutlers sell little rotten apples about the size of walnuts for five cents apiece. I have nothing of great interest to write you, but as always take great delight in writing to you, and I always do write when I have an opportunity. John Gilmore said to me the other day, "Bob it's a good thing you got a wife to write to." Why? Said I. "Because," he replied "You occupy all your spare time in writing to her and don't get into bad habits." I think he was about right. The greater part of my spare time is occupied in writing letters& (when I can get books or papers) in reading.

We are still bivouacking at Canal Bayou. We have been at work, ever since last Sabbath, on the roads between here and Richmond. Our Regt has made a good corduroy road about two miles in distance through the woods. Do not know how long we will remain here to "work the roads". I think we have "worked out" our "poll tax" and "Uncle Sam" should give us "clear receipt" for this year. Seven Transports attempted to "run the blockade" at Vicksburg last night. Six got by without receiving any material injury.

One – Tigress sunk soon after passing the batteries. *Col. Shedd went within four miles of the "Burg" & saw the spouts of flame from the cannon of the batteries. A great many officers went down to witness the spectacle. The cannonading commenced about midnight & lasted an hour and a half or two hours. Heavens! What a roar they made! The whole earth seemed to be shaken! These boats, that passed are to be used to ferry our troops across from Carthage to Warrenton or Grand Guld. Thence our men will go to the rear of Vicksburg and cut off all its communication with the rest of the world. Our troops are sanguine of success.*

It is reported, and generally credited, that Gen. McClernand has a Secesh force of 8,000 or 10,000 "hemmed in" on this side of the river a few miles below Carthage. Gen. Osterhaus Division started out in the advance yesterday to capture them. He was skirmishing with them nearly all day. They expected to open on them to day or to night with artillery. We heard a few reports of artillery this morning in that direction.

Gen. Grant & Gov. Yates passed here to day. They stopped here and took a lunch. I was not aware that it was the Governor who was with Gen. Grant, so I paid no attention to him. He expressed his dlight at seeing the Illinois boys and to see them looking so hearty. Gov. Lad of Ohio is also in these parts, somewhere looking to the interests of the "Buckeyes". It is thought they are here, in anticipation of a battle, to attend to the sending of the wounded to the hospitals of their respective states.

Mrs. Gen. McClernand passed us while at work on the road last Tuesday, on the way to her husband at Carthage. She is quite young & beautiful. She is a daughter of Old Quartermaster Dunlap & a sister to the Gen's first wife, also a sister of Lieut. Col. Dunlap of the 29th Ill. Regt. You have seen them at Cairo. A lot of our boys were in the bayou at the roadside when she passed. "They were rafting rails across & swimming & nude as our first parents in the garden of Innocence. She could & perhaps did see more than a dozen of Emaline's Scarecrows. I think she'll live over it!

We have good times foraging here. Each Co. details a couple every day to get fresh beef, pork, mutton & etc. They go to some plantation get what they want then press a nigger, mule and cart to haul the spoils to camp. To day John Cannons & John G Clark went off on a foraging expedition. Afternoon they returned conducting an old badly seared nigger riding the poorest most miserable blind mule you ever saw hitched to an old screaking cart, that has not been greased since the revolutionary war, with three little slab-sided shoats of "razor breed" so poor they had to lean against the fence to squeal. They assumed quite an air of triumph and satisfaction with their success and strategy!

Jo. Stanley, of Co "C" who was taken prisoner at Abbeville last winter, while on picket with John Gilmore and Russ Paxton has been exchanged and is in New Orleans, waiting a chance to get to the Regt. Capt. Now Major Wilson rec'd a letter from him recently, with the above information.

One Brigade of Gen'l. Quinby's Division passed through here to day on its way to Carthagee. A very strong force will be sent there as rapidly as possible. The weather is excellent for operations, but rather warm for comfort. My health is very good & since I quit chewing tobacco I am getting fat! Occasionally have to take a chew to prevent castiveness. Dunk is at Millikens Bend taking care of our tent & etc. God Bless you. Your loving & constant Husband, Robert.

By the 24th of April the 33 Illinois had moved further south and was helping unload supplies from transports that had run past the batteries at Vicksburg. Another member of the 33rd, Judson Gill, wrote to his wife of this experience. Unfortunately part of this letter has been lost to time but still provides excellent insights to the event.

Apr 24th 1863

Dear Sophi –

We are about 30 miles below Vicksburg on the river. Our camp or another stopping place is on the plantation of Judge Perkins now a member of the rebel congress. You probably have heard in this through the papers of the running of the Vicksburg blockade by river of our gun boats and seven transports. Two transports, The "Henry Coley" and the "Tigress" were sunk. The "Empire City" was disabled and floated down and last night I helped to unload her. She was loaded with forage and rations. Her pilot a brave fellow from the 32nd Sea who volunteered for the occasion was mortally wounded in the bowels by a fragment of shell that burst in one of the smokestacks. I saw him die yesterday. The Benton – flag ship – received a few shot in the side by a 120 pounder. It passed through her iron skin 4 ½ inches thick and entered about a foot into the …

(missing content)

But then – look out. Never mind, even, I'll bring you a shelter tent or a rubber blanket so you'll have "where to bag your head." I heard this morning that the 22nd Iowans were to send out a mail at noon so I came down to the bank of that grand old humbug Mrs. Sippi where our field desk had been left by the raft and where I am now seated under the shade of a small tree writing a sonett to the Little Maden to send with their mail. I expect we will get a mail occasionally and I will write as often as I can find opportunity to write and mail. Nelse is in good health and sends his compliments. Remember me to all.

Yours forever

Jud

George Deal's 20th Ohio had moved forward to Millikens Bend at this point. Two other regiments of his brigade had been sent further south to build roads for the army moving through the wetlands to the point where it would cross to the Vicksburg side of the river. His "ghost writer", H. J. Souder, warns Deal's wife to stop sending discouraging letters to him at the front. Inaccuracy regarding numbers of troops for both combatant forces abound.

Camp near Milikenes Bend, Louisiana
April the 20th, 1863

My Dear Wife,

 I again take the pen to write you no…. (where) we was where we are and how we are. I am well and …. What is put. I think all of the boys is well as far as I know that is here. I am sorry to tell you that I am close to Vicksburg and expect a big fight soon. We are in Louisiana on the banks of the Mississippi river. The 20th regiment and the 30th Illinois and the 18th Ohio has gone or most all gone to build roads or cut a road through so we can get at Vicksburg. Some say our troops has got eighteen or twenty thousand surrounded on this side of the river. If that be so, we will have them soon or they will have us but it is impossible for them to take us for we has one hundred or one hundred and fifty thousand here.

 I received your letter a few days ago and it was wrote on the 4th of April. I was glad to hear from you and was glad to hear you was well and the rest also, but you said you there was to be a draft here. All I do hope is that it will fetch out some of the butternuts in the field. I think it will bring them to limerick or limber or some other way so I do hope the draft will come and fetch some of the north rebels. You said you was afraid I wasn't going to come home in the fall. It may not be the case but if I can I will. That is if as the war may be over before fall. I hope it will be but it don't look like it now but I don't think they will hold out much longer nor I don't think they can much longer.

 You stated that they was a going to tear down the house over me. If they do, I don't think anymore of them then rebels and I think if they can't get me a house for you to live in, I think they haven't much but I think that they will before they let you suffer. You stay there till you get somewhere to live. You wrote something about my step-mother. I am glad to here she was well but sorrow to here papa's been sick (all) winter. I hope he is well by this time.

You stated something about George Fowler had a team. I am glad he has got a team. You wrote some verses. I hain't good to making verses but I think the dove will come to the nest and to your arms for I no I want to be with you as much as you do with me. Now don't go on and fret about me for as long as I keep my health, I can do my duty I think so or more to. Now don't fret about me for I will come home just as soon as I can.

Now I, H. J. Souder, will right a little advise to you and that is I don't think it is advisable for you to write any discouraging letters to him for fear is a soldier gets discouraged it is ten chance to one if he ever gets over it. Now don't write to him for to desert nor to run off or to come home any soon than I can. I will come home just as soon as I can that is sure but I hope I can come home on a furlough in the fall but it is doubtful if wee or I get to come home then. George he is a bully for cocks or any other man or woman and so am I so I must quit scribbling to you in such foolishness. I will draw this letter to a close so write soon and I will write for him again soon but you musn't get out… with me not writing to you for I have to get my letters wrote for me and you know I can't get on€ wrote every time when I want to but I will write for George every chance I get. I am a cooking for 28 men and that is all I want to do but I will write as often as I can for him. I wrote three letters today and I hain't tired yet so I must quite for this time.

Direct your letters to Milikenes Bend, Louisiana, 20th Ohio regiment, Company K, in the care of Capt. Kaga vis Memphis OVI and it will come alright to me. So no more at this time but remember I am you friend and your husband till death. So good by Sarah.

Deceit as a Tactic for Success

To assure success Grant needed to keep Pemberton and Johnston confused and off balance so they could not consolidate their forces against him. He designed three diversions at this point to accomplish this objective while landing his main force at Grand Gulf on the same side of the river as Vicksburg.

One division was sent to demonstrate towards Greenville, Mississippi 100 miles above Vicksburg. Another division of Major General James McPherson's Corps was dispatched to join Sherman at Young's Point in order to keep Confederate attention fixed there.

The most important feint was performed by a large cavalry raid lead by Colonel Benjamin Grierson. From his base in Lagrange, Tennessee, just north of the Mississippi state line, Grierson conducted a raid that covered 600 miles in 16 days ending in Union controlled Baton Rouge, Louisiana the first week of May. In route he had destroyed railroad tracks on all three of the main railroads in Mississippi, while destroying immense amounts of Confederate supplies. However, his most important accomplishment was that he had occupied almost all of General Pemberton's attention. This drew as many as 20,000 Rebel troops away from the river in an attempt to hunt Grierson down and end his spree of destruction. Grant called it one of the most brilliant cavalry actions of the war.

As these diversions were beginning to unfold, on the Confederate side of the river John Douthit (52nd Georgia) was settled into the humdrum duty of garrisoning the works with no expectation for a fight any time soon.

Vicksburg Miss   *April the 16th 1863*

Dear Companion

I this morning take my pen in hand to let you know that I am in common health at this time hoping these lines will come to hand and find you all well. I have nothing new to write you at this time. I received two letters from you not very long since which I wrote. Glad to hear from you. There is no prospect of fighting here nor of our leaving here that I know of. The weather is very warm here when it is dry and when it is raining tolerable cool. If you see Harriett tell her that Davis is not very stout. If the cow that Harriett has will do her any good let her keep her. that is if you do not need her yourself. So do the best you can until this cruel war ends. So nothing more at present only remains your husband until death.

John M. Douthit.

Confederate Defensive Works to the east of Vicksburg (Library of Congress)

George Burns of the 34th Georgia remained oblivious to the Union plans as well. He acknowledged that they had moved from the opposite side of the river in a letter to his wife of April 17th. He also talked about gunboats and transports running past the batteries at night but he still had no idea of what lay ahead. He is discouraged that his unit is not being ordered back to Tennessee where living conditions were much better.

Vicksburg April 17th 1863

My Dear wife I can inform you that I am well as to health. I have been troubled for some days with Rhemmatism in my limbs so at times I can hardly walk. I hope this will find you all well. I was highly set up with the hope of going back to Tennessee but my hopes are all gone. They have sent Thousands of other troops off from hear and others are ordered but nothing said about us going. Vaughns brigaid was ordered to Tenn and yesterday then the order was countermanded. The yanks have mostly left hear. Last night about 12 o'clock our batteries commensed fireing and such a roar I never heard. It lasted 2 hours. 8 boats 6 gunboats and 2 transports went down past in spite of them. We burnt one and disabled 2 or 3 others. All is quiet this morning. The boats went on down the river.

I want to come home worse than I ever did in my life but alas there is no chance. I look in the future. I see no glimmer of a hope for peace. There is no chances for furlows. Oh the long – long months. How slow they will wear away this summer. I dream of being at home walking about with you and leading my sweet little babe by the hand and her jabbering to me. I awake only for new troubles. I was dreaming this last knight when the big guns waked me up. I want to see you all so bad but I try to be as cheerful as possible. I wish you to be the same. I have got no letter from you since I got my trunk of provision. I had the best mess the other day. I went to town and got me a dozen eggs and some buttermilk. I had boiled eggs butter and milk. You ought to have seen me eat them shore. I send you a present in this letter. A fine comb. It was made in our regiment. If you get this keep it till I come home if I ever get home. I paid 50 cents for this. Tell mother I will send her one as soon as I can get one. I would have sent her one to day but he had more but this finished off. I woul have sent you one worth one dollar but he had non finished off. We will get 4 dollars per month more than we have been getting. I will get 16 dollars per month. We will draw in a day or two for two months. I will send part of it home if I get a chance. I will close. Write often to me. I remain your loving husband. G H Burns

To Mrs. Nancy Burns.

I did not close this till the mail come to day thinking I would get a letter but none come. I have got nearly fat on your goodies. God bless you. Long may you live to misiter to the poor soldier. Never mistreat one as long as you live. G H Burns

Burns writes to Nancy on the 22nd that they are moving soon, perhaps to Grand Gulf, but he hopes to Tennessee. The rank and file are still unaware of Grant's intentions at this point.

Vicksburg Miss

Apr 22th 1863

Dear wife I am well at present. All to my joints. They are better. I read your kind letter which was mailed the 12th. I read one The same day from Milly and Sarah Wilson. I was glad to hear from you all one time more. I sent you twenty dollars yesterday. Sergeant John Hopper was sending some home to his wife at Tilton and I thought it would be a safe plan to send it with him as the man was going strait There. You go or send to his wife in Tilton and get it. I just drawed 24 dollars this time. I will draw 40 in a week or two and I will send you some more. I wont start money home from hear by mail. We will leave hear in a few days somewhere but I cant find out where. We are going some think we will go to Grand Gulf 80 miles down The River. Some thinks we will go to Tennessee. I hope we will come back to Tenn. Still write to this place if we move I will write where we are gone. Times are hard hear. Tobacco is worth 2 dollars per plug. I could sell that you sent me for a dollar per plug but I would not take 10 dollars for it. I don't kneed any clothing but socks and I can make out without them a while yet.

I send you a song ballad sung in the Tune of ..O heaven sweet heaven home of the blessed. I long to be there and its glories to shear and lean on my saviors breast.

I think it pretty. You can sing it to the baby. I send you some other little presents. You can do what you please with them. I did not mean for you not to go to Tennessee. I want you to go and see your folks but not move there. If ever I get back in one or two hundred miles of home you shall come to me if you want to have. I must close. Write. I get but few of your letter but still write. Your loving husband   *G H Burns to Nancy Burns*

Keeping the Enemy Guessing

So far everything was working in his favor but Grant had one more deception to play in order to keep Pemberton in the dark as long as possible. Pemberton was aware of Grant's force across the river from Grand Gulf and had ordered reinforcements from Vicksburg to move in that direction. To counter, Grant ordered Sherman to move a strong body of troops north of the city on April 29th. Sherman loaded 10 regiments that were still across the river from Vicksburg upon transports and moved across the river with one final feint against the city's garrison. Making as much of a display as possible, his demonstration north of the city duly impressed General Stevenson who was in command of the immediate defenses of the city. Stevenson sent an urgent request to Pemberton for reinforcements as he was positive this was the main attack force.

It worked. Pemberton recalled the forces he had just sent south to help thwart any crossing at Grand Gulf. This weakened both his forces in the vicinity of Grand Gulf while exhausting the troops compelled to make two forced marches, coming from and then going back to the Vicksburg defenses.

John Douthit confirmed in his letter of May 2nd, 1863 that Grant indeed had the enemy confused. The 52nd Georgia had been moved up and down the defensive line and they were preparing for attacks from the north, south and center as far as he could tell.

May the 2nd 1863

Vicksburg Miss

Dear Companion,

I write you a few lines to let you know that I am still alive and in common health hoping these lines will come safe to hand and find you all well. I started a few lines to you and sent it out by Lieut. McClure a few days ago. The rail road is torn up so the mail don't go out nor come in. Consequently we have had no mail in several days and have not written any letters for some time which will account for your getting no mail. There is considerable excitement here at this time. There was some fighting below here yesterday in which we got the best of it. We are expecting to leave here this evening or in the morning to go below though we may not go. We just got in this morning from above. We went up five or six miles above Vicksburg night before last. It was reported the Enemy was landing up there. It is thought here they will attact us both above and below and in the center all at the same time. And if they do we may have some tolerable hot work to do. I have subscribed for a news paper printed at this place which if you get it regular will give you most of the news about this place. I will send this by the hand of Wm. Blalock. I will also send you fifty dollars in it which you will use to the best advantage you can. I will Say to you do the Best you can with your stock. The Lord only knows whether I will ever live to get home or not but I shall live in hopes so as long as I live at all. Tell Harriett that Davis is in common health. He is getting a good deal stouter than he has been. I think he will get stout enough to make every (a very) good soldier all without it is on long marches. I don't think he will s(t)and a hard march. Charley Henson is done better than he has been.

Write to me when these lines come to hand and let me know how you are getting along and let me know whether you get the money or not. Give my best respects to all inquiring for me. I think the train will be running through in a few days so we can get our mail. ....

105

On May 6th, Sargent Douthit wrote his last letter home. He was taken as a captive later, during the surrender of Vicksburg on July 4th and died in a prisoner hospital in New Orleans on July 23rd.

May the 6th 1863
Vicksburg Miss

Dear Companion I write you again to let you know that I am still alive and in common health at this time hoping these lines will find you all well. I have nothing very strange to write you at this time. I received a letter from you yesterday bearing date of April the 18th which I was glad to receive as it was the first that I had received for several days though I could not expect letters to come when there was no mail. The mail was stoped on account of the rail road being torn up. You stated that you had not heard from me in some time. I wrote regular as long as the mail went through and sent a few lines by LIeut McClure to be mailed at Atlanta. I started you a letter with fifty dollars in it by Wm. Blalock two or three days ago. The Regiment left here day before yesterday. They are now ten miles below here at Warrenton. I did not feel very stout and the doctor said I had better not go so I am still here but think I will go to the Regiment tomorrow or next day. As for war news there is plenty here but I suppose you can hear plenty of that without my writing any though you may listen for a big fight from this place before long or in this country. So nothing more only remains your husband until death. John M. Douthit.

Write soon and often

Frank Cassidy, 26th Iowa Volunteer Infantry, wrote home to his parents on May 2nd. In a letter full of questions regarding the total lack of communication he has had from his family he mentions the results of Sherman's feint north of Vicksburg on the 29th. The news, as we have often seen, is incorrect as far as the outcome was concerned. This is the only surviving letter from Cassidy during the Vicksburg campaign. He was later killed on August 9th, 1864 near Atlanta.

"*Millikines Bend Lousianna*
May the 2 1863,

Dear Father and Mother
   I once more take my pen in hand to write a few lines to you to let you know that I am well hoping if these few lines ever reach you they will find you all enjoying that inestimable blessing health. Yesterday was my birthday and I had a very lonesome time. The weather is warmer down here now than it is in Iowa on the 4th of July. We have moved 12 miles to a place called Millikens bend, we have a very pleasant location on the river bank 25 miles from Vicksburg. Our forces have gained haines bluff with a heavy loss of men, the Rebbles lost but a few. They are a fighting at the back (of) Vicksburg and up the yazoo for the last three days. There is a boat load of wounded come up the river this morning. We are under marching orders but where to I do not know. I have not received a letter from home since the first of April and this is the 10th letter from me to write since I got one. I wrote to Jim Hirwan and 6 home and got no answer. I don't blame Jim for not writing because I suppose he is buisy but I don't think Margaret is so buisy but what she can write. I know if Mag has not changed her ways greatly she has plenty of time to write.

        I sent twenty six dollars home with Patrick Dempsey and I have not heard from him or the money since he left here with Capt. Heavey. They started from here the 20th of March. Chris and me sent our overcoats home. we sent them along with James Mendermotte things. He sent them to his brother that lives in Center Grove. He was to leave them in Charlotte. There was a likeness rolled up in my coat if you did not get them you go after them. Enquire for Thomas Mendermotte. I am going to send 10 dollars home the first chance I get. If anybody going up I want you to write as soon as you get this letter and let me know if you got my bounty and if you got the money that I sent with Pat Dempsey. as soon as I can hear from this letter I will send you ten dollars more. Well I guess I have told you all the news that I can think of. John Durman is dead. He died in St. Louis. The rest of the boys is well.

Christopher Kirwann has been sick but is getting better, Mike McLoughlin is in Memphis, Thomas Coaty is gone up the river.

I must now bring my letter to a close by sending you all my best respect and I send a Jolly shake hands to Linnarse.

Francis

Cassidy   *Good bye for a*
while   Write soon.

Crossing the River

The same day (April 29th) as Sherman's demonstration above Vicksburg, Porter began the naval bombardment of Grand Gulf. His objective was to silence its guns and enable McClernand's XIII Corps to land on the east bank of the river. Unfortunately, after several hours of shelling it was clear that Porter's fleet would not subdue the enemy, so Grant concluded to find another landing spot that would allow his force to capture Grand Gulf from the rear. Based on intelligence provided from a captured slave, McClernand's troops were transported approximately 8 miles further south where they disembarked, unopposed, the next day at Bruinsburg.

The only route to Grand Gulf from Bruinsburg was an inland course through very rough terrain of heavily wooded ridges. These conditions made movement difficult and highly favored any defender. To reach Grand Gulf McClernand's men would march along two roads about 12 miles northeast through Port Gibson then another six miles northwest to Grand Gulf.

Between the troops sent to quell Grierson's raid and the recall of reinforcements to Vicksburg, Pemberton's commander at Grand Gulf, General John Bowen, was hard pressed. He had forces numbering only 5,500 compared to Grant's 20,000. While Grant had the advantage of superior numbers, Bowen anticipated his movement and positioned his forces in advantageous blocking points along the two roads McClernand's corps had to use. The ensuing battle at Port Gibson was well fought by Bowen. He held out as long as he could before realizing further resistance would end in the complete demise of his smaller force. In the end he had lost a third of his fighting force in order buy just one day of time.

Port Gibson was in Grant's hands and Bowen was no longer strong enough to defend Grand Gulf. On May 7 Bowen withdrew his troops leaving the town to Grant who now had a secure beachhead on the same side of the river as Vicksburg. He ordered all rear echelon troops including Sherman to move up to the river crossing with all haste.

On May 8th Osborn Oldroyd, a fellow soldier of George Deal in the 20th Ohio, wrote briefly of the unit taking up the march again on the Mississippi side of the river. He mentions the locals coming out to view the "Yankees" while the Union soldiers foraged along the way.

" May 8 1863"
On the march

We were ready to continue our march, but were not ordered out, some white citizen came into camp to see the "Yankees" as they call us, of course they do not know the meaning of the term, but apply it to all union soldiers. They will think there are plenty of Yankees on this road if they watch it. The country here looks desolate. The owners of the plantations are "dun Gone" and the fortunes of war have cleared away the fences. One of the boys foraged to day and brought into camp, in his blanket a variety of vegetables- and nothing is so palatable to us now as a vegetable meal, for we have been living a little too long on nothing but bacon. Pickles taste first rate.

Osborn Oldroyd

Moving Quickly to Take Jackson

According to original plans agreed to by Washington, once he was secure on the Vicksburg side of the river, Grant was to send a corps south to cooperate with Major General Nathaniel P. Banks in capturing Port Hudson. Only then was he to combine both his and Banks' troops against the main stronghold. However, Banks had diverted some of his forces to the western side of the river on a mission that made any joint effort impossible for at least another month. Grant knew he had to move quickly in order to keep Pemberton and Johnston confused regarding his plan as well as prohibiting them from joining forces and outnumbering him.

As long as Port Hudson stood in defiance south of Grant's beachhead, supplies from New Orleans could not reach his army. Having anticipated moving away from a line of supply at some point, Grant made the only decision that made sense to him. He would move immediately with his entire force which would subsist off the land. He sent word to Washington of the change of plans, full well knowing that by the time the war department received the report he would be well advanced in his movements. The nearest telegraph in Union control was 400 miles away. He figured that positive results generated by that time would keep the politicians at bay.

Pemberton knew he was at risk and requested reinforcements from General Johnston in Tullahoma Tennessee. Johnston had forwarded two brigades but could spare no more. He recommended that Pemberton unite all of his units in order to defeat Grant outside of the Vicksburg defenses. This was the same strategy he had recommended to Davis and Pemberton back in December. He argued that while this might risk losing the city temporarily, the primary mission had to be to destroy Grant's army.

Grant knew he needed to keep Pemberton from doing just that. His next move was to move rapidly northeast to Jackson where he intended to destroy the two brigades already there as well as the two in route from Johnston. Then he would destroy the rail junction there to keep any other reinforcements from easily getting in his rear.

Seth Hall, 8th Iowa, sent this letter to his wife describing a plantation house he had entered and the number of plantations they had burned over the last few days during the campaign.

Grand Gulf Miss
May 8th 1863

Dear Wife

Our Division arrived hear last evening. we are all reasonably well. we are 55 miles below Vixburg & on our way to Jackson Miss. It is saposed we will have fighting to do 20 miles from hear. their was a battle hear a few days since & some 800 or 1000 prisoners taken by our troops. I see the 13 Regt & took dinner with James. I never see them look better. I have seen 40 or 50 plantation dwellings burned in the last 2 days half of which must of cost at least from one to two hundred thousand dollars each. I was in one of the buildings before it was fired. their wer 30 fine sofies beside every room was covered with the finer carpet 4 pianneys & furnished with the finest spring botem cushened chairs. also many of the rooms had mirrors on every side 5 feet wide & 10 feet long. there is no use for me to undertake to describe the destruction. it _____ to my _____ & I say go in & lay the land in desolation we have traveled some 90 miles in the last 6 days on about ½ rations aloud one tent & one teame to the Regt

Yours truly until Death S. E. Hall

I receive yours just before leaveing which was very exceptable

Playing Pemberton against Himself

The Northern commander also took advantage of the fact Pemberton was building entrenchments west of the Big Black River indicating that the Confederate commander thought Grant would move directly toward Vicksburg. In order to sustain Pemberton's belief, Grant sent a diversionary force to keep that thought in Pemberton's head. Between this feint and Sherman's earlier feint up the Yazoo against General Stevenson's Vicksburg garrison, Pemberton was totally confused about where the Federals would strike. That being the case, and not heeding the advice of Johnston, Pemberton moved out to meet Grant with 20,000 men, leaving 10,000 behind, instead of consolidating all of his troops to enhance his chances of winning the impending confrontation.

On April 29th, George Burns sent a letter home to Nancy to tell her that the Yankees were on their side of the river and that he knew the next week would be treacherous and frantic. It was a distressing report but he expected to give the enemy a strong fight. He was also running low on tobacco and asked that she send some quickly. If she could not he would have to quit due to the high cost.

Vicksburg Miss
Apr the 29th 1863
Dear wife I take this opportunity to write you a few lines to let you know that I am well. Captain Blackwell is going home this morning at 7 oclock so I have but few minutes to write. I have got no letter yet from you . We have had no mail for several days. The Yankees cavaldry mad(e) a dash down from Holly Spring and got the Railroad at Newtons Station between Maredian and Jackson. They burnt the Depot commissary store and hospital. They also burnt two bridges but their stay was short. General Lowrary got after Them. They left in a hurry. They are trying to flank us and get behind us. Part of our brigaid is gone up the road now to watch them. They are landing on this side of the River below hear. We heard a distant cannonaiding all day yesterday. Supposed to be fighting between them and our forces down the River.

We are back on our old camping ground at town again. We are with the Reserve Corps. There will be stiring times hear within the next week. The Yankees are going to make a desperate effort to Take this place. Write quick to me. Let me know if you got your money I sent you. I Think the mail will come *Through in a few days. If any one comes through from there hear and you can do it send me some Tobacco. I cant get any hear for less than 1.45 cents a plug and a bad article at that. I have 3 plugs of that you sent me and one plug besides. When that gives out I must quit for it will be 2 or 3 dollars by that time. Do the best you all can. I will do the same. If we fight we will give them a powerful fight before we will let them cut us off from home. This is what they are trying to do. I must close for the present. Your loving husband*

G H Burns To Nancy Burns

Pemberton Continues to Misread Grant

With Grant's diversionary force heading toward the Big Black, reinforcing his belief of Grant's intentions, Pemberton erroneously moved to the works being constructed there and waited for Grant. Grant, however, moved directly toward Jackson with his main force. In his way was a 2,500 man brigade under Brigadier General John Gregg. Pemberton had earlier ordered Gregg to move up from Port Hudson and positioned him at Raymond, Mississippi. Pemberton presumed this would put Gregg on Grant's right flank as he approached the Big Black works. That, in turn, would enable Gregg to make a flank attack on Grant as his line moved toward those works as expected.

Instead, on the morning of May 12th McPherson's 10,000 man XVII Corps ran head on into Gregg's much smaller brigade. The battle began in dense woods east of Raymond along 14 Mile Creek. Gregg's effective tactics, aided by the terrain and the great spirit of his troops, held the Federals in check for a time. At one point they even threatened to break the Union lines, but in the end McPherson's troops were too many for them. By the end of the day Gregg was in retreat for Jackson and the pursuing Union Corps was enjoying the picnic lunch the townspeople of Raymond had prepared for Gregg's troops as a thank you for their salvation.

Thomas Wolfe, regiment unidentified, wrote to the family of John Groves telling them of his death at the battle of Raymond.

In Camp near Vicksburg 14
May 18 1863
Mr. Groves,

I have the sad duty to write to you by request of your son. Which was the last. Your son John Groves was killed in Battle of Raymond on the 12th of May in the Battle of Raymond. He was shot in the left Eye and past through and coming our at the back of the head killing him instantly. We mourn the loss of one so good and brave. We suffer with you his parents and kind sister of his. We have some letters that I will open that are left and if there is any thing in them I will return them to you. You will please to let my parents know that I am well and oblige me. I will close this for we are ordered to march. Excuse this for there is no ink. Yours respectfully

Thomas Wolfe

Richmond Tries to Avert Disaster

In Richmond, as the reports from the front continued to worsen, James Seddon, the Confederate Secretary of War, had ordered Johnston to proceed to Mississippi immediately and take full command there. Johnston arrived in Jackson on May 13th and had perhaps 12,000 total troops at hand. Grant was rapidly approaching with two Corps totaling at least 20,000 men. Johnston wired Richmond to let them know he was too late and could do no good. He then ordered Gregg to remain as a rear guard with two brigades and began a withdrawal to the north.

As McPherson's corps advanced toward Jackson from the west, a torrential rain fell, delaying an immediate attack. The Rebels used the time to strengthen their defenses so that when McPherson was finally able to push the assault resistance was intense. Undaunted, the Union soldiers continued to press the assault until the 24th South Carolina gave way in front of them, thus breaking the Confederate line.

Sherman's corps advancing from the south arrived about this time and had no problem sweeping the few defenders in his front. Soon the northern army had control of Jackson, the state capital.

Grant arrived shortly after and ordered the destruction of all the industry and supplies in the city that could support the war effort as well as the destruction of the two rail lines that converged in the city. This was done rapidly and efficiently by Sherman's Corp.

George Thomas was part of the 53rd Indiana Infantry serving as Regimental Quartermaster. On May 18, 1863 he wrote to his wife Minerva letting her know they had crossed the river in Grant's wake and were moving into the interior of the state to serve as garrison forces at some point there. He is encouraged by Grant's victories so far and the occupation and destruction of Jackson.

May 18 1863

Dear Minerva,

You will see from the above that we are fare (far) in the southern confederacy. I wrote to you from near Youngs Point. If you did not get the letter I will simply say here that there was no incident worthy of note on the trip down. We arrived at Youngs Point the 14th marched across the point to the river below Vicksburg where we embarked yesterday for this place. We got here last night and debarked this morning. We have gone into camp where we will be used to garrison points for a time. Col Gresham says the 1st Brigade when it arrives is to garrison this point. Ours will go farther out. Such seems to be the program at present. But the interest exigencies or necessities of the service may change it all. Nothing is certain or fixed in the army.

You will certainly have all the news I can give you long before you get this. But news is very encouraging. This is the point from which Gen. Grant started for Jackson Capital of this state. At port Gibson a point some ten miles of this place he had quite a battle and defeat of the rebels. Again when near Jackson he encountered a force said to be ten thousand rebels going from Port Hudson to reinforce Vicksburg. He defeated them with great loss to the rebels. At Jackson he had another battle. We have not yet got particulars, that is the relative loses on each side. But he took the place and has destroyed all rail road communications with Vicksburg. I feel the utmost confidence that Vicksburg will be reduced or evacuated at a very early day. Having a large army there with scant supplies with their communications cut off is a state of things that cannot be endured long. Necessity will force them out of their strong fortifications either to evacuate or fight on equal terms. To evacuate would be disasterous. I donant think but that to fight would be more so.

I have but little idea yet of what aspect the interior of the country wear where it has not been held by troop of one or the other side. I suppose however that there is something in the way of agriculture going on. But along the river from here to Memphis so fare (far) as I saw it is one scene of desolution. With one solitary instance I did not see an acre of ploughed land and in that instance the owner of the farm had left and all the able bodied negroes had left but a few old men and women had remained and were trying to raise some corn. This people surely never realized what war was until they brought it upon them selves. Most terribly are they suffering for their idea of independence. The weather is now clear and the sun shines hot but there is generally a breeze that makes it pleasant in the shade. The nights are cool enough to sleep comfortably under a pair of blankets. *No more today. Write often whether you hear from me or not.   If you get no letters it will be owning to the uncertainty of the mails. But I think they will reach you some time.*

Remember me to all the family

Your affectionate Husband

George Thomas

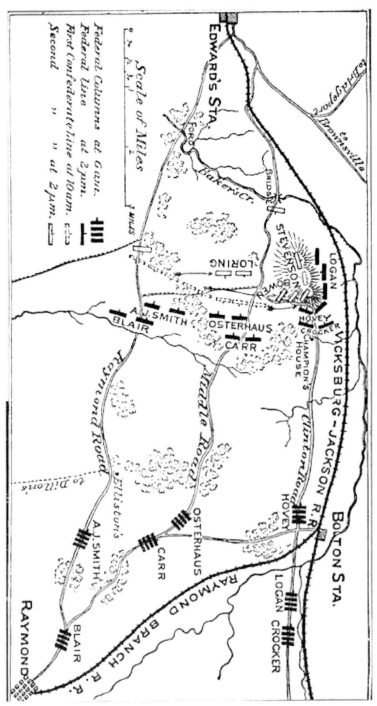

The Battle of Champion Hill - (Library of Congress)

Champion Hill and the Big Black

The mission at Jackson accomplished, it was time to move towards the prize of the campaign, Vicksburg, itself.

Now, Joseph Johnston sent dispatches to Pemberton ordering him to move toward Johnston's position at Clinton, Mississippi, 21 miles northwest of Jackson, in order to join forces while hopefully hitting Sherman's Corps from the rear. Pemberton was still determined not to leave Vicksburg unprotected and decided to send a force south to cut Grant's line of communications instead. Since Grant had intended upon continuing the campaign with or without a supply line since the beginning, Pemberton's move worked in his favor. Grant had also intercepted a copy of Johnston's orders for Pemberton to move to join him. Grant countered with orders to McClernand to move in Pemberton's direction and intercept him in route.

Upon receiving a second order from Johnston to proceed to Clinton, Pemberton recalled the troops he had sent south, ordering them to countermarch and join Johnston. Half way back, these troops were indeed intercepted by McClernand and McPhersons' corps at an area defined by a hill on the Champion farm.

Pemberton's force held the initial high ground on this hill, which was indeed a good defensive position. His three divisions were placed as follows: Stevenson's division on the left, Bowen in the center and Loring on the right. The line itself resembled a fishhook with Champion Hill being the prominence at the bend in the hook.

The battle began in the morning at the southern point of the opposing armies' lines. There Major General Andrew Jackson Smith's Federal 10th Division of McClernand's Corps came under fire from Loring's artillery as he approached from the southeast on the Raymond Road. As skirmishers were deployed and engaged, the fight grew hotter. Grant ordered McClernand to assault the hill to the north (right) of his line of battle. While McClernand demurred and delayed his attack, one of his divisions took action on its own. Having heard the guns of Major General John Logan's division of McPherson's Corps on their right, the Twelfth Division under command of Brigadier General Alvin Hovey pressed the assault on the hill where they gained control late in the morning. In response, Confederate General Pemberton ordered Bowen and Loring to move to this critical piece of ground and regain it. Bowen moved as ordered but Loring refused to move his forces in support of Bowen due to the bulk of McClernand's troops massed in his front. McClernand also continued to delay pressing the issue in his immediate front until late in the afternoon.

Bowen's move to reinforce the breach created by Hovey gaining the crest of the hill was ultimately foiled by reinforcements from McPherson's Seventh Division. Brigadier General Marcellus Crocker was in command of the division that day and he added their weight to the contest, pushing Bowen's troops to the brink. It was at this juncture that McClernand finally sent in Osterhaus's Division, hitting Bowen's right flank. Bowen's men were broken and Pemberton was forced to abandon the ground, leaving scores of casualties, artillery and the offal of an army behind.

Pemberton's route of retreat now took him to the railroad bridge over the Big Black River near Bovina. Earlier he had prepared earthworks on the east side of the river. Now he positioned a fresh brigade of Tennesseans as well as Bowen's remnants in those works as the rest of his exhausted and demoralized army crossed the river to safety.

In the confusion of the retreat, Loring's division was cut off from the balance of the Confederate army and forced to retire toward Jackson, ultimately joining General Johnston's force. Grant had lost 2,400 men. Pemberton lost over 3,800. Add the loss of Loring's 6,500 men and Pemberton's army had been reduced by over 10,000 troops.

On the morning of May 17th McClernand's Corps reached the Confederate defenses on the Big Black. Brigadier General Michael

Lawler deployed his 2nd Brigade of the Fourteenth Division on the northern end of the rebel line. Impetuous and eager, Lawler advanced his men without orders. Had the Confederates been in better condition this could have been a fatal mistake but they were so worn down and dispirited from their campaigning and recent defeats that they broke and made for the bridge. Pemberton was forced to burn the bridge before many could get across. As a result, over 1,700 of his soldiers were captured while over 200 were killed and wounded. Another 2,000 lost from his ranks at a cost of less than 500 casualties to Grant's now rampaging army.

Pemberton ordered his force back to the defenses of Vicksburg, 12 miles behind him to the west. He had been outwitted and outfought at every step of the way and now had no choice but to hunker down behind the works at Vicksburg and hope for relief.

Samuel H Byers' book "Fire and Sword" included this excerpt on the battle of Champions Hill. He participated in this battle as part of the 5th Iowa, 3 Brigade, 7th Division, XVII Corps under General McPherson.

Page 71

"Since we crossed the Mississippi I had marched & carried my rifle all the way-had been in every skirmish and engagement. Sometime I tramped along with my company B of Newton, sometimes I went with the extreme left of the regiment. I was no more heroic than all the others in the command, but I was fond of the risk and the excitement of Battle.

Page 72

May 16

"On the morning of the 16th my regiment was up and getting breakfast long before daylight. The breakfast consisted of some wet dough cooked on the ends of ramrods; nothing more.

Troops were hurrying past our bivouac by day light. Once I went out to the roadside to look about a bit. It was scarcely more than daylight, yet cannon could occasionally be heard in the far distance, something like low thunder. As I stood there watching some batteries hurrying along I noticed a general and his staff gallop through the woods, parallel with the road. They were leaping logs, brush, or whatever came in their way.

It was General Grant hurrying to the front. Shortly came the orders "Fall In" and we too were hurrying along that road to Champion Hills. By ten O'clock the sound of the cannon fell thundering on our ears, and we hurried all we could, as riders came back saying the battle already begun. As we approached the field the sound of great salvos of musketry told us the hour had surely come. The sound was indeed terrible.

At the left of the road we passed a pond of dirty water. All who could broke ranks and filled canteen, knowing that in the heat of the fight we would need the water terribly. I not only filled my canteen, I filled my stomach with yellow fluid, in order to save that in my canteen for a critical moment. Just then there was in front of us a terrific crashing, not like musketry, but more like the falling down of a thousand trees at once. Our brigade a small one, was hurried into line of battle at the edge of an open field that sloped down a little in front of us and then u to a wood-covered ridge that wood was full of the Rebel Army. Fighting was going on to the right and left of us and bullets flew into our own line, wounding some of us as we stood there waiting. There was an old well and curb at immediate right of my regiment, and many of our boys were climbing over each other to get a drop of water. Soon bullets came faste, zipping among us thicker, and thicker. We must have been in full view of the enemy as we stood there, not firing a shot. Our line stood still in terrible suspense, not knowing why we were put under fire without directions to shoot. Zip, Zip, Zip came the Rebel Bullets and now and then a boy in blue would groan, strike his hand to a wounded limb or arm, drop his gun and fall to the rear or perhaps he fell in his tracks dead, without uttering a word. We too, who saw it uttered no word, but watched steadily, anxiously at the front."

122

" *Six thousand Blue and Gray-coated men were lying there in the woods Dead or wounded, when the last gun of Champion Hills was fired.*"

Judson Gill (33rd Illinois) provided details to Sophi on the closing of campaign approaching Vicksburg and the opening assault on the Confederate main works, including casualties suffered by the regiment.

May 23rd 1863,

My Darling Sophi –

We have just passed through an active and bloody campaign. The bloody fields of _____ Hills, Raymond, Jackson, Champion Heights, and Black River Bridges have marked our path and wreathed the brows of many worthy soldiers with laurels. I wish I could write in full but I can't now. Suffice it to say that at Black River Bridges Co "B" was the first company over the enemy's breastworks and as a matter of compliment we put-in charge of the captured artillery and small arms. 3 cannon and 4500 stand of arms. We came with them as guard to Haines Bluff. 8 miles north of Vicksburg on Yazoo River where we now are. The battle of Vicksburg has been raging fiercely for 5 days until today. There has not been much shooting today. Yesterday a general charge was made but most of our line was repulsed. Our Division got into the ditch in front of the enemy's works and were still in it at last account. Captain Kellogg is killed and Col. Lippworth and Hyde Norton slightly wounded. Our entire loss is very heavy – probably four thousand men were killed yesterday. I suppose you are glad I am not there but I never felt as bad about anything in my life. We are loading the artillery tonight and I think we will go to the Regt. Tomorrow. Everything has looked today as if they were preparing for a general pitch in tomorrow. This campaign has been a complete success so far; we have whipped the enemy in the successive battles – taken over one hundred pieces of artillery and now we have them penned up in Vicksburg and they must surrender sooner or later. Grand Gulf and Port Hudson are ours and when

Vicksburg falls the river (will be) entirely open. One man in Co "B" lost his right arm at Black River. That is all the serious wounds. Some killed.

Love to all

Jud

The following note was written above the script on the top of the letter as an after thought:

This is rebel ink and paper. It is a shame That I cant write more but I will try to do so soon. Our commissions came to us on this battlefield at Black River all right.

On February 1st, 1863 Captain J. R. Gregory wrote to the Adjutant General of the Confederate Army in Richmond for approval of his recommendation to promote private W. L. Foster to the position of Chaplain in his regiment. In that role, Foster authored a most comprehensive missive on the siege of Vicksburg.

Headquarters 35th Miss.
Camp Simmons Feb 1st 63

General,

> *A vacancy having occurred in the Chaplaincy of the Regt by the death of the Rev. Mr. Tho. Haynes, I have the honor to recommend for appointment to that place the Rev. W. L. Foster of Co. C.*

I have the honor to be
Very Respectfully
Your obt. Servant

J. R. Gregory
Sr. Capt. Commanding 35th Regt. Miss. Vol.
General S. Cooper
Adjt. & Inspect General
Richmond, VA

W. L. Foster, now the chaplain of the 35th Mississippi Volunteers in Moore's Brigade, Forney's Division, Army of the Mississippi, shared his experience. On June 20th, 1863, two weeks before the fall of Vicksburg, he began writing a long letter to his wife, Mildred. He was motivated to share as much of his story of the campaign as he could with her for fear that he might not survive the siege. Each evening when he had a few minutes peace from the hospital duty he performed, he would continue to scribe his memories of the entire campaign and siege. His letter was over 50 hand-written pages beginning with his brigades' movement from Warrenton back to the works of Vicksburg, following Pemberton's defeat at Champion Hill. The letter has survived almost in its entirety and is shared here in its entirety as befitting the timeline of events. This excerpt is the description of those initial events, starting with his recollection of the retreat after the Battle of Big Black and his own brigades march back to Vicksburg.

Vicksburg,

Miss., June 20 1863

My dear Mildred:

   When I wrote you last, I told you that the storm was gathering in the West. It was not long before the enemy landed at Grand Gulf, after considerable resistance, and took possession of Fort Gibson. Gen. Bowen's Division grouped over Big Black, not far from its entrance into the Mississippi River, and endeavored to check the enemy in their progress. An engagement was brought on and our forces beaten back before overwhelming numbers. At this time our Brigade was stationed about Warrenton which is on the river eight miles below Vicksburg. In a few days after Bowen's defeat, some of his troops passed our camps worn down and exhausted from repeated forced marches. The enemy had been pursuing them, hanging upon their rear, capturing those that were unwell or too much exhausted to march and causing our men to push forward with all their might. It always makes me feel bad to behold a retreating army. There they go, covered with dust, with a swinging gait, hungry, thirsty, tired , sleepy and discouraged. I heard one remark that "he had not slept for two nights". The victorious enemy moved on with exceeding rapidity. They seemed to march straight upon Edwards' Depot. A portion of their forces took possession of Jackson attempting to swim across – others are shot while crossing by a close pursuing foe. They take a stand in some entrenchments on the West side of Big Black. The victorious enemy, like a rushing whirlwind, drive them out of the very ditches. They retreat in utter rout, broken, shattered and dispirited. What a helpless thing is a defeated army! What an utter wreck of former power and strength. How impossible to recover and rally! Gen Loring's Division, in endeavoring to cover the retreat is cut off and forced to retire towards Jackson.

While this battle was progressing, our brigade was quietly occupied above Warrenton. Our Regiment was protecting a very important battery on the River. On Sunday morning, the 17th of May, we could hear distinctly the artillery on Big Black. For half an hour it was exceedingly rapid. Our minds were in deep suspense as to the result. Presently we saw a cloud of black smoke rise up in the distance in the direction of the firing. We knew that it was the railroad bridge across Big Black that was burning. Then for the first time the dark suspicion crossed our minds that we were defeated and compelled to fall back beyond the river and to burn the bridge, for as yet we had heard nothing reliable as to the result of the battle. The smoke in the distance soon died away and the firing of cannon ceased and all was quiet again. It was now my regular hour to preach. A good congregation soon collected around my tent and I endeavored to preach to them on the shortness of life. It was no doubt the last sermon that several ever heard. No sooner had we dismissed the meeting than we received marching orders. In a few minutes we were on our way to Vicksburg. Lieut. Breck and myself walked along together; talking about our prospects. When we reached a high commanding point, from which we could see a large portion of our brigade moving on in their winding way, Lieut. B. remarked, "It makes me feel sad to look upon that army". "Why so?" I enquired. "Because", said he, "those men will soon be disarmed and on their way to *some Northern prison". I rebuked him for his despondency and replied: "No sir, they will soon be shouting victory, victory, while pressing a routed foe". It yet remains to be seen who is the true in their position and now for the first time we learn of our sad defeat on Baker's creek. We converse with men who were in the fight and they confess that they were badly beaten. With deep curses some denounced Gen. Pemberton as a traitor and as having sold the place. A strong and muscular Missourian swore with flashing eyes and compressed lips and a frowning brow, that if Pemberton surrendered Vicksburg, his life would pay the forfeit. The despondent said: "Vicksburg is gone up – it will be taken by storm". Upon the whole, the army was discouraged; that is, the portion that had been engaged. Forney's Division was fresh and buoyant and hopeful... (to be continued)*

News was not always accurate and, perhaps in the name of morale, false information constantly plied the telegraph and rumor lines. James Shaver (Confederate Regiment unidentified) had spent time in Mississippi before moving with his unit to Tennessee. His letter of May 25th to his mother falsely shares that the Federal troops have been beaten back with heavy loss near Vicksburg and 10,000 captured. Still, amidst the hardships of war, he manages to shift his thoughts to the "the girl he left behind him" for a moment, returning to news of the war. Then another girl, from Georgia this time, comes up in his thoughts.

Camp Bell. Buckle May 25th 1863

Dear mother

Once more I have the happy opportunity of communicating with you although it has been but a few long days since I wrote I know have the chance to send a letter by one of our company that is going home of Furlough. I will give you his name. It is Henry Meacham he is some connection of Aunt Linnie Crisswell & he was wounded at the Battle of Murfreesboro on that awful & long to be forgotten by the boys that was there. Dear Ma it looks like fortune has spread her downy wings over me & has kept me from all harm thus far & I do hope that my life will be spared so

127

that I can return to my distant home in the west. I am writing but I don't know whether it will ever be able to reach you or not if it dos you may know that I will not forget you all. I hope we may yet be able to spend many long & pleasant days together then I could tell you something of a soldiers life. Sure but it is enough now to let you know that I am still in the land of the living & doing what I can for myself. Well I am getting on finely but I tell you the boys have been giving me Sut about my gal. Well I have had a very bad cold for a few days & they accuse me of grieving but I have out lived it & all is well. to tell the truth I don't have any idea that I should have married her for you know that I never was in much of a hurry about marring. if I had of been I guess that I could before the war broke & I was old enough. I guess that I will be old enough when I get home if ever I should but I think I can work for you a long time & then be young enough to fly around. I don't think old age has hurt me any yet. There is a hard battle going on now at Vicksburg. I understand & I learned yest. that we had captured 10 thousand of the Feds & drove them back for 5 miles. It is telegraph news though I hope it is so. If the Yanks fail to capture the city & army we have there I think they will quit that place for good & always. They have made so many Signal failures though they was all around the place at the commencement of the fight but old Joseph E. Johnson of Virginia run in rear of them with considerable force. We have been looking to be sent from here but I don't suppose we will now. No I don't wat to go to Miss. Any more. Not that the fighting is any harder than it would be here but this is a healthier country to live in. I have written a long letter to Aunt Carrie S. Jones but I haven't got an answer from her yet. I think it is time for her to write & if she don't I shall send her one more & quit but I will give her fun for I know that any of them could write to me at any time & it only takes 2 days to go from here to Blountville. Well ma, I hardly know what use to write for it is so seldom that I write. I had a yong Ladie last evening in Georgia to send me word that I must write to her and I think I shall as she has been highly recommended to me by those that has a right to know. I sent her my compliments a few days ago. She lives near Calhoon Georgia. She is said to be young & handsome & her father well of(f) in this world. So don't you think I might do well to see her some time. But however, home is my *first view when ever the opportunity offers favorable. I think the time long to be away from you all but still I hope the horrid & cruel war will soon come to a close. It certainly last longer than next year some time for the time will soon be here now to elect another …*

Robert Hamilton and the 33rd Illinois also fought at Champions Hill. As with each of Hamilton's letters, this one to "Dearest and Ever Loved Kate" was more accurate and descriptive than the "telegraph" news young Shaver had heard.

> *"Camp in the Field"*
> *Snyder's Bluffs, Miss.*
> *Tuesday June 2nd 1863*

Dearest and
> *Ever Loved Kate:*
> > *Since last writing we have been out to Mechanicsburg and Satarshee on a line on reconnaissance. Several Brigades started from around Vicksburg last Tuesday night, May 26th, and marched till near day break before resting. We reached Mechanicsburg Friday, May 29 and our advance had a skirmish there and drove the Rebel cavalry across Big Black. Mechanicsburg is 40 miles N.E. of Vicksburg. I will write you a full account of our expedition soon. I wish to give you a brief account of our battles at Champion Hill & Bakers Creek. The next day after the battle at Raymond, we marched to Clinton – a little village on the Vicksburg and Jackson R. R. and ten miles west of Jackson. Here we found an amount of cigars & tobacco, also some Secesh clothing. Of course the boys helped themselves. Thursday, May 14th we set out for Jackson – our Brigade in the rear of the division and train. Rained like fury, but we marched on heedless of the torrents that were pouring upon us. We heard the rapid boom of canons ahead of us & expected soon to be engaged. We arrived at the scene of action about two o'clock P.M. and found that the rebels had retreated toward the north in the direction of Canton. We were ordered to take through the woods*

and over fields on quick time to cut off their retreat if possible. But the Enemy having a start of being on the road while we had to go a long and about way and over hills, hollows, fields & through woods they succeeded in getting away before we reached the road. We then returned to the Division which was encamped about __ miles west of the city. We got to see the part of the city, but like Moses we saw it from a hill but were not permitted to go in. Crocker's Division (Quimby's old Division) did most of the fighting at Jackson. He captured several pieces of artillery and stores for the _____. I have never heard the likes of either side but I saw a good many dead scattered on the field, both friends & foe. The __ Iowa Reg. lost many, by charging upon the enemy when the Rebs opened a masked battery & killed quite a number. They did not falter however so they took the battery. The next morning we started for Vicksburg. Camped a few miles west of Clinton. Saturday, May 16th we resumed our march till about ten o'clock. We came to a halt. Soon we heard occasional shots from muskets, about ½ mile in front which became gradually more rapid. We then knew there was skirmishing ahead. We were ordered to move forward. We found that the enemy had taken a position in a long tongue of woods open fields on each side. These woods were full of hills and hollows which afforded the rebels with shelter & hiding places. Logan's Division took position in an open field, to the north of the woods. Hovie's Division held the center & his lines were East of the woods and bent around the _end_ of the _tongue._ Osterhaus, I understand, held the left and Logan's a position on the south side. Soon as all got in position we were ordered to advance. Our Brigade marched over the hill behind which we had formed and across to another hill. Here we were ordered to lie down on the crest of the hill within two hundred paces of the Enemy who were posted in edge of the woods behind a fence. Their bullets sung over us & struck near us. Chancey Kimmel and several others wounded while lieing here. We were not allowed to fire a gun. McAllister's Battery was to our right & several yards in front of us, shelling the woods. Soon the rebels rushed out of the woods yelling like yahoos to take the battery. Every piece was double shotted with grape & canister. When within fifty yards of the battery we were ordered to give them a volley by the right oblique, and at the same time every piece showered its contents into the ranks of the advancing foe. Quick as thought they broke and fled to the woods. Our Co. and most of our Regt. Found a bank that afforded us good protection. The enemy fell back to another hill in front of us and took up a position in deep gullies that had been washed by the rains. Here we fired at each other for two hours until most of the boys had fired away all their cartridges when we were relieved by the 68th Ohio. Moses Flory was wounded while here. We then fell back after being relieved and filled our cartridge boxes. Soon the Enemy were seen massing in front of Hovey's Division. The 34th Ind. Was to our left & was hardly pressed. We were ordered to support it. But while advancing several of our men were killed & wounded. Here Adjutant Kerton, Stephen Laye (of Co. "B") and others were wounded & Capt. Killed. The 34 Ind. supposing we came to relieve them fell back. We were in line along a fence another fence joined this at right angles to us just at the left of our Regt. No troops were placed in position along that fence & soon we were attacked in front, on the left flank and an oblique fire from the rear. We were then ordered to fall back to a hollow about 75 paces to our rear. The artillery then opened on them over our heads and drove them from that corner. Soon we advanced again but the Rebs did not make any more stands. They kept on till they had crossed Big Black. Our Division captured 11 pieces of artillery & 1300 prisoners. Twenty five pieces 8000 prisoners were captured altogether.

Grant Consolidates his Forces

By the close of the battles for Champions Hill and the Big Black, Sherman's Corp, which had been charged with the destruction of the rail lines and other materials in Jackson, had caught up to the army. This meant that Grant had his full complement of forces reunited. He ordered Sherman to advance to the Bluffs north of Vicksburg as quickly as he could get there. Soon Grant joined him atop the Bluffs that had eluded Sherman in December. As the entire Union army enveloped Vicksburg, Sherman remarked to Grant that "This was the end of one of the greatest campaigns in history."

Robert Hamilton detailed the advance of the 30th Illinois on Vicksburg following the battle of Champion Hill and their expedition to Mechanicsburg in a letter to his wife, Kate, dated June 5th.

"Camp in the Field"
Near Vicksburg, Miss.
Friday June 5th 1863

Dearest and
> *Ever Loved Kate:*
>> *I was the recipient of a sweet letter yesterday from you dated May 24th. I was truly rejoiced to learn of your continued good health and that your eyes were getting so much better. My own health is very good but I am literally <u>worn out</u> by the hard marching we have endured within the two months past. I had rather follow one of McCormicks reapers as the Secesh. We left Snyder's Bluffs yesterday morning & arrived near the fortifications of Vicksburg a little after noon where we found Dagget who is (transferred) to the Regt. from Grand Gulf. He is in good health. Dr. Holstien is in charge of the <u>"Mary Ann"</u> hospital at that place. I suppose he (the Dr.) named the hospital in honor of Aunt Mary Ann. That was the hospital Dunk was in. We drew new clothing yesterday which was very, very much needed, for we were the dirtiest, raggedest & <u>lousiest</u> set of men you ever saw. Had you seen me before I drew my new clothes you would have been ashamed to own such a dirty ragged man for your husband. Wore*

a shirt just a <u>month</u> *without getting it washed & a pair of drawers* <u>two</u>
months. The roads were generally dusty, we slept on the bare ground, so
you may know how <u>clean</u> *we were. We did not stop for errands while on the*
march to wash and when we <u>did</u> *halt we had the assurance of remaining ten*
minutes. Vicksburg is all closely penned - how long Pemberton will <u>hold out</u>
in his position to thousands. Grant is getting heavy siege guns in positon to
bear on the enemy's locations. Grant is also throwing up rifle pits out about
eight miles from here on the different roads converging here, to guard
against an attack from the rear. It is well enough to look out for Bragg &
Johnston's forces. I hope and pray we may be successful in capturing the
"Maiden City" as the Rebels papers style Vicksburg. May God help us. The
enemy are said to have made two or three sallies from the forts; either with
the intention of cutting their way out or capturing some of our batteries, but
they have been repulsed & <u>more</u> *than driven back inside breastworks. They*
generally make the attempts after night.

I will now go back and bring up briefly a narrating on the doings and
meanderings of our Regt. after the battle of Champions Hill. Saturday night
maybe about a mile from the main battle field some after dark we saw an
immense fire in the direction of Edwards Station. Presently we saw frequent
flashes that looked like explosions. We found out afterwards, as we then
surmised that the Rebs had a train of cars loaded with ammunition & being
pressed so closely by our troops they were obliged to destroy the train.
Hence the fire and explosions. Early Sabbath, the 19th, morning we heard
cannonading in the direction of Big Black Bridge. Soon our division took on
the number to reinforce McClernand if necessary. After two or three hours
the firing ceased. The news soon came back to us that McClernand had been
successful in capturing seventeen pieces of artillery & about 2500 prisoners.
Of course the news was hailed with evident satisfaction by the boys. A great
many stragglers of the enemy were picked up, they being scattered
everywhere through the woods & ravines on the roadside. Some of our boys
without guns took several prisoners and some with empty guns captured a
few rebs. Most were captured seemed to be well pleased. They represent a
glorious state of affairs in their army. We found letters written the eleventh
of May by Secesh troops in Vicksburg to their friends and relations their

stating that they were allowed ¼ lb of meat per day for rations ever since the Yanks had crossed the Miss. River. Sabbath night we encamped near Big Black. Our Pioneer Corps built three or four pontoons during the night. Next day, Monday 18th, we crossed, Bivouacked within five miles of Vicksburg. Tuesday, May 19th we moved up with(in) ¾ mile of the fortifications & remained there until Thursday, 21st, when we moved up within sight of the works.

Vicksburg is Cut Off

Joseph Johnston was beyond frustration with Pemberton, ordering him to abandon the city and march his forces to the northeast in order to save the troops, if not the city. Pemberton again refused, stating that he would hold the city as long as possible. Despite his losses he still commanded approximately 30,000 men compared to Grant's 45,000. With strong works surrounding the city it would be enough to defend Vicksburg. The 10,000 men he had left behind under Generals Martin Smith and John Forney were fresh and ready for a fight. Those fresh troops were moved from their southern positions to the northeastern works in order to defend the most threatened area.

Shortly after the turn of the century, The Print Shop, Vicksburg Mississippi, published the book Yankee Bullets, Rebel Rations –By Gordon Cotton. Cotton included this quote from Lucy McRae Bell from a June 8, 1912 article in Harper's Weekly titled "A Girls Experience in the Siege of Vicksburg."

"Vicksburg, however, put on her war clothes, and cannon were rushed to the river-front; forts sprang into sights in a short time "whistling Dick" the old Confederate gun, stand in defiance. Louisiana and Tennessee troops commanded the river front, My mother, so comfortably fixed in a large suburban house with a friend, considered herself safe, suddenly, one day, *there flashed through the town the news" The Yankees are coming" My mother fearing to be left in the country, decided to go back to Vicksburg. Packing trunks with clothing and what articles of value she could take, she called a Negro whom she owned, and said "Rice I will want the dray and surrey ready to make an early start for Vicksburg tomorrow morning."*

Chaplain Foster's epic letter to his wife picks up the description of the atmosphere as the Federals approached and state of readiness for what was to happen next. The defenses were not adequately constructed at this point to resist every form of likely attack.

"…The line of defenses around Vicksburg began about one mile and a half above the center of the town, extending in crescent form around, and ending about two miles below on the river. Our lines at the most remote point were not more than a mile and a half from the river; their whole extent on the outward circumference not much short of five miles. On either hand there were two lines – On the center but one line of defenses and this consisted of a very inferior ditch about four feet wide and as many deep. The places constructed for the batteries were strong earthworks, with the usual embrasures, none of them casemated. There were no ditches cut for purposes of retiring and no obstructions to cut off an enfilading fire.

Behind these works our army, consisting of about 20,000 men, took their position on Sunday evening, the 17th. The question now was 'Will the enemy come' – 'Will they try to take the place by storm?' The impression, as far as I could ascertain, was, that the Yankees would not attack us in the ditches. Some thought they would fall back upon Jackson, fortifying that place and then operate against us by cutting off our supplies. Others thought that they would certainly make an assault and were anxious for them to try it. The despondent expected to see the place carried by storm and thought there was no hope for us. On Sunday night all slept on their arms, opposite their place in line of battle. On Monday morning the question became still more pressing and interesting, "Will the enemy come", "When will they be here?" During the forenoon flying rumors came in that the enemy had crossed Big Black and were coming rapidly on – that our advanced pickets were driven in. Then came the startling intelligence that Snyder's bluff was vacated and that all our splendid siege pieces had been spiked and fallen into the hands of our victorious foe – Thus the whole Yazoo Valley was in their possession and we could be cut off from supplies in that direction – Besides they could now so easily supply their own army, having possession to this valuable inlet to the great river.

On they come, driving in our scouts and pickets. In the evening a cannon is heard not far distant on our left. Ominous sound! As the loud clap of thunder gives warning of the coming storm, so does the resounding cannon ever open the fierce battle. A few hours later the distant popping of small arms is heard – This sound becomes nearer and more frequent – Now and then the cannon chimes in. Towards sunset our pickets are driven in near our entrenchments and the enemy's sharpshooters advance boldly. Rapid skirmishing begins on the left and gradually extend around towards the center. The impudent foe is indeed encircling us. Night comes on but the small arms do not cease. The risky sharpshooters, under cover of darkness, endeavor to secure a closer position. That night was a solemn night for the soldier. None but those who have had the experience can tell the feeling of the soldier's heart on the night before the approaching battle; when upon the wings of fond imagination his soul visits the loved ones at home – and while he thinks of a lonely and loving wife whose face he may never look upon again and who may never see his form any more on earth, his heart bleeds and dark forebodings fill his mind. Then, when he lies down upon the cold ground and looks up to the shining stars above, the gloomy thought crosses his mind that it may be the last time he will ever look upon the shining heavens and that those same stars which now look down so quiet upon him, may behold him on the morrow night a lifeless, mangled corpse. If he be a child of God, he will commit his soul to God and implore his protection. If a wicked man, he will review his past with remorse and the future with dread and will form a weak resolution to do better from that day if God will spare his life through the battle. By the break of day all expect the dreadful… several pages missing from the original…" (to be continued)

Positions of Grant's three corps for assaults of May 19, 1863 (Hal Jespersen www.cwmaps.com)

Initial Assaults on the Rebel Works

With all three of his Corps in positon around the Confederate works Grant believed that the beaten enemy would be too dispirited to put up much of a fight. He was wrong. His attack on May 19 was met by an enemy that was behind strong works, buoyed by fresh troops and high in morale.

Grant had ordered all three corps to attack. McClernand positioned to the east and McPherson to McClernand's north. Both became bogged down in thick woods, ravines and difficult terrain. Soon they were pinned down under a murderous fire and their advances halted. Sherman, further yet to the north, was able to get Colonel Giles Smith's brigade as far as a ditch just north of a strong enemy position called Stockade Redan, but they too became pinned down. Under cover of darkness, troops moved back to their lines knowing that Vicksburg would be a much more difficult and bloody fight than anticipated. Grant had lost nearly 1,000 men, Pemberton only 250.

2nd Lieutenant William C. Porter of the 55th Illinois, of Sherman's Corps, described their assault on the Stockade Redan, May 19th in an excerpt from an undated report.

"A call for volunteers was made to act as a storming party in our recent charge on the enemy's works. The call was made in our regiment by Col. O. Malmborg (55th Illinois Infantry), and responded to promptly by 12 men and myself. Being the ranking lieutenant, I assumed command of the different volunteer detachments from the brigade and reported to Captain----, Thirtieth Ohio Volunteers, in charge of the storming. At 10 A.M. precisely we started, and proceeded rapidly, occupying but three minutes from the ravine to the bastion. Just as we entered the ditch, a captain and a lieutenant from the Sixth Missouri were shot by sharpshooters on our flank, severely wounding both. I immediately assumed command, and with the colors firmly planted on the parapet by a private of the Eighth Missouri, all I then could do was to prevent the rebels from carrying them in (which they tried) and wait for support which we did not succeed in getting. Some men of Ewing's brigade came up, but not sufficient to warrant my thrusting them over the ramparts to be either slaughtered or taken prisoners. We remained in this position, exposed to the fire from the flanks of the enemy, and a direct fire from the skirmishers of the First Brigade, till 430 p.m., when about 30 of the eleventh Missouri with their Colonel, major, and 2 lieutenants, succeeded in reaching us with their colors, which they planted alongside of ours. The bearing of the two color-bearers was all that bravery and true

courage could do, waving their colors in defiance of enemies and traitors, marching straight and unwavering to the fort through the most murderous fire I ever experienced. The rebels, in trying to dislodge us, commenced to use 12-pounder shells, burning the fuse and then rolling them into the ditch. We succeeded in throwing back three with our bayonets which burst on the inside, causing the same effect they intended on us. One shell , however exploded, killing Serg. Richard Haney, Company F, fifty-fifth Illinois Infantry and wounding 4 privates severely. At about 7:30 p.m. I received verbal orders from Major- General Blair to fall back, which we did, but not till I had all my wounded safely removed. "

> *William C. Porter*
> *2nd Lieutenant 55th Illinois Company E*

Following the failed assaults of the 19th , Grant immediately put his men to work constructing siege works and a road from the steamboat landing at Chickasaw Bluffs now in Federal hands. This facilitated a line of communications for what was now a crucial need for supplies and food.

On May 22nd Grant ordered a more coordinated attack on the Confederates. Every artillery battery in the northern army, as well as Porter's gunboats, bombarded the Confederate lines for four hours attempting to soften up their works.

At 10 A.M. the cannon fell silent and all along the line, Union troops advanced at charge bayonets. The battle was hard fought on both sides. At the Railroad Redoubt, in the approximate center of the Confederate defenses, two of McClernand's battered regiments made the top of the works but Confederate counterattacks were able to seal the breech and eventually push them out. All along the rest of the line, Union troops were pinned down and receiving incredible fire from the enemy.

By early afternoon Grant saw that the assault was doomed to fail. However, McClernand reported he had two rebel forts partially in his hands and requesting that Grant needed to push hard all along the line in order for him to complete the victory. Although Grant didn't believe McClernand's claim, he nonetheless sent more troops to McClernand on the outside chance that victory might be had. He also urged Sherman and McPherson to renew their attacks. The result was merely to increase the Union casualties with no further gain. In the end, Grant's army lost 3,200 men while the Confederates' loss was less than 500. This was the highest loss of the campaign for Grant who determined that the Confederates would have to be starved out in order to prevail in this contest.

Robert Hamilton's letter of June 5, 1863 detailing the advance to Vicksburg continues with a description of their assault on the Confederate works on May 22nd which sadly included casualties from friendly fire. He then describes the settling in of the siege and the banter that commences between opposing pickets. He concludes with flowery words of his devotion to his "ever loved Kate".

..Friday May 22nd was the day appointed for storming the breastworks. Scalers & firm lines were needed for scaling the works. Our Brigade was in the reserve of our Division. We wound around through the hollows and cropped ridges in rifle shot of the looming redoubts & rifle pits of the enemy. When within 300 paces of the works we were ordered to lay down first behind the crest of a little ridge and await further orders. At ten o'clock an advance was made upon the formidable works all around the lines. Our artillery opened a terrific fire on the enemy and our infantry moved confidently towards the works. We were in position to be spectators of the terrific scene. Our men kept on in the face of a galling fire our hearts beat with high hopes that they would succeed. But soon we could see our lines to the left waver and fall back. Then they would rally and try it again. Our anxiety was wrought up to the greatest intensity. They advanced until within twenty or thirty paces of the breastworks when they halted. They dare not advance & the men dare not raise their heads above the rifle pits, or their lives would have paid the penalty. So thus they lay doing nothing till

darkness set in, when commenced the grandest display of fireworks I ever beheld. Spouts of flame issued from the thousands of muskets – vast <u>sheets</u> of fire…

Missing page..

…and did that day. But few of the enemy would stick their heads over the fort till about ten o'clock when they were _____. They then opened a heavy fire on us. Some of our boys receded over into the _____. Soon they reformed with something that was not <u>running.</u> They lit the fuse of twelve & twenty four spheres and threw or tossed them over the fort toward us. They rolled down the slope until they were stopped by the little ridge of dirt thrown up in front of us. The first two or three that exploded made us feel decidedly <u>streaked</u> but aside from making a big noise and scaring us did us no damage. We lay between our own batteries and the rebel fort. Soon as the "rebs" commenced to throw the hand grenades at us our artillery opened a rapid fire. We got interested in watching the cannon balls (which we could see distinctly) from our cannon. Soon we saw one coming whirling spirally & strike in the ground about twenty feet below our Co. The next one from the same gun whirled similar to the first and struck in Co "B: - mortally wounding two men slightly wounding four others. Robert McMann had one leg and one arm shoulder & body badly bruised. Jordan Somers had both legs shot off ____. They were the worst mangled men I ever saw. They died in an hour afterwards. Well this was one case. We expect to see some of our men laid low & wounded by the <u>enemy</u> but to be killed by <u>our own</u> men is too much. Some of the boys unwounded ran back down the hill in a hollow. I did not like to stay there & born the risking shot by our artillery, but I was not going to leave my post without orders. Soon Col. Shedd ordered us to fall back in the hollow. We did so in the face of a heavy fire of musketry from the enemy, but thank God none of us were hurt, except a slight wound received by Sergt. Steele of Co "E". I had passed through three bloody battles but I never had such feelings come over me as I had that day when I saw our men murdered by our artillery. I had rather go into a battle than to have to repeat the ordeal. We learned afterwards that it was the fault of the ammunition that the balls fell short. The gunner cried like a child when he learned what he had done. The ammunition was damaged. The artillerists did not like to use it but they ran the risk to <u>save us</u> as they thought. Our sharpshooters are in rifle pits near the works and annoy the enemy a great deal. In the evenings some very interesting conversation is carried between the rebs & our men. Our boys ask them how they fare on mule meat. "O very well!" responds a Reb. "Aint you about out of sassafras tea?" "No! Got lots of it." "Any whiskey in Vicksburg?" "Plenty of it." Then Mr. Reb asks a few questions. "When are you going to take Vicksburg?" "Oh, were in no hurry, we're going to take our time to it." A thousand other questions and alike satisfactory answers are given. Then they try their skill at shooting; each being the target for the other. But as it is generally after night or late in the evening, their marksmanship is rather defective and seldom attended with any serious result.

In my next I will give you a brief account of our trip to Mechanicsville & Satarsha God willing. My Dearest I trust that God will soon reunite us. I feel hopeful! I love you above all things earthly. At times I fear that I love you with a devotion bordering on Idolatry. God knows I desire to see you above any person living. I trust God will bring me home through this war & return me to you alive, my home & kindred in peace & safety. God bless us, shield us from every evil influence, lead us into the paths of uprightness & permit us to spend many happy days in each other's society & God's service is the prayer (of) your thrice loving constant and adoring husband Robert

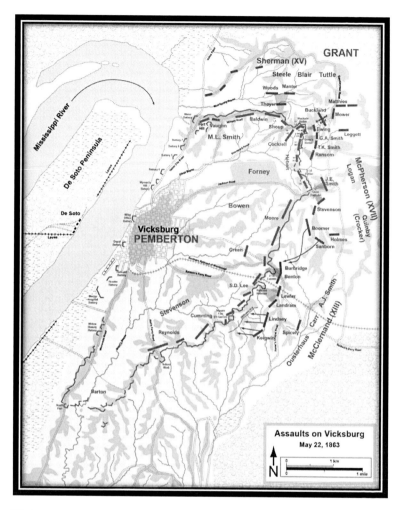

Union Assaults on May 22, 1863 (Hal Jespersen www.cwmaps.com)

James Carlisle's final surviving thoughts from his parole camp diary reflect his view of these initial assaults by Grant as his 34th Mississippi regiment defended the soil of their home state. Written after the surrender, a few dates are incorrect but the descriptions are telling.

"....Early on 19th May the artillery on both sides open with rapid, heavy firing. Our lines running from near the Yazoo to the Mississippi River

(forming the perimeter of a circle) on the South East side. At the commencement of the battle we had small redoubts on the crest of hills forming a chain of works which in many instances were joined by ditches dug after the fight commenced. Heavy fighting. On this day the Feds came boldly up to our works; their ranks swept down by the awful hail of lead. Their appearance at a distance resembled the assemblage of myriads of black birds, soon their well drilled squadrons filed in sight. Bravely on they came, flushed with victory, drunk with wine. Our first shots would cause many to right about face, others to throw up their hands falling on their backs in death, others still to fall to the earth for protection, whilst some straggled in broken groups up to the ditches we occupied, there to be mangled in horrid death. Night stops the carnage. We lose only 60 killed and wounded in the 17,500 reported inside the area which, by-the-by, was two miles long and 1 to 1 ¼ wide according to the winding of the River.

On the 20th heavy fighting again. Shot and shell raining incessantly over our unprotected heads. A repetition of the 19th.

21st but little done, occasional firing.

22nd the same. The Federals are making their approaches, throwing up their works.

On the 23rd the Grand Fight of Fights is fought. Their artillery is in position. Ours is soon disabled. Nothing but infantry to defend our works. Their solid columns invest our works. Advance all around the circuit of 7 miles in many places in triple files. The horrid din of battle grates upon the ear of the few who are contented to sit in danger and look idly on. Charge after charge is gallantly made and bravely repulsed. Cotton bags are used by our forces (relying I suppose on the New Orleans 1815 tradition). These are soon burned by the Feds, being an element of weakness to us, since they rolled down against our cannon which were separable and destroyed the carriages. Many places the ditches on the outside are filled with the Yankee dead. Several standards of theirs are planted on our works. Their brave bearers never returned. Father met son. Uncle met nephew and brother met brother in deadly strife. *The same state, the same family afford the material for the contending armies.*

At night relatives would anxiously inquire for each other and schoolmates tenderly ask for each other; visiting to and fro was inaugurated and many were the old sweet associations of by-gone days called up by the unholy meeting in opposing armies. Many entreaties were urged by both parties for their friends to quit fighting against them, but both parties remained inexorable. On the principle that where the affections had been the warmest and tenderest, if a wound or unfortunate irruption of feeling is given or caused so much the more intense is the bitter feeling of revenge stirred up and hatred engendered.

24th. Little occurs to enliven the already monotonous battle. Shelling constant until evening of 25th when we are allowed to breathe a few moments by our authorities petitioning the Yankees to perform the act which distinguishes humanity from brutality – to bury their dead.

What a spectacle is here unfolded. The dead and wounded who have lain 3 days in a hot summer sun. Flies and insects have spread themselves over their mangled cavies. One poor fellow said he had been wounded 4 days ago. His thigh was broken …"

Chaplain Foster's fervent letter to Mildred continues after a number of missing pages with his recollection of these initial attempts to storm the works by Grant's forces.

"… (First Charge)…Pound rifle shell struck him on the left thigh, inflicting a most severe flesh wound, and then passed down on the same leg, tearing off the entire calf. The same fatal shell had struck a private, removing almost entirely one hip. The doctors worked and dressed these awful wounds while I endeavored to remove the dust from their hands and faces – for they were covered with dirt. An ambulance soon arrived and they were carried off to our Brigade Hospital. The private died on the way. This was a terrible blow to Capt. C's company and fell with stunning effect. His men felt their great loss and their awful danger.

Second Charge. On Thursday, the 21ˢᵗ, as soon as light dawned, the usual sharpshooting began, only more rapid and more dangerous. The enemy were now planting their batteries all along the line and shelling became every hour more intense and destructive. Their furious missiles would explode over the heads of our brave men and fragments strike down into the ditches, killing and wounding them while lying on their faces. Here come the litter bearers again, bearing their groaning burdens. Who can it be? A man well advanced in age, who has a grown son in the same company, is severely, and as it proved afterwards, mortally wounded by a shell. A fragment passed through his knee, shivering it all to pieces, while his shoulder was also sorely wounded – The old man bore it with so much patience – You bear their pain some meekly, without scarcely a word of complaint. His wound is bandaged and he is sent to the Brigade Hospital.

Towards evening heavy cannonading was heard upon the right. It seems like a half dozen batteries have opened upon one point. The firing is so unusually rapid and fierce that it begins to attract the attention of the whole line. Now, the batteries of the enemy open all along the line and the sharpshooters increase their fire – but on the right the cannonading is hottest. Will the enemy make another effort to storm our works? The cannonading now subsides but the fire of small arms grows more rapid and now whole volleys of musketry, with one continuous roar, break forth. Another charge is made. In solid columns the persevering foe presses upon our right, endeavoring once more to force our lines. Our men, as before, reserve their fire until they approach near, and then pour forth a perfect storm of Buck and Ball, so that the enemy fall by hundreds. They fill up the broken ranks and press on but they stagger before the deadly fire. Their men will not advance and turn and fly from certain death – But upon one point they concentrate a powerful force. They press with great fury and an Alabama Regiment is driven out of the ditches. The Yankees plant their flag upon our works and send back for reinforcements. They take possession of our works and for two hours hold their position. Volunteers are called for to retake the works. Enough readily respond, and they with a single dash and but little loss, drive the enemy from the lost ditches, killing and capturing several. Thus for the second time they have failed in their efforts to storm our works. They become discouraged from their failure and heavy loss, while our men gain confidence.

On Friday, the 22nd, the day opened as usual with the popping of small arms and the booming of cannon. The enemy had succeeded in planting more batteries and their sharpshooters had gained positions nearer our lines. Their first parallel had now completely encircled us and upon every commanding hill was planted a powerful battery. Having failed in storming our works upon the left and then on our right, we were beginning to think that they would abandon the hope of taking the place by force and would be satisfied in laying siege to the place and in annoying and wearing out our people by continual firing and unceasing watching and exposure. But our persevering foe was not willing to give up such a glorious undertaking until he had made another proud effort; so in the course of the forenoon an unusual heavy firing both from the sharpshooters and the artillery was opened along the whole line and continued for about one hour. Our brave men had to literally lie cleaving to the dust to avoid the worrying minnies and the bursting shells. While the firing was kept up along the whole line, it seemed to be more intense about the center. Upon the center, every available battery was turned and the very hills made to tremble with the awful fire. The breastworks were torn down over the heads of our men and many were borne away frightfully wounded. Our cannon that would dare to fire were either dismounted or forced to retire. Now, about the center, the enemy cease their artillery firing, while the skirmishers increase theirs. They are forming for a last desperate charge. They come with short ladders to scale the works where they are precipitous. They stimulate their men by every means possible. They promise every man a reward of land and money that crosses our lines. They form as usual into a column, six deep, and through the winding valleys and by artificial channels they make their way into a few hundred yards of our lines. Now with rapidity they advance. Now our cannon pour the deadly grape upon them – But on they come. Our men, as before, reserve their fire until they approach near. Now, they raise their heads above the works and into the bosoms of the foe's crowded ranks

147

pour forth a withering, consuming fire. They fall back in confusion. Again they rally their men and make another charge. The same storm of death drives them back. They come the third time but meet the same awful fate. They fall back in confusion and dismay, nor can they be induced to make another effort. This ended the last and most desperate effort the enemy made to carry our works by force. Their loss was very heavy. The hillside was strewn with their dead. It so happened that every attempt made to carry our works fell upon Forney's Division, which was fresh and had not been in the other engagements. Our loss was comparatively small – Most of those that were killed or wounded were shot in the head. After this repulse the enemy abandoned all hope of taking the city by direct assault. Their only chance was the slow process of starving us out but we felt confident that Johnson would come to our relief before this could be effected. As for myself, I regarded the city as safe…." (to be continued)

Seth Hall, 8th Iowa, described a truce called in order to bury the dead in his letter of May, 26th. He added comments on the physical condition of the Union troops after the arduous and continuous campaign to reach and surround Vicksburg.

In rear of Vicksburg May 26th /63

Dear wife

I have just received yours of May 1st & May 4th and was exceeding glad to hear you wer all well & too that Mrs. Sam Ward was so hily (highly) favored. I am reasonably well. Irwin is still in the hospital also M. R. Stephenson. he has been bleeding at the lung. have not herd from them for 3 or 4 days. the rest are all reasonably well. our Regt. Is now in front saporting a no. of Batterys. yesterday the Rebels sent in a flag of truce to bury the dead hostiztys (hostilities) wer then seased for 4 hours in which time the Rebs & our men met both for the same purpos without arms, shuck hands & convened together as brothers & their was brothers and nabours met & had then interesting chat. but when the 4 hours was up each party returned to their own rifle pits of defence. skirmishing is going on all the time I think their has been near 2000 of our men killed & wounded hear *since the commencement of the fight. we are being reinforced. our strength is probably 75,000. we sapose the Rebel 40 or 50,000 they are so well fortified we have don them but little harm so far. the 5 & 13 Regt. Are both hear but I have herd nothing from them yet. they are on the extream left of the left wing & we are on the right of the center. tell Nate I got letter when at Grand Gulf. tell him to do as he would with Bootens Classics as if they were his own. when I can get time & material I will give you all the particulars of our march & fighting. we marched 18 days constantly the weather was very hot & the roads very dusty we have had a hard time & more. we have not had an opportunity to wash or chang a garment since the 1st of the month and we are very durty. I think I would keep the little boys out of school until the Scarlet fever had subsided. hug them for me & do the best part for them you can & talk to them about heaven & their creator. impress their minds as they may know & learn from whence they came & to wher we are all tending & must sooner or later appear. I have sent you $30.08 since I left St Louis. have you got it. write often & beleave me yours truly until death S. E. Hall*

I will write as often as I can. depend on this. Lieut. Ward surmised right in regard to Kennon being put over us. all is well that ends well. leaveing the results in the hands of the Supream ruler of the univers hopeing his not our will be don

S.E.H.

McIntire Lash McCanel Are all right Barber was left at Duck Point well

Jared Sanders regiment, the 26th Louisiana, had been in reserve inside the defenses of Vicksburg when the Union Army made its appearance and drove the main force back into the defenses of the city. His diary recorded these events during these first days encountering the enemy face to face from the Confederate works.

Sunday, May 17th '63

Great excitement in town, the 26 regiment ordered to pits on the lines of fortifications below the city. Heard of the battle at Big Black which is disastrous to us. Slept in trenches.

May 18

Ordered into town at 10 o'clock. Very dusty. Saw very many soldiers returning tired out from the last battle field. Everybody looking <u>blue.</u> It is now a foregone conclusion that we are to be besieged by the approaching enemy. Rumors place the Yankees within a few miles of our works. Now will be tested the <u>state</u> of preparation in which the defenders of Vicksburg have placed the city – how much provisions – how much ordinance stores they have in the city.

Marching orders again! Ordered to the line of works above the city. Got on line of works running toward Snyder's Bluff – heard enemy's guns before we got in our place. We are outside of (our) regular line, 4 o'clock P.M. About half past five Yankees advanced, infantry came up and began firing on us. We are replying whenever they show themselves. Lay down to sleep on the ridge.

One man in Company K wounded slightly.

May 19

Ordered in to take our position in works at 3 o'clock in the morning. After changing & moving about, at last found the position in which we are told our regiment must occupy. Not a sign of pits to get into & enemy in edge of woods firing upon us – 300 yards distant. I marked off our pits, & put Company "B" to work. All the regiment now doing same. _____ is "sun up." Great (shame) this work was not done long ago.

I was sent to town for stragglers from the regiment – returned & found our pits deep enough to protect the soldiers. One man killed in Company A in digging his trench. Sharpshooting & cannonading commenced before 12 o'clock. Very heavy. I think enemy will charge _tomorrow._ Very hot in pits. Went to woods 20 yards in rear to shade. Gen. Shoup, Bislund, West & etc. there. Cannon ball cut a limb down & came near falling on West & myself. _Two_ charges made between 2 & 6 o'clock in evening were repulsed! Col. Hall was wounded. John Smith wounded, standing on my left. First man hurt near me was on my left at Chickasaw Bayou! Lieut. Ternier killed, also poor Capt. Felix Winder was shot 25 minutes of 6 o'clock P. M. He was near Major Martin & West, the ball passed through his heart. A manly, high souled, generous man. His words were – "I am gone, I am gone"!

May 20

Lay down expecting heavy work on the morrow. Into our works before light. Sharpshooters commenced before daylight. No charges near us today. Yankees badly punished yesterday. Suffered much in pits from sun & dust. We need cross pits much.

May 21

Up and in pits by day light. Very heavy light artillery fire upon us all day.

William Anslum, Company "B: wounded in arm and two others in regiment. Slight sprinkle about 12 o'clock.

Our provisions are brought at night for the men. Enemy seem to be fond of flaunting their miserable old flag close to our works. An adventurous Yankee has planted one within 100 yards of our line & has dug him a _trench_ from which to shoot. At night walked up where the charge was made yesterday. In the charge they crowded up behind a house close to our men, & there many fell. The stench of the dead was awful!

May 22

Batteries commenced shelling at 2 o'clock & we got into our pits. We were sleeping on the roadside. Lieut. Arrieux, Company C, killed at twenty minutes of seven this morning. Shelling during day. The enemy charged on our right in sight of us. And in our front, at the same time, were *running under the hill to make a charge on our regiment. About five o'clock they came up the hill to our left in full view. They would run up until they were tired & then fall down, jumping up they would strive to reach our works but the fire was too severe for them and in twenty minutes they were repulsed.*

Dave Gregg also killed today. I understand our loss was 3 privates today.

Went to Vicksburg to wash. In the charge one Yankee came up with a pipe in his mouth. Very coolly he stooped behind a stump within 20 years (yards) of us but there very soon ended his life of which he was so careless.

May 23

In pits still. We are looking anxiously for <u>Joe Johnson.</u>

No fighting around line today. Our men went on field & got guns & trophies of the fight.

Sunday, May 24

Sharpshooting early. Man in Company F had head shot off by cannon ball. At midnight an <u>informal</u> truce, for their dead was stinking & we hallowed to them to come over and bury their dead, both parties promising <u>"not to shoot."</u> Had a talk with captain & an <u>adjutant</u> of the 9th Iowa regiment. Told me Vallandigham had been sent South. He was confident of taking Vicksburg. The dead burst as they were moved. What an awful thing is war – how callous & heartless it makes us. Wee begin to see the dead & dying with almost no emotion, & we soon forget them. – Oh! May God soon give us victory & peace!

Brigadier General Ralph P. Buckland commanded a brigade containing the 93rd Indiana Volunteer Infantry. Buckland's official report described his Union brigade's movements and actions between May 2 and 22nd in his official report to headquarters.

Headquarters First Brigade, Third Division, 15th Army Corps
Near Vicksburg, Mississippi, June 8, 1863

In pursuance of directions from division headquarters, I have the honor to submit the following report of this brigade from the 2nd to the 22nd of May inclusive. As this brigade was not separated from the division in the march from Duckport to Jackson, Mississippi, it is not deemed necessary to give in detail each day's march. We commenced our march from Duckport at 10 A.M. on May 2 with two teams to the regiment, taking five days' rations in haversacks and teams, and 100 rounds of ammunition per man in cartridge boxes and teams, leaving tents, baggage, and all but very few cooking utensils behind. We reached Hard Times and crossed over to Grand Gulf on the 7th, but were not able to cross our teams which contained all of the rations we had.

During the night, word was sent to me that the commissary was prepared to issue rations of hard bread but when applied for early in the morning all of the hard bread had been issued to the other brigades, reserving none for mine. Notwithstanding this unjustifiable conduct of the commissary, when the command 'forward' was given, every man was in his place and my brigade moved promptly forward, without transportation nd with empty haversacks, not knowing where the next meal was to come from. Other troops, having gone before us, it was difficult to procure provisions on the road. Every effort was made to supply the deficiency, but many of the officers and men suffered extreme hunger.

We encamped that night at Willow Springs, where we remained until 4 P.M. the next day. A stock of fresh meat was procured, but very little meal, not enough for one tenth of the command. Having no cooking utensils, the soldiers cooked their meat on sticks and as best they could. We reached Rocky Springs sometime after dark on the evening of the 9th, where we remained until the morning of the 11th. Here the commissary brought up some rations of hard bread and meat, and issued three-fifths rations for three days. This scanty supply of hard bread was a great relief and a great luxury for the soldiers, who renewed their march on the morning of the 11th, refreshed and in fine spirits.

At Cayuga, the 95th Ohio under Col. McMillen was ordered to Hall's Ferry on the Black River to guard that crossing, but the road the colonel was directed to take took him to Baldwin's Ferry where he hound a few of the enemy's pickets, which he drove across the river. Col. McMillen returned to the brigade with his regiment on the evening of the 13th, having made about 12 miles extra marching which was very severe on this men.

May 14: Today, according to the regular program of the march, my brigade was entitled to the lead but by order of Gen. Sherman, Gen. Mower took the advance and my brigade the rear, Gen. Tuttle's division being in advance of Gen. Steele's. On the march, Waterhouse's battery, which had been assigned to my brigade, was ordered forward and when the advance encountered the enemy's skirmishers near Jackson, was ordered into position. My brigade was ordered into line of battle in the rear of the Third Brigade, and advanced in line across an open field, crossing a ravine, which proved to be deeper than was supposed. After crossing the ravine, Gen. Sherman ordered the brigade to follow the batteries by the right flank. The batteries again being ordered to take position on the right, and the other regiments to support the batteries on the center and left. This point was in range of the enemy's batteries, which were served with admirable precision.

Here the 93rd Indiana had had two men killed and eight wounded, one mortally, since dead; the 114th Illinois had one killed and two wounded, Waterhouse's battery, two men wounded. This was the first time these two regiments had been under fire but the officers and men behaved with the coolness of veterans. Not a man left his post. Col. McMillen with the 95th Ohio was ordered to reconnoiter the enemy's position on the right where he found the enemy's rifle pits unoccupied and thereupon marched into the city and the rear of the enemy's batteries, taking them by surprise. Col. McMillen captured six guns, one captain, three first lieutenants, two second lieutenants, and 46 enlisted men. The 95th Ohio had the honor of being the first to enter the capital of Mississippi.

Having marched my brigade within the enemy's works, I was ordered to encamp in a grove near the road leading out of the city westward. We went into camp and the men had got pretty comfortably fixed for drying their clothes, having marched most of the day in a drenching rain, when I received an order to post my brigade along the rifle pits, in position to man them in case of an attack. This was pretty hard for men who had marched all day in the rain with very little to eat, the rain still continuing in intervals. The order was obeyed and submitted to with less complaint than might have been expected under the circumstances. The next morning my brigade was ordered to proceed at once to destroy the railroad leading from Jackson to Vicksburg. We had not a tool of any description and could procure none from the provost marshal. I borrowed four axes of Waterhouse's battery, one for each regiment, and took up my line of march in accordance with orders, trusting to luck for tools and rations. Passing through a Rebel camp, we had the good luck to find five or six axes and as many picks and with these we commenced the work of destruction, and before night we had completely destroyed several miles of road.

We encamped that night about four miles from Jackson, surrounding our camp with a chain of pickets. During the day I sent out a foraging party, who collected an abundance of cattle and sheep; but we had no bread. The next morning we renewed the work of destruction, proceeding toward Clinton, which point we reached a little after noon, and awaited the arrival of the division, having totally destroyed six mile of railroad by piling up the ties, laying the rails across, and burning them. At Clinton, the regimental teams joined the brigade with ammunition and a very small supply of hard bread. WE did not get into camp that night until sometime after midnight and were ordered to be ready to march at daylight.

We arrived in the vicinity of our present position on the afternoon of the 18th, the 93rd Indiana, Col. Thomas, being ordered to take a position on the direct road to Vicksburg, and hold it until relieved by the advance of Gen. McPherson's corps. Co. Thomas was relieved and joined the brigade during the night. At 2 P.M. on the 19th I was ordered forward to support Gen. Blair inhis charge upon the enemy's works. I advanced my brigade by the right flank, according to orders, the 72nd Ohio leading, the other regiments following closely as follows: 95th Ohio, 114th Illinois, 93rd Indiana. I was directed by a staff officer of Gen. Blair to the position I now occupy, who directed to put three regiments on the right and one on the left of the road. I advanced with the head of my column along the road under the severe fire of musketry from the enemy, to the position indicated. Just as the three leading regiments had got over to the right of the road, Gen. Blair sent word that he wanted two regiments on the right and two on the left, which necessitated crossing the 114th Illinois over to the left, under a heavy fire from the enemy. The movement was made by Col. James W. Judy (114th Illinois) in gallant style, with a loss of one man killed, and nine wounded, two mortally, since dead. The 72nd Ohio had one man killed, and 12 wounded, Lt. Col. Crockett, commanding, being himself slightly wounded. The 95th Ohio had two men wounded. The 93rd Indiana, on this day, had one man killed and five wounded.

My brigade was in position as follows: the 72nd Ohio along the ridge, left resting on the road, the 95th Ohio in rear of the 72nd, the 114th Illinois along the ridge, right resting on the road on the road, and the 93rd Indiana long the ridge on the left of the 114th Illinois. About dusk, Gen. Blair's troops in advance retired, leaving no troops in the advance of my brigade. I immediately ordered pickets and guards to be thrown out to the front. My brigade remained in this position, being the advance at this point, until the evening of the 21st,

when my brigade was withdrawn, except the 93rd Indiana which did not withdraw until the morning of the 22nd. From the evening of the 19th until the evening of the 21st, my brigade maintained this front line, keeping up a constant fire of sharpshooters duringthe day and throwing forward guards at night, and having several men killed and wounded.

On the 22nd, my brigade was again ordered to support the troops of Gen. Blair. The 72nd Ohio was ordered to take position on the left of the advance of Col. Kilby Smith's brigade,where it remained until evening, when it rejoined the brigade, who had taken position on the same ridge, on the left of the road, previously occupied by the 114th Illinois and 93rd Indiana.

I am proud of my brigade. During this long and tedious march, not in a single instance has any regiment been behind time. My thanks are also due to my staff officers for the faithful performance of their duties. I must here say a word in praise of the line officers of the brigade. Deprived of all transportation, even for provisions, they have endured fatigue and hunger *without complaint, setting a noble example which has had a beneficial influenceupon the conduct of the men. Upon the subject I refer to the report of Lt. Col. Crockett, 72nd Ohio Volunteers. I venture to say that, owing to the circumstances beyond my control, my brigade suffered more from want of food than any other in this army; yet I doub whether any reached the end of the march in better condition or better spirits. I repeat, I am proud of my brigade.*

Respectfully submitted,

R. P. Buckland, Brigadier General commanding First Brigade

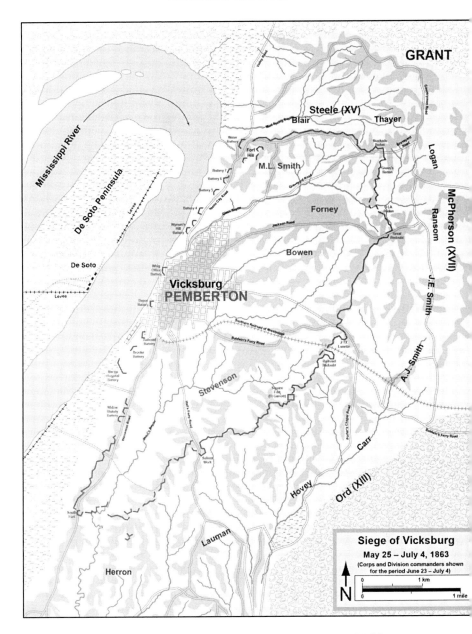

Union and Confederate Positions May 25 – Jul 4, 1863 (Hal Jespersen www.cwmaps.com)

The Siege of Vicksburg

Grant Determines to Starve the Rebels into Submission

Even though Vicksburg was still in Confederate hands, Grant was already being lauded by the press and his superiors for his successful campaign that brought him to its doorstep. Washington was ready to provide whatever he felt was needed next. First and foremost, Grant needed reinforcements. The Union perimeter around the Confederate works was nearly eight miles long and his forces were stretched thin.

These were readily sent and soon Grant's army was over 70,000 strong. Vicksburg was completely sealed. The siege plan was straightforward. Grant would starve the rebels into submission while constantly bombarding their positions and the city. All the while he kept his troops busy moving their trench lines closer and closer to the enemy works, applying relentless pressure.

The first part of one surviving letter written by Andrew Bush of the 97th Indiana Volunteer Infantry to his wife Mary exists from the campaign. It contains a description of the method by which the Union troops moved their trenches ceaselessly forward during the siege. Later in the war he would write a compelling series of letters during Sherman's March to the Sea.

June 4th 1863

Headquarters Fourth Division Fifteenth Army Corps:

Dear Wife I am hapy to inform you that my health is good altho my chin is pretty Soar yet where the Rebel Shot struck but is getting well fast; Trusting when this note comes to hand that it may finde you and all the friends enjoying good health and in fine Spirits without feeling uneasy about our personal Safety. Samuel and James are in good Health but as all our Soldiers are very much fateagued and care worn with long watchfulness for they have been skirmishing with the Rebels for eight days and sometimes they get up a pretty Strong and Stuborn fight. Our boys are working on the Vexburg plan fight behind their breastwork in day time and at night role barrels fild with earth toward the enemys breastwork and throw up fresh works which keeps them on the watch nearly all of the time. We are not loozing very many men Concidering the amount of men engaged. But the rebels have lost heavy on several occasions on the twenty eight they threw most of their forces on our Corps making an attempt to turn our right flank but they did not Succeed as it happened; they came like mad Deavils with deafing Chears but our boys held their fire until the enemy came within twenty paces of our lines. When they let Slip at them which foiled them up nicely and made them lumber to the rear with about three thousand less than they came with; Oh Mary this may be cheering news to those at home who never for one moment take a thought of how fast our nation is winding its road down toward ruin; it no doubt cheers the hearts of many when they hear of us gaining a grate victory which it Should but do those ever think of what it … (balance missing)

The 26th Louisiana's Jared Sanders continued reporting daily in his diary from May 25th through June 14th as the siege progressed. His diary portrays the difficulties he and his men face daily while noting the advance of Union trenches towards their line on an almost daily basis.

May 25

    No one hurt today in our regiment; for the first time since the siege has such been the case. Flag of truce at 5 o'clock, & we had a few hours of rest & _free_ breathing. During flag of truce a sharpshooter, seeing most of our men had returned in pits, & me standing in full view on the parapet, took a _deliberate fire_ at me – the ball passed harmlessly by. It was an infamous act. Their men were in full view, & one of my men hallowed to them – "If ye do that again we will fire a volley into ye & it will take all day tomorrow to bury ye're carcasses!" He was an _____.

May 26

Lieut. Guion acting <u>Inspector General</u> on Gen. Shoup's staff – appointed yesterday.

Close infilading fire today. One man wounded in Company H. Heavy bombardment of town by mortars. Read Yankee Memphis paper, <u>Bulletin,</u> of 19 May. Yankees active in front digging rifle pits.

May 27

Gunboats & mortars bombard town. An iron-clad, the "Cincinnati," tries to silence upper batteries & is sunk. Sharpshooting & cannonading all around lines as usual. Enemy place their flag close under our works to draw our fire. They all fire on our flags when they are put up. Ours is shot all to pieces. I think Johnson cannot possibly do anything before the 31ˢᵗ of this month.

May 28

Good news from Johnson; he is organizing a force at Canton. This is official. We hear Lee is on Arlighton heights & K. Smith in Lafourche. We hear <u>so many reports.</u> Two men wounded today. Col. Marks of the 27ᵗʰ Louisiana wounded today. Was on picket.

Our lines are from three hundred to four hundred yards apart, & men talk to each other sometimes. Last night one hallowed out "Hall old <u>reb</u> are ye sleep?" They do not <u>revile</u> us as much as when they first appeared before us confident of driving us from our works at the first charge.

May 29

Very furious bombardment all around our lines. Thomas Mason, Company B, wounded in left leg by shell, leg was amputated – poor fellow! One man killed & seven wounded in the regiment today. At 5 this evening the most furious cannonading around our lines since the siege.

May 30

Heavy cannonading at 8 this morning. Occasional firing during the day & very heavy firing from 5 until <u>sunset</u> – this is the daily routine. The boys call this "evening firing" their "<u>dress parade.</u>"

The soldiers suffer so much from confinement to pits all day. Our generals expect a night attack. If enemy were to increase occasional shots at <u>night</u> we would be much worried by it, for wee lay <u>low</u> in <u>daytime,</u> and scamper about at night.

Sunday, May 31

The last day of the month & no Johnson <u>yet.</u> Sunday & I thank God I am spared to see the holy Sabbath again. From the 17 until the 31 I have been among the dead & dying & yet have I been spared.

May the last of June find the siege raised & Vicksburg be still ours!

Was in town last night to wash & get clean clothing. In passing the road I saw dead horses & men on the road side killed by the enemy's rifles & (see the shell fall in a) part of town. They throw Parrot shell from the rear of the city into the Mississippi river.

The city grave yard was filled with camps; & as the work & stirring about of a besieged army is to be done at <u>night,</u> the haste & life in that solemn place was in sad contrast with the many <u>marks</u> that told of the dead. The moon was shining calmly down upon me as I made my way to the peninsular in front of the city the Yankee bombarders, 6 in number, were throwing monster shell in meteor-like course and with a terrible explosion throwing their pieces in every direction & some times demolishing buildings upon which they fell. Few houses, if any, are occupied; the inhabitants have caves in the hills with which Vicksburg <u>fortunately</u> abounds.

No one of the 26 hurt today. The Yanks now & then amuse us with a charge when they get a good drubbing – much to our delight.

June 1 1863

Very warm & has been so since our occupation of this place. Soldiers for water have to run over the hill to the hollow under fire of the sharpshooters. Our cry is "Oh, for Johnson or night"! lay in pits & read all day. Lieut. Guion reported for duty to Gen. Shoup. No one hurt today.

June 2

Bombardment all day - & very heavy fire near night. The days are <u>very long</u> now & nights very short. The enemy work constantly _____ the way. Night falls at ½ past seven & day breaks at ½ past three – very light at 4 o'clock.

Last night the enemy charged our right about 12 o'clock, rolling cotton bales ahead of them & were repulsed with great loss. This is first night attack. No one hurt in 26 today.

June 3

Not a great deal doing along lines. We are in constant danger from accidental shots. This is quite a school for patience. We are shut in from the world & are a <u>constant</u> target for the hostile soldiery outside. No one of the 26 hurt today. We can hear constant bombardment of Vicksburg. Our position is to the left of Jackson road about three quarters of a mile, & about two miles from the city – air line.

June 4

The enemy's main force has gone to look after Johnston no doubt. The fire was not heavy during day-time, but at night they shoot constantly at us – which <u>worries</u> us <u>much</u>. Heretofore in front of us the enemy have never fired during the night.

One man in Company H wounded. Beadel of Company B had his hat shot to pieces by cannon ball but not hurt – wonderful escape. The enemy have dug rifle pits within 75 yards of our lines.

June 5

Firing as usual, & we bored as usual. Lieut. Navarre wounded. Man in Company H wounded. Martin Fight, Company B wounded through side of head on picket. We fired on enemy's fatigue party digging pits close to our works. Not as many <u>rumors</u> as usual today. Went into town. Saw Bob Royster. No shelling while I was there.

June 6

Very warm; everything as usual…. Sat up late to look at flight of enemy's shell thrown at a battery 75 yards on our right. They burst very close to us. We have become accustomed to them. Yankeees over the way hallowed to us "Played out" – "Played out." And again one said "Old Rebs are ye all <u>dead</u> yet?"

June 7

This is a day of rumors. Kirby Smith has run Banks into New Orleans – taken Baton Rouge & New Carthage. What <u>humbug</u> rumor! Price has taken Helena & 60 siege guns. The enemy shoot every night now to get our grub wagons and are coming close to us – shooting pickets & etc. Shells are bursting now over our heads. Man in Company F wounded. Lieuts. Guion & Dick West pay me evening visits in my trench.

June 8

Yankee sentinel in front of the 26ᵗʰ captured. Our sentinels were posted on one side of a log & he was on the other – so he gave up. He was very non-committal & would tell nothing favorable to us. Yankees are digging rifle pits up the hill side which runs to our works. We are trying to drive them away but it is now <u>too</u> late. Very warm. Capt. L. E. Nee A.Q.M. (Acting Quarter Master) payed me up to June 1ˢᵗ, 1863. I have now $470 & a note of <u>Capt. Bateman</u> for $100, & one of Lieut. Dubois for $50.

Yankee was facetious last night and hallowed over to us that we had a worthy <u>general</u> over us now. Our boys asked who it was & the Yankee said "Gen. Starvation," which was a cause of much merriment on their side.

Read last of the Barons. Admired Earl of <u>Warwick</u> greatly a man of unbounded soul & principle. Our pickets ran the Yankees out of their rifle pits near us. Fatigue party commenced a palisade 40 yards in front of us on our left. Yankees posted men & drove them off. I was sick with fever last night.

June 9

Very little shooting this morning. Lieut. Denisson went to city sick. Fired at our position all night. If they were to try and enfilade us with <u>cannon</u> & <u>rifles</u> we would suffer much more. Last night two or three men wounded on picket – which is dangerous business now.

June 10

Heavy lightening last night in northeast – and this morning a very heavy rain. Our pits a perfect <u>mud hole</u> – awful time! Looks like it would rain for a week. For two weeks there has been a great deal of lightening & no rain. Quit raining at 3 o'clock. Had a fever again. But I wish to pass this siege without having been absent one day & hence I will <u>stick it out.</u> Rained again at dark. Covered over head & ears & took a soldier's unquiet rest. Rained, & prevented the enemy from shooting much today.

June 11

Poor <u>Joseph Evan,</u> Company B 26 Louisiana Volunteers, killed this morning at 6 o'clock. He was standing in pits & was shot in head with two balls – entering above right eye. Said nothing when he fell & was carried to regimental hospital senseless – died shortly after. Joe's mother was living at <u>Mrs. Bowman's</u> when last heard from. He was an only son of a poor widowed mother. As a soldier he had few equals – intelligent, brave, & never hesitating on duty or complaining. His officers regret him much. If I live I must see his poor mother after the war. Enemy enfilading us with an 8 inch gun on our left. Soldiers begin to draw quarter rations of <u>pork</u> today – <u>beef</u> is all gone.

165

Rumored that our fleet has taken <u>New Orleans.</u> What an absurdity. Stood up after dark to stretch my <u>limbs</u> & see the flying bomb shells thrown over the city to kill sick soldiers & women & children. There are so many unrecorded dead & among our noblest, that we should raise, when better times come, cenotaphs in each parish to their memory.

June 12

Put up palisades last night. No firing at our regimental pickets. Heard bugles of the enemy for first time. Beautiful day. Eight inch shell ____(killed one man in) Company F, in two – it took a fatigue party to pick up his remains. Lieut. Martin got a letter through lines by a courier. What war news he brought has not transpired.

June 13

Went to Vicksburg at 7 o'clock. Visited <u>Miss Gibbs.</u> Sent a letter to Cousin Jared W. Sanders in New Orleans which Miss Gibbs promised to send out by a wounded Yankee. Soldier in Company F killed, two others wounded. Lieut. Guion, <u>Bateman</u> & I dined together. Had a fine dinner – ham, chicken, steak, greens, okra & green corn – finishing off with <u>pie.</u> No firing at night. Returned to pits at 4 o'clock much refreshed.

Sunday, June 14

Last night was the most quiet since the siege. Saw Gen. M. L. Smith riding by his lines before day. Soldier in company C killed.

Chaplain Foster likewise continued his saga with an extremely detailed description of the first week of the siege including his personal terrifying experience regarding the constant bombardments. His recounting of his first walk through of the brigade hospital is graphic and bone chilling.

"…Change of base. Since our baffled foe could not take the place by force, he now endeavors to annoy our men by a more severe fire. They plant other batteries still and their sharpshooters dig trenches still nearer our line and make their constant firing more galling still. On the next day the firing

upon and over our Regiment was very severe. Their new batteries opened a cross fire upon our battery and since they had not acquired the range and overshot the mark, their shells fell over in the hollow where the Surgeon's Quarters were. Dr. C_____ and myself were lying by the side of the hill when those batteries opened upon us. At first the shell would explode above us and at either side; but at every shot they approached nearer, until our situation became exceedingly perilous. With rushing fury they would pass in a few feet or our heads and then with crashing sound explode, hurling the flying fragments in every direction. Close to the hill side we would lie, not knowing but the next fire would take off our heads. Presently one exploded just behind us, covering us all with smoke and the fumes of Sulphur. After the loud crash was over, we heard the deep moans of a man severely wounded. Who could it be? Was it one of the doctors that were with us? Upon looking around, in a few steps of us, there we discovered a soldier shot through and through the body with a ball from one of those loaded shells, weltering in his blood, hardly able to move. The place was too hot to dress his wounds there for the fire had not abated in the least, so he was borne higher up the valley and his wound examined and dressed. Poor fellow! He had come into the valley after a canteen of water and he was shirking from his duty by staying for hours on the side of the hill, thinking it was safer than in the trenches. Had he been more faithful, his life might have been saved. The post of duty is the post of safety, as well as the post of honor. He was carried to the hospital and lingered for several days before he died. The surgeon now thought about changing his quarters – but could not find a place suitable while all the valley was more or less exposed. Their troublesome batteries ceased after awhile and we had comparative quiet in our quarters. But we were not allowed to enjoy repose long. Towards evening the same crossfire opened upon us, overshooting our works and ranging up and down our valley. Now they come nearer and nearer. Every man hangs close to the hill side. Some get at the root of large trees. Capt. Wilson, our Commissary, rides up hitches his horse about seventy steps in front of us and seeks shelter with us under the hill side. A shell now explodes upon our right and now close by on our left; now one just behind us and then another in front; now they burst above us. How awful the rushing, howling sound of those rifle shells as they pass with the speed of lightning close to your head and then burst with thundering crash in your very ears. They come like howling demons of destruction, rejoicing in death and carnage. What is poor frail man when opposed to such missiles of war? Can his strength and courage avail him anything? Can he fight against the lightnings of heaven? Can he resist the swift thunderbolt when hurled from the hand of the Almighty? Where may he withstand the mighty missiles of war? What heart is there that quails not in the face of such danger? What face but turns pale in the presence of these bursting furies? Surely the demons of hell could not have invented a more terrible and frightful engine of destruction than these exploding bombs. If all the furies of the lower regions were turned loose upon earth to terrify and destroy the children of men, they could not with all their screams and howlings and frightful noises equal these terrible machines of death. Now, one of these howling monsters explodes right in our midst, but fortunately a little in front of us. The Captain's horse is struck down; he falls upon his haunches, pierced through with a piece of shell. His entrails protrude. He groans and moans with pitiful cry and tries in vain to rise. The firing grows hotter and hotter. We hold a counsel as to what is best for us to do. Shall we remain or shall we retire. We conclude it is safest to remain, for we had the shelter of the steep hill side and the valley all around is exposed. But no sooner had we come to this conclusion than a shell burst in our very ears and sent its sulphurous fumes in our nostrils. It seemed like to remain was death. A hundred yards below would carry us out of the range, though in making this distance we would be without any shelter. For one I determined to get out of the range for I was doing no good there. Others determined to pursue the same course. Leaving our shelter we passed down the valley out of the range of that dreadful crossfire. New batteries opened and the whole valley was filled with Minnie balls. Most of the men in reserve had made excavations, dug in the sides of hills, which afforded them great protection. When the firing ceased the doctors again had a consultation about changing their quarters, for the carriers said it was the most exposed position in the whole valley and when they passed they generally went at full speed, but owing to its convenience to the Regiment and to water, they agreed to remain there and to dig caves for protection. On the same evening I visited the Brigade Hospital where the most of our wounded were carried, and since my business was now with the wounded and dying, I thought I could do more good there than by remaining at our Regimental Hospital for as soon as the wounds were dressed they were removed to some Brigade Hospital.

The Wounded. This hospital, which was called Hospital No. 1, was situated about a quarter of a mile behind our lines. The building where the sick remained and where the cooking was done for all, was situated on a high hill, a beautiful resident. The wounded were placed in tents on either side in deep hollows. As I entered one of these valleys, a most horrid spectacle greeted my eyes. Every tent was filled with the wounded and the dying. There they lay, poor, helpless sufferers; some groaning from excessive pain, others pale and silent through weakness and the loss of blood. As I approached the surgeon's tent, my eyes fell upon the bloody table upon which amputations were performed. Upon it had just been laid a suffering victim – a man from our Regiment whose knee had been shattered by a piece of shell. They were applying chloroform to his mouth and nose. He now becomes insensible and seems to rest in sweet sleep. The surgeon, whose duty it is to perform the bloody job, rolls up his sleeves and takes a drink of brandy to strengthen his nerves. A tight cord is passed around the leg – then the gleaming knife cuts through the flesh all around – a flap of skin and muscle is turned back – then with a strong stroke the knife cuts down to the bone and next the saw with quick stroke completes the job and the leg is removed – the artery having been tied with a small cord, the flap is then turned down over the stump and a few stitches complete the job. The leg is thrown on the ground, where lay other limbs, hands, fingers, etc. All this time the poor soldier lies sleeping, unconscious of his loss or pain. He is then borne off to his bunk, where he must lie for weeks upon weeks, unless, indeed he be carried to his grave, which was the case with more than half upon whom this operation was performed. This was the first case of amputation that I witnessed and it made a vivid impression upon my mind. The poor boy did not get over the influence of the chloroform for that day; in fact he was stupid and drowsy as long as he lived. He survived for seven or eight days and died.

On passing through the hospital what a heart rending spectacle greets the eyes! Here we see the horrors of dreadful war! It is not on the field of battle amid the confusion and clamor of arms, where the sulphurous smoke and the thundering cannon drowns the cries and mangled bodies of the dead and wounded victims – but in the solemn hospitals where the wounded and dying are conveyed that the awful horrors of war are depicted. The first sight that greeted my eyes was most appalling. There lay a man with the frightful countenance, scarcely human so much disfigured he was. His hair, eyebrows and eyelashes singed off and his face blackened and burned to a crisp with powder. His mother could not have recognized him. Every feature was distorted – his eyes were closed and water running from his scalded mouth. He belonged to some battery – the caisson had exploded, scattering death and ruin all around. His groans are pitiful and low and plaintive. He can only lie upon his back. There he lies and there he must lie for weeks unless death comes to his relief. Passing along still further on, without mentioning common wounds, I beheld a youth, not more than seventeen, with his eyes and face most uncommonly swollen. A ball had passed just under his eye, entering his face and lodging there in the bone, which could not be removed. Both of his eyes were closed – Not a groan escaped his lips – With difficulty could he eat or drink, in fact he could subsist only on soup and fluids – he could not chew solid foods. There he lay, day after day and week after week, so meek and resigned, while not a murmur escaped his lips. He could not change his position.

Still further along my attention was arrested by a strong, athletic, noble looking young man who was wounded by a Minnie ball passing clear through his mighty chest. His chest was heaving and his heart palpitating so as to shake his whole body and his whole frame agitated by this fatal wound. What can manly strength and muscular power avail against such missiles of death? The strong as well as the weak fall helpless victims. There lies another, shot through the jaw. His mouth lies open and his tongue is tied back. Here is another scalped on the top of his head – his jaws are locked and he soon dies with convulsions. Another is wounded in a peculiar way – the ball enters his ear passes but – goes down through his shoulder, lodging in the vital parts of his body. There are several with their legs amputated who are destined to lie for weeks in one position, unless indeed, as it often happens, they are carried to their last resting place. Here are several with their arms out – There is one with his whole underjaw torn off and his shoulder mutilated with a shell – he soon expires. Here is one with his arm and leg both amputated. What would life be to him if he could survive? There is one who has had a pair of screw drivers driven into his jaw and temples. He floods his bed with his blood. Another had his hand torn all to pieces, with a thumb and little finger left. One is pierced through the bowels and suffers a thousand agonies before death comes to his relief. Why should I proceed any further? Every part of the body is pierced. All conceivable wounds are inflicted. The heart sickens at the sight. Low groans proceed from some of the suffering victims, while others with clenched teeth remain silent. The weather is excessively hot and the flies swarm around the wounded – more numerous where the wound is severest. In a few days the wounds begin to be offensive and horrid! The vile insect finds its way into the wounded part and adds to the pain and terror of the poor sufferers. Nor, can this be avoided, unless a nurse were detailed for every man – but there is only one allowed for every eight men. Those that can hold a brush in one hand must use it constantly and those that are helpless must suffer. Never before did I have such an idea of the cruelty and the barbarism of war. The heart sickens at the sight. Poor Cap. Coopwood, his wound was the most awful I have ever seen. His whole leg deprived of nearly all the flesh.

On Saturday there was a shower of rain. I was curious to know whether the enemy would cease firing during the rain. Instead of that they rather increased it, no doubt getting a view of our men as they would arise to adjust their blankets. The harder it rained, the more frequent their fire.

Now it is Sunday morning. On account of a severe cold and sore throat and general weakness through dysentery, I could not preach. But there is no Sabbath quiet here – War knows no Sabbath. I thought of the quiet Sabbaths at home and contrasted them with the noise and din of war that was now raging all around us. I thought, will I ever see those peaceful days again. Here we were shut in by a powerful foe – prisoners. There was no rest for our brave men – nor did the enemy take any. It was a day of no spiritual comfort to my soul. How unnatural is war. Thus the first week of the siege had ended. The enemy had made three grand assaults on our works and had signally failed. Will not Johnson come to our relief before another week is ended? Some of us felt sanguine that he would come. His cannon had already been heard in the rear it was thought. It was rumored that we had only ten day rations of bread. Our only hope was from without and Johnson's name was no doubt reported thousands of times every passing hour. The rations for our men were sufficient during this week, though not full rations. The men were cheerful. The desponding had gained courage by our successes and the sanguine felt more confident. Even the strong prejudices against Pemberton began to soften down. As for my part, I expected to hear Johnson's cannon thundering in the rear almost as confidently as I expected to see the rising Sun and I expect to see Grant's army sent whisking up the great river and I imagined how pleasant it would be for us to go and examine the enemy's works and how happy we would be when free once more and no longer molested by shot and shell. During this week many of the enemy had fallen to rise no more. This loss must have been heavy. Also several of our brave men had been sent to their long rest...." (to be continued)

The Noose Tightens

Eventually the Federal lines came to within a few yards of the Confederate defenses. In moments of less peril, soldiers from opposing sides would joke and taunt each other. Pickets would get together with their counterparts to share coffee, tobacco and news about relatives on the other side. They always returned to their posts though, ready to bludgeon each other in the next moment should the tentative truce be broken.

Tens of thousands of artillery rounds were fired into Vicksburg by both Grant's land based army and Porter's gunboats on the river. While the primary targets were Confederate defenses, so many shells landed in the city that buildings were unsafe for civilians as well as military personnel. The population dug caves in the hillsides for protection. Some were mere bombproofs used during heavy bombardments. Others were "lavish" multi room structures that were now the "permanent" homes of the well to do families for the foreseeable future.

Another excerpt from the book Yankee Bullets, Rebel Rations –By Gordon Cotton, included these interviews with Mary Jane (Smith) Bitterman who endured the siege while using one of these caves. In 1851 at the age of 15, Mary Jane Smith married 21 year old John Bitterman. He was a Pennsylvania carriage maker. He moved to Vicksburg to work his trade. The Bittermans lived on Jackson Street one block away from the Old Court House. Through her husband's foresight, this cave was outfitted in a manner much more luxurious than most. In 1906 Mary Jane recalled her life in a cave.

"Unwittingly and unintentionally I became a sharer in the uncertainties of cave life during a long period in the Civil War. My husband was employed in the Quartermasters department in this city and had sent my little son and myself to Bovina, where with my mother we were entirely safe. My anxiety for my husband was really the only personal uneasiness I felt, and when there was a lull in hostilities I would go into the city to see him. On one of these visits he urged that I had better return to Bovina, and I purposely loitered until I missed the train upon the appointed day. The second day also I arrived at the depot too late, and fully made up my mind that I would leave the next day, as my husband's anxiety for us was evident.

It seems that the federals were congregating in such numbers around the Big Black section, that troops of soldiers were being sent to circumvent their entrance to the city, and the train accommodations were insufficient for all the soldiers and I was barred emphatically. We returned to our home in Jackson Street, the two story brick adjoining the Dreyfuse Store but remained there a very short while, as its central position made it eminently uncertain and insecure. My husband superintended the excavation of a cave which would be about the most certain place of safety; in anticipation of the events that he believed would follow as the war progressed. The cave was most comfortable and our life in it was far more pleasant than most people would imagine. A hall way ran the entire length of the four bedrooms arranged on either side, and which were arches cut into the solid wall of ground. Beyond the hall was a large square room; used as a dining room and continuing from this was a continuation of the hall that led to another entrance into the other side of the hill. During a fierce firing and bombardment it became urgently necessary for us to seek the shelter of our cave. A slight cessation in the middle of the night gave us about as opportune time as those turbulent occasions could. Across from our house was a large vacant lot, and a number of mules were in the enclosure. As we were leaving our home that night a shell whizzed by immediately above our heads, and striking in the midst of the mules killed four of them. A small piece of exploded shell which scattered in every direction barely touched the skirt of the little negro girl who was with us, and she was seized with an agony of fear. The piece, small as it was, imbedded itself into the base of a wooden fence, thus showing the swift momentum and force which they traveled. My little boy found splendid diversion in watching the shell flying through the air, and when one would explode in close proximity he would exclaim in ineffable delight "by ding, there's another one."

Well our journey was short and uneventful; we had previously fitted the cave with the articles of housekeeping and were comfortably fixed. Our beds arranged upon planks that were elevated on improvised stands, planks covered the ground floor, and these in turn were covered with matting and carpets, the walls surrounding the beds were also covered with strips of carpets, so all possible dampness was by a little care entirely eliminated. The wall carpeting was made adherent by small wooden pins or stubs."

174

William Christy was an artillerist for the Union Army. As one of those relentlessly pouring shells into the Confederate positions he wrote a very soul searching letter to his father on May 31st He relates the most dangerous experience he had encountered and his concern for his character, as a result of the abject fear he felt at the time.

May 31st
Camp Close by Vicksburg

Dear Father,

I will try in this letter, to describe one of the grandest sights I ever saw. This morning at three O'Clock the batteries of Gen. Grants Army at this place, oppened at once on the doomed city of vicksburg and the effects of such a sight almost defies description. The line extends some eight miles round the besieged town. There is artillery enough on this line to shoot from one to the other. Now just stand with me on the point where the battery is placed, and see the vivid flashes of the guns, like lighting, and the showers of the shell, as they made there quick curves through the air, hissing and hurtling, and finally exploding with a report almost as loud as the gun. The air waved like the sea, and vibrated with a horse murmering sound, while the valleys were filled with the loud thundering sound of the detonation of the firing of the morter boats on the river and the flash of there shots, were seen on the background exactly like lightening, but still there is one phase of the scene I have not spoken about. that is the burning of the fuse in each shell, while they are going through the air. The fuse burns, with a blue light, and looks to say the least very devilish, and I have no doubt the secesh thought so. We kept up the cannonading for over an hour, and made some excellent shots. Tom and I worked on the gun together, he as four and I as three, so you see when there is anything going on we are generally close together and we were volunteers at that. There was not much danger in the dark from the rebel sharpshooters. But we have to stand our ground in the daytime, and then we have to dodge the bullets frequently. I have been doing the duties of driver no. 3, ditto also on the gun, and I don't see as there is much danger at the gun as there is driving. Now you must think me a coward but I will try to give you and the boys an insight in my feelings on the occasion of my first ride full in sight of the rebel fortifacations within rifle range. On the first day of the siege, we were ordered to a point on the left of the main road, from Jackson to Vicksburg, and in front of the largest fort on the works. Now I had stood my ground on the open field, and did not feel very shakey on the legs, but to be mounted on the back of a horse and know that there was not only hundreds of men that would shoot at you like they were shooting at a turkey, with a cool deliberate aim. But at the same time just such a thing as you were drawing after you, only larger if anything, made me feel very nervous, I assure you. But still there was not a man near me would have thought that. I really would have liked to have run away, I drove my own team with precission, and even directed the other drivers how I thought we could get along over some parts of the ground (it being very rough) to the best advantage. We had got our guns in position and got our horses and limbers under shelter of the hill, and beginning to feel that we had not so much to fear when we found out that our officers in command had not got our howitzers in the right place, so we had to take the same ride over again and ride up to within five or six hundred yards of the enemy works, in the open range of his batteries and sharpshooters. Father I was desperate, desperatelly afaird (but thank god) only of myself you know my bump of firmness is large and it is well for the christies, it is so, or I really am sure I would have run away, could you have seen my inner self. You would have seen a very strange trial of strength. How I reasoned with my self about my duties as a soldier. How a deep trust in the goodness and mercy of god would speak up in me to keep me true to myself and Country. I can only give you a faint Idea of what I felt and really suffered in that ride. But the battle was fought and praise be to god he gained the victory over me and I am considered good coin anywhere as far as soldiers is concerned, and really now I do not think I will ever feel so again. So now you see the confessions not of a great man, but of a poor weak fellow that scarsely knows how to live after trieing it now for nearly thriti-three years. In my letter to A.D. Christie, I gave you an account of the appearance of the country and so I have nothing new to say about that. Therefore I will have to fill up the balance of this sheet the best way I know how. Lately I have been in the habit of digging away down in too myself, as are all men *like me. In any way one respect as far as thinking is concerned or the methods of thinking is every one as erratic in there modes, not that (I) am in the least excentric that is to be noticeable, but at the same time I am so well aware of my weaknesses and yet it seems I do so little in the way of mastering them. There must be some thing fundamentally wrong in a character such as mine or at least in my surroundings, when I was more easily impressed with greater or lesser good, than I am now not that I can say anyone is to blame for me being just as I am myself. For in looking over the past I see nothing but a great many shortcomings in every respect on my own part, in all circumstances and a wonderful forbearance on the part of all with whom I have come in contact. Tis true I have been often miss judged through mistake of others and my own. And it must be that there must have been some reason on account of my own action or they would not have judged just as they did and acting accordingly. Now about the money I am really sorry that I have caused you to feel just as it seems to me you must have done when you wrote that letter to Tom in which you abuse me unmercifully, and talked so foolishly about me and Poor Cousin Jessie, it surly cant be mother saw that letter before you mailed it. Now you may not relish this little bit of advice much, but still it is about all the scolding I will give you whenever you feel again (which I hope wont be very soon for my own sake) just as you did when you wrote that letter. just ask Mother what she thinks you had best do. And I'll be bound you will do well to take her advice. Do with the money just as seems best to you. don't loose a cent on your wheat if you help it on my account, and if you do make yourself whole out of my funds, I regretted having asked you the question about David Bertie, in connection with anything of mine before the sunset on the day it was written not that I thought of the past, or what he has been to both of us, but I saw the folly of it in another way altogether. now when you write to me give me bread, even if you have to think to do it for I am very hungry, I will certainly write to mother soon. Father give me some clue to my self if you can for as sure as you live I am at fault or won't give way to the solution. Write soon give my love to all and believe me your Affectionate son Wm. G. Christie*

Conditions inside the Confederate lines were deteriorating but both soldiers and civilians had faith that Joseph Johnston would attack Grant's rear and break the siege. Johnston was indeed in Grant's rear, having reoccupied Jackson with some 30,000 men. But he was also convinced that he could not coordinate with Pemberton on a meaningful assault that would enable Pemberton and his force to break out. Additionally, Grant had positioned three divisions, one from each of his corps, in defensive positions on the Big Black in order to thwart any such plan. And so, while Vicksburg languished, Johnston did nothing.

Chaplain Foster continued his missive sharing his observations and thoughts regarding the second week of the siege. He spares no details in writing what he believed may be the last words his wife may see from him. Included in this segment are descriptions of the bombardment from mortar boats, a fight between the Confederate batteries and a Union gunboat, and more on the front lines. Then it's back to the hospital and the fate of the wounded.

"…Second week. On Monday morning, the 25th of May, a flag of truce was sent from our General to the enemy requesting that they would bury their dead, for their dead bodies were becoming very offensive, since some of them had been killed nearly one week and the weather being hot, decomposition was very rapid. The enemy did not seem to be very anxious to inter their slain, hence we were under the necessity of making this request. The flag of truce was received and the request granted. Presently the firing began to cease on the center of the line and gradually extended from right to left until quiet reigned along the whole line. What a relief! For nearly a week our ears had been greeted by the continuous sound of small arms and cannon. Not a moment in the day passed but brought with it some report. The stillness seemed unnatural but was very welcome. Now, the enemy make their appearance, coming out of their trenches and hiding places. They are numerous as a swarm of blackbirds in the winter season. They come out as numerous as the ants from a freshly stirred up nest. Some of them with spades and shovels approach to perform the solemn work of burying their

fallen comrades. They dig ditches near the dead and then roll the putrid bodies in – sometimes with a blanket for the winding sheet – sometimes with nothing but the clothing in which they fell. A little earth is thrown over them and they are left unmarked, unknown, to sleep until awakened by the last trumpet which we all shall hear on the great Judgment Day. While this sad work is going on, the enemy and our men approach near enough to hold conversation. The Missouri Regiments from each side begin to inquire for friends and relations. Old friends, once friends, now meet and extend the welcome hand. A brother meets a brother – bound by such ties which no relation in life can sever. They now meet as deadly enemies arrayed against each other in fatal strife – but still, born and nursed by the same fond mother they can but love each other. In another quarter they try to quiz each other. Says a Yankee – "How far is Joe Johnson in the rear?" The Confederate replies, "Where is your $300.00 bounty and your sixty days furlough?" For it is said that the enemy promised every man who would break through the lines, the above reward. Neither side secured an answer. Another western man cries out: "I say, I want to borrow some coffee and pay back when Johnson comes up in the rear". The Confederates make no answer to this cruel taunt – for no coffee has passed their lips for months, and they feel that Gen. Johnson may not come to their relief soon. The enemy are not allowed to come up to our works but are kept back at a distance sufficient to prevent them from over-looking our fortifications. The most of the day was thus occupied. The time at length arrived at which the truce expired. Back to your trenches now, men! Get down now from the high hills and exposed places. – To your guns, you persevering and unrelenting sharpshooters. – Separate now, ye brothers and relations and old friends and resume the miserable work of killing each other. Ye artillerists of the enemy go now to your guns that have now for the first time grown cold during the daytime in the past week. The storm is now coming – the storm of death – the cruel and bloody tempest of war. Let all seek shelter from the missiles of death. The whole line is now cleared, not an enemy is to be seen. Our brave men lie low in the trenches. The crack of the sharpshooters rifles break the stillness – another and another. The firing extends along the line. The booming cannon break forth once more. The firing increases – the whistling Minnie –

the rushing cannon ball and the bursting shell proclaim that the work has again begun. Our ears are greeted with the same old sound and the same suspense and disagreeable emotions fill our minds. Night again comes on and the firing ceases, except the booming of a cannon occasionally or when some wakeful sharpshooter fires at some dusky object in the distance as a pastime for the weary and lonesome watches of the night.

The Bombardment. The persevering foe gives up all hope of carrying our works by assault. As yet there had been no firing from the river in the rear upon the city. The stillness and serenity of the twilight is now broken by an unusual sound. A dull heavy sound falls upon the ear. Every ear is directed now to the rear. Now a tremendous explosion takes place high above our heads. It is a mortar shell! The wide throated mortar has opened upon us. In quick succession another follows and then another. The air is filled with them. Several mortar boats, within easy range, now shell at the devoted city of hills. They cannot possess the place, so they will endeavor to destroy it. Heretofore the women and children had been safe in their houses. Now, no place is secure in the town – houses are no protection against these mighty monsters of death. Now there is confusion and bustle amongst the citizens of Vicksburg. There is hurrying to and fro with the women and innocent children. They must leave their comfortable homes and go to their dark, gloomy caves. Better to live in a cave than to be slain in a fine house. Most of them have caves in the steep hillsides, which they dug during the long bombardment to which the city was previously subjected. To these gloomy caves must they retire for security. The enemy envies us our quiet nights and by the time the firing in our front begins to subside, they open upon us with mortars to drive away sleep from our eyes and disturb our repose. Their large mortar shells, thirteen inches in diameter and weighing about two hundred pounds are sent clear across the peninsula and reach nearly to our lines in the rear, passing over a distance of four miles. Within their range was all our wagon trains, all our hospitals and even some of our arsenals. Their firing was directed to different parts of town. Their fuses were shortened or lengthened, so as to throw them in the heart of the city, or to throw them in the rear. The appearance presented by this bombardment at night was grand and terrific to the last degree. Directing the eye to the river you first see a small light, about the size of a star, darting like a meteor through the air, ascending higher and higher in its progress. This you see before you hear the report, so much faster does light travel than sound. In a few seconds you hear a dull, heavy report in the distance. The spark of light, which is caused by the burning of the fuse, ascends higher and higher until it threatens to reach the very stars. Now it reaches the summit of its orbit and begins to descend on a curved line toward the earth. Nearer and nearer it approaches. Now a rushing sound greets your ear – like the coming tempest when the clouds roar with wind. The falling star now descends with fearful rapidity and the noise becomes more furious and terrible. It seems as if it will fall upon you head. You look with suspense and intense anxiety, expecting every moment the dreadful explosion. Now it bursts with tremendous crash and sends its howling fragments singing through the air. They fall all around, bearing ruin and destruction in their path. Another light is seen in the distance. Listen now at the dull sound. See it ascending with almost lightning speed up to the very clouds. Now it begins to descend. Look out! It is coming directly towards us. Hold your breath now, it is about to explode! The storm comes fearfully near. Fall down behind the cliffs and hills and hide from the rushing, falling mountain. It strikes the earth without exploding and shakes the very hills and makes the ground tremble like an earthquake. Instead of falling upon our heads, it fell a quarter of a mile distant. All night long they continue their bombardment. The hospital to which our wounded were carried was in full range of these mortar shells; also in reach of the Minnie balls and cannon shot from the lines; but it was convenient and all parts of the town were more or less exposed and the deep hollow afford some protection.

On the 27th an unusual heavy cannonading was heard on our left. The guns seemed to be of heavier caliber than usual. The firing was most rapid for artillery. It turned out to be a combat between one of their gun boats and our upper water battery. The gunboat, with a full head of steam, approached fearlessly and proudly. A shot from our splendid rifle cannon told her to halt. – But she heeded not the challenge, but with a defiant air and open portholes draws up in easy range, turns round her broadside and makes the bosom of the old Mississippi tremble with the shock of her big guns. To your guns now, Ye Confederate artillerists and punishes the insolent foe that dares defy strength. Our battery accepts the challenge and every gun does its part. With keen and cracking report, peculiar to rifle cannon, the voice of our guns can be distinguished from that of the enemy. The waters all around tremble and no doubt the fishes terrified at the unusual noise and shock, retire from the field of conflict. The resounding noise rolls up the mighty river and echo takes up the sound and rolls it further on. The gunboat is enveloped in smoke – a cloud of smoke rests over our batteries. Who shall be the victor? A contest so hot and so furious cannot last long. Surely, the boat is sunk. Soon the batteries will be dismounted. Unless our guns are soon silenced the boat must go down. The boat now trembles before our terrible fire. A fatal shot now passes through a vulnerable part – She totters under the fatal stroke. She turns her course and begins slowly to move off. Our shot pursues her with unrelenting violence. Now she careens to one side – her hull fills with water and slowly she settles down in the water and sinks to the bottom. The friendly waves close over her form – nothing but the chimney and the highest part of the upper deck remains as marking the spot where the conquered victim was buried. The object of the enemy was to carry our upper battery and then plant guns upon the commanding points and force our lines near the river on the left – for our water battery was exceedingly annoying to them and could silence any guns they planted within range.

To the lines again – but how are matters now progressing on the lines? The enemy, baffled in their efforts to storm our works, now turn their attention to planting new batteries. They do this on every hill, right in the face of our works. Their sharpshooters approach nearer and nearer. So numerous are their heavy guns that our batteries are virtually silenced – Only occasionally do they dare open fire. Then they bring down upon themselves the concentrated fire of the enemy's surrounding batteries, so that their cannon are exploded, the carriages broken to pieces – guns dismounted. Besides the increased fire of the sharpshooters, killing our artillerists and compelling our pieces to retire for protection. In fact our artillery was of but little service to us – so superior in number and caliber were the enemy's guns. We would not prevent them from approaching nearer so that they planted their guns in our very faces, just as near as they desired.

Their sharpshooters become more annoying this week. They learned the range of our ditches and killed our men while lying flat in the trenches. One poor fellow in our regiment was lying down fast asleep, not knowing that he would never awake again in this world. A ball pieces (pierces) his head and without a struggle, or scarcely a motion, he dies. Another one waiting to retire to the rear, but thinking it too tedious to go down the trenches and enter the ditch leading out for that purpose, and supposing that he can go over the exposed point, which is but a few steps, without danger, makes the attempt. He pays for his daring – a ball pierces his body and he falls mortally wounded. The dirt is being continually knocked off from the parapet by Minnie balls. Then more shells – that can go anywhere – keep the men in constant dread for they are continually exploding around and killing and wounding somebody. There they must lie under the scorching sun, without scarcely a breath of air. Day after day they must endure its sultry beams, with only an outspread blanket to keep off the rays, which also excludes the air. There they must endure the drenching showers of rain and lie in the mud day and night.

On a certain morning before day, during this week, we were aroused from our sleep by the most terrific cannonading that ever greeted my ears. The whole air above us was filled with streaming lights, carried by burning fuses and the bursting of shells, more frequent than the lightning flash on a stormy night, almost converted the night into day. The whole air around was continually filled with solid shot and shell. Over the valley of our hospital it seemed that a hundred were passing every moment. A constant rushing and continual bursting filled the atmosphere. The firing of their artillery was as rapid as brisk skirmishing with small arms. It seems that the enemy were endeavoring to frighten our men out of the ditches. It extended all around the lines. They had now mounted all their guns and they were showing us their power. Those in the trenches lie low and those without hug close to the hillsides. Those on the outskirts of the town, near the lines, creep back deep into their caves and the mother hugs her children close to her side. The shells burst all around our men, flashing in their very faces and filling the air all around with the fumes of Sulphur. The top of our breastworks are in some places leveled with the ditches and our men become more exposed. Do they leave the ditches? Are they frightened out of the works? Like heroes they stand this appalling fire and bear patiently all the fierce wrath of the enraged enemy. Some have slept their last sleep and live not to see again the sweet light of the day. Several shots fell in the valley amongst the wounded but fortunately no one was hurt. This heavy firing did not last longer than half an hour. It was too frequent to continue long as the guns would soon become too hot to use. It subsided about the dawn of the day. Then the old mortars chimed in again for it seemed that they had ceased during this severe cannonading, but it may have been that the noise of these monsters was only drowned by the heavy firing on the lines.

Here comes the sad ambulance. Within one heard doleful groans – the bottom is bloody with newly shed blood; with great pain to the sufferers their mangled bodies are borne along to the tent prepared for them. Another ambulance approaches – more wounded. We look with anxiety to see if any of our friends are in the number. Thus it was during nearly every day until our hospital was filled. How our men suffer in those rough ambulances. Some of them were simply small wagons without any springs. Just to think of a wounded man with broken limbs and mangled body being borne on such a rough, jolting vehicle as this. Every step is filled with pain and agony to the poor sufferer. No wonder they groan under such circumstances. It is a wonder that they are as patient as they are.

During this week a great many of our wounded in this hospital died. The first ten days generally decides whether the wound will prove fatal or not. The weather was so warm that many died who might otherwise have recovered. More than one-half of the cases in which a leg was amputated proved fatal. In nearly every case where a leg was broken by a shell, death was the result. The case which I have described, whose limb I saw severed from his body, survived several days. Every day I would carry to him a cup of buttermilk and he would express much gratitude, for he could not do anything and he subsisted on what I brought him and a little loaf of bread. He never seemed to have recovered from the effects of the chloroform. His eyes ever have a sleepy, drowsy expression. He was as patient as a lamb, for he was a child of God. Day after day he lay on his back, troubled and perplexed by the swarming flies – disturbed by the bursting shells. Gradually he sunk, growing weaker and paler, until he found relief from all his pain in the sweet sleep of death. I have described this case because it represents the condition of hundreds and their sad end.

Poor Capt. Coopwood, his end is drawing nigh. Ever since he received his awful wound he has been willing to converse upon the subject of religion. I talked with him freely and he seemed desirous to place his thoughts on the future and endeavor to make some preparation; but his pain was so great, his body so restless and his mind so confused that he often complained that he could not collect his thoughts and place them upon our subject. I exhorted him to look up to Christ and trust in him. Said he: "Parson, my mind is too weak". What a poor chance has the unpardoned sinner to make his peace with God when death is staring him in the face? His mind is confused, he is filled with terror – there is so much to do and no little time remaining that the mind shrinks back from the task. How few ever make their peace with God in their dying moments? As yet the Captain had entertained some hope of recovering. One morning I called in to see him and saw a great change had come over his face. His pulse was fluttering fast. Mortification had begun and was progressing rapidly. He felt the change; he called me close to his side and told me his fears and requested me to ask his doctor if there was any chance for him. I did so and was told there was no hope in his case. I went back to the Captain with a sad heart, afraid almost to tell what was the opinion of the physician – but upon his request I informed him that he must die and watched closely his countenance. He was not surprised for he had already felt the approach of death. O, what a moment that must be when the truth flashes across the sinner's mind that he must soon stand before his God! During all this day and the coming night he was sinking rapidly. The next morning when I came around to see him he was suffering intensely. He said to me: "I am passing away". He would use the same expression to his friends around, "I am passing away". He then pointed to his servant, who had been faithfully watching by his bedside day and night. I turned around and the tears were running from the boy's eyes, running down upon his cheeks and falling to the ground – he sobbed like a child. No doubt he loved his master. The Captain said that he hoped that his sins were forgiven. He now said: "O, that I could now go" and a few minutes after he shut his eyes in death.

I will mention another case which was deeply interesting to me. You remember that I noticed a large, stout, young man who was wounded in the breast. His wound at first was regarded as very dangerous, if not mortally wounded. I had passed him several times but he had not as yet spoken to me. He found out by enquiring that I was a Chaplain and he sent me word that he wished me to converse with him. I readily consented and found him very serious and determined to seek the Lord whether he survived or whether he died. He did not seem to think that he would die. He would request me to pray for him, saying that he had been a very wicked man and that he had a praying father and mother in Texas (for he was a Texan and was a Lieutenant in Walls Legion). Every time I returned to see him he would enquire of me if I had been praying for him. For some time he seemed to be doing very well and strong hopes for his recovery were entertained. But one morning when I called to see him his pulse was very much excited and his heart was bounding and leaping as if it would break through its prison. His breathing was very difficult. His fate was sealed – inflammation had begun and he cannot survive but a few days. I enquired of him how he was progressing in making his peace with God. "O", said he, "I am making no progress at all; I feel no better." Then he would close his eyes and pray. Deeply did I sympathize with him, for he had but a short time to live, but all I could do was to command his soul to the mercy of God. And the coming night he sent for me. As soon as I saw him I discovered a great change in his countenance – his face was radiant with joy – his eyes beamed with delight and a sweet smile was on his lips. He caught me by the hand and said he had made his peace with God – that he was happy in the Lord. He then requested me to pray with him. During the exercise he was deeply engaged and expressed great delight. Then he called up some of his men and said to them: "You have now seen what we have been doing – When you write to my father and mother, tell them what your eyes have seen and how I died rejoicing in the Lord". I remained near him all night – slept in hearing distance at his request. The next morning he was still rejoicing and gave every evidence of being a converted man. He died during the day, I trust in the triumph of the faith of Christ. No doubt the prayers of a pious father and mother were heard in his salvation, though they were far away and he died in battle. How their hearts would rejoice to hear that their dying son had laid hold upon Christ in his last moments.

Ah, the sufferings of the wounded! The whole air in the …

Page Missing

… long day?" Here we see the need of Christian patience and fortitude. What is there in this awful condition to sustain the heart of the wicked man? Here we see the horrors of war – the cruelty of this barbarous evil. Oh, Liberty, how precious and costly is thy price! Thus has it ever been. For this precious boon the best blood must be shed and untold sufferings endured. When the battle is fought we rejoice in the victory but we are too apt to forget the anguish and suffering of the wounded. How much better to perish at once on the battlefield than to linger out a miserable life for days after receiving a mortal wound. During this week our wounded men died rapidly – four or five every day at this hospital. Wrapped up in their blankets and placed in very inferior boxes they would be placed in shallow graves in the adjoining hollow. Sometimes the name would be marked – sometimes only a rude board and a small mound of earth would tell the spot where the unknown dead lie. Though no tear is then shed over the grave, yet far away hearts will bleed and tears will flow from the eyes of mothers and sisters and wives for those who are sleeping in the valley – unnoticed, unhonored and unsung. 'For every grave shall make some heart desolate'.

It was during this week that the first courier from Gen. Johnson reached our lines after much difficulty and danger. He came down the Yazoo in a small canoe – then down the Mississippi River – having been fired upon frequently. He brought the intelligence that Gen. Johnson was organizing an army at Canton and that he would soon come to our relief. This news was extended down the whole lines by order of Gen. Pemberton. How it cheered the hearts of our brave soldiers. Already were they encouraged and greatly lifted up by their repeated victories over the assaulting enemy. Now they felt that deliverance was at hand; that in a few days the thunder of Johnson's cannon would be heard in the rear and that with a strong force he would break the lines of the investing foe. No one now doubted but that Vicksburg would be successfully defended.

The rations of our men were now greatly shortened; in fact, reduced to one-fourth. Still they bore it cheerfully but complained of great weakness. Their rations were cooked by a detail and sent up to them in the trenches. Day and night they must lie cramped up in the ditches – drenched at times with rain, remaining wet until dried by the sun; then exposed to the hot rays of a burning sun. Towards the end of this week such hardships and exposure and the scanty diet began to tell upon our garrison. The cheeks became thin, the eyes hollow and the flesh began to disappear from the body and limbs and the whole appearance was haggard and careworn. Yet they were cheerful and did not complain. A few of them at a time were allowed to retire to the valley behind the lines and rest awhile but it was but poor resting for the shells and Minnie balls were as dangerous here as in the trenches. Many of them preferred lying in their places in the ditches. Some would read their Testaments – Others would sleep half the day. Thus would they quietly pass their time while the storm of war was raging over their heads and about them. Now the monotony of the scene would be rudely broken by the sudden death of one of their comrades, or a fearful wound inflicted by a bursting shell. They were refrained from firing and the enemy daily drew nearer our lines…." (to be continued)

Behind the Union works opposite Vicksburg, George Deal was one of the troops sent to block any potential attack on the army's rear by Joseph Johnston. On June 2nd he wrote to his wife and mentions a seven day march behind the lines to ward off Johnston's anticipated threat.

June the 2nd, 1863
Hanes Bluff near Vicksburg

My Dear Wife,
I once more take my pen to write a few lines to answer your kind letters I received from you. I was very glad to hear from my family once more and was glad to hear you was all well but was sorry to hear you had to live in so bad a house as you wrote. I am well and hearty but nearly wore out. We have been a marching for seven weeks most of the time and my feet is awful sore and has had blisters all over the bottom. I was at the battle of Snake crick near Raymond and then I was at Jackson, Mississippi and then was at the battle of Champion Hills and they was all hard battles and good (men) killed but I escaped all of them.

I would've wrote to you sooner but we had no chance of sending any letters home since we was on the march but this morning we can send a letter. So I got my old friend to write for me and that is H. Souder. I haven't wrote any to my family since we have been on this march. You wrote something about thanking me for writing for George Deal you husband. He always comes to me for a paper before he goes any other place. I can get and do all I can for him when I can. (Previous comments were from Deal's writer, Henry Souder:) I am glad you got that money I sent you. I was afraid it wouldn't get through but it is alright. I am sorry you have to live in such bad a house. I think some of the neighbors ought to fix the house a little for you.

I come here at Vicksburg and commenced a fighting and stood in a line of battle for seven days and then there was part of the time very heavy canoding (cannonading) and still they are at it. They have bigger canoding and ..... A little every once and awhile. we have them surrounded and this is the fifteenth day the battle has been here but our brigade has been (on) the site here all the time. We went on a march out after old Johnson. He was a coming on our backs but he was sorry for it. We run him. We was gone seven days. Some hard marching too. Oh I hope the war will be over after Vicksburg is taken.

I would like to see my family but it is out of the question. I will come home just as soon as I can and I write to you as often as I can and that is all I can do. Now don't fret for me for I have had good luck so far and I do hope I will come out as well as I have. You mentioned something about me a seeing the elephant. I have seen the tail and I think I will see something else soon.

Direct your letters to Vicksburg, Mississippi, 20th Ohio regiment, Company K, in the care of Capt. Kaga. I hain't sure this letter will go to you for there has been order against it. I will write soon again and I want you to do the same.

So good by my dear wife. This from your beloved husband. So no more, George Deal

Union trenches in front of Vicksburg (Library of Congress)

Captain Judson Gill's 33 Illinois was in line before the Confederate works of Vicksburg. His men were assigned picket duty. He mentions the informal arrangement between opposing pickets not to fire upon each other. He also tells of being awakened from a dream by a rifle ball hitting the stump next to his head. Clearly, while the Union troops seemed to be in less persistent danger than the Rebels, their positions were still in constant danger from Rebel sharpshooters.

June 7th 1863

Dear Sophi –

Still we (Co B) are all alive and some of the boys show symptoms of approaching bilious fever. In fact three of them have been taken

191

sick with that disease in the last three days. We are strengthening our works and part of the line is slowly advancing by means of tunnels, trenches etc. Sharpshooters are all the time exchanging shots and some cannonading by our gunboats and land batteries. The enemy returns but very few cannon shot either from scarcity of ammunition or because they can't use their guns on account of our sharpshooters who make it a special duty to kill every gunner who shows himself. Our pickets hold more or less conversations with the rebel pickets every night – except when prohibited by orders. I am Brig. Off. (Brigade officer) of the Day today and shall tonight station our pickets within 40 yards of the rebels. It is a point of honor with the pickets not to fire on each other unless there is some unusual demonstration.

Today I received yours of the 28th all informing of Mothers visit to B_ etc. I was glad to hear that father came too because I know it will do him good. He gets lonesome and downhearted at home and a visit abroad makes him so much younger. I was afraid they came before the house was done so that you could not have a good time. How do our mothers hitch & your mother always seemed more like my own mother before we were married than any other woman I ever saw. They don't look alike nor act alike but somehow it seems as if their feelings and sympathies are something alike. Do you think so. They don't "Think about little things" some? Yes indeed! Often forget – the cannons and muskets that are continually belching was and turn my thought to the most simple things at home. I even wished the other day that you had sent me a piece of your calico dress. I wanted to see what it was like and fancy how you would look with it on. I had a funny dream the other night. I must tell it. We had been ordered up at 3 in the morning to get out of the range of our siege guns that shoot over our heads at the enemy and are dangerous to our own men. We went a little way down the ravine and I lay down on the side hill with my head on a root – and fell to sleep. Dreamed I had gone home and you and I were on a visit to Toulon. It was Sabbath and we went to church. The same old familiar church in whose choirs I have sung ever since I was a boy and the same old preach preached from "Let not your heart be troubled, etc." After church we went home with Abby Gardener – you will know her some time – took dinner and were in the parlor enjoying ourselves highly. Abby was playing upon the piano and singing "Ever of Thee" when the piano broke and I awoke. The worse which I had suffered was the breaking of the instrument was the striking of a rebel bullet on the root about a foot from my head. I rubbed my eyes, raised up and found I was alone. The company having gone back with Kelsi (?) to their quarters. I cursed the scoundrel that spoiled my dream and leisurely returned to my "hole in the hill". I wont say that I wished the dream were true, because I wouldn't be anywhere else in the world at this time right here if I had the powers, but I will say that I wished that all but the last part of the dream would come true "and that sight early". One of the boys just tells me that this is the Sabbath. It is 4 P.M. Good Bye

Love to all. Yours C. Jud. Gill

As part of continual Union reinforcements making their way to the front around Vicksburg, Captain Joseph Young, 97th Illinois Infantry, wrote two letters home during his deployment towards Vicksburg. Upon his arrival at the front he would join those detailed to protect the rear against any possible attach by Johnston.

June 2, 1863

Dear Wife,

I have not rec'd a letter from you since that one you and Mr. Cater sent together. I am looking for One every mail but have not got any yet. I will write as soon as we land to let you know where we are.

I have had some fotographs taken of which I will send to the Children One a peace. You have my likeness. I will send one to your Mother and One to John Young and One to Elizabeth. I think they are not good picres. The artist said they was the best he could do under the circumstances. I had 13 taken for three dollars and if any of my connexion wishes the Balance they can have them by you informing me of the fact. I wish you to write soon for

I am very anxious to hear from you and the children. I have not Rec'd a letter from you and I have but little to write. I will close for the present, I Remain your husband until Death. I would write moore but I can not think of any thing that would interest you.

Joseph Young

Elizabeth Young

Memphis Tenn
June 7, 1863

Dear Wife

I have landed here this evening after a hard march of fifty miles. I am in first rate health and in fine spirits. I hope you are all well and harty. I have not Rec'd a letter from you since date 17th May though I think I will get one tonight. It is said that the transports is awaiting here to convey us to Vicksburg and we are all Ready for I think that will End this war and I would like to have a hand in it before it closes. I want you to write reagular direct as you did before. I have to go to setting my tent and I must close by saying to write often and as soon as I land I will write again I remain your husband until death.

Joseph W. Young

Elizabeth Young
Excuse my short letter for it is haste that makes me quit.

George Thomas, 53rd Indiana, wrote home to Minerva on the 10th of June expressing great confidence in the final outcome of the siege and the lack of casualties being suffered by his regiment although they were at the front opposing the Confederate lines. How different from the torturous depictions from inside of the Rebel works.

In Rear of Vicksburg
June the 10th 1863

Dear Minerva,

There is nothing transpired in the way of news since I wrote you last some three days ago. The rebels still occupy Vicksburg and our forces are still adhearing to the policy of keeping up a close siege without attacking them in their fortifacations. Then (as I have written before) if they get no assistance from outside the city it is only a question of time how soon the place must fall. They never can come out and fight with the force they have. I doant suppose it is deffinately know(n) how large a force they have but it cannot be anything like equal to our own. We all think that the supplies they have in the city are near exhausted. What few reach our lines give the same report. But there are but few coming in now (because) the pickets are so vigelant on both sides. There are but few causalities. Our regiment is on picket duty about every other day and yet there has not a man been touched yet. At some parts of the line pickets of the rebels and our own are said to be within thirty or forty yards of each other. But each party in rifle pits. If one of either side shows himself above the pits he is in danger.   There has been a good deal of rain falling today. The first for some days. It is still raining late night. There has been some heavy thunder this evening. Our camp is situated in a very deep gorge between two high bluffs. The rain as it falls runs off of the side hill down this narrow valley and overflow the most of the encampment today, rendering the tents entirely untenable. When the water ran down they moved them on to the hill side. A few of us had been inconvenienced in the least.   We have has some quite warm weather. But I have experienced quite as hot weather in June at home as we have had yet. But I doant pretend to think but what we will have a fair greater degree of heat yet.

No more tonight. Write Often

Remember me to all

Your affectionate

George

husband

Thomas

Shortly after Thomas penned that letter, Jared Sanders (26th Louisiana) recorded another week in his diary as the Yankee troops continue to tighten the noose around Vicksburg.

June 15

Cloudy & sprinkling. Bateman & Denisson rejoined their company.

On picket – went within 25 yards of Yankee rifle-pits under fire from their rifle-men. Heard enemy charged our lines on right on day before yesterday.

June 16

Up all night on picket. Slept until 12 today. James Johnson, Company B, killed by sharpshooter at ½ past 5 o'clock this evening. He was a brave & gallant soldier. The sharpshooter & himself both fired at same time. He fell with his gun empty as soon as he pulled the trigger. The enemy's 6 inch guns' enfilading us worries us much….

June 17

More shooting today than usual. Enemy charged on right yesterday. Saw large bodies of enemy on hillside moving off. Looks like it would rain. Made a place to get into during rain by covering 12 feet of pits with wood covered with dirt. Have my bed inside of the ditch. By the 27 of this month expect to be out of this.

June 18

Very thick fog to-day until late. Saw a paper to-day – saw one also on the 13th – the <u>Citizen.</u> Can hear the enemy singing hymns in their camps. What incongruity, an invading horde burning & devastating the land with unrelenting vigor at the same time having the sacred name of God upon their lips!

June 19

Beautiful day. Very quiet last night. Commenced giving rations of flour to our men. The 19th – last month we dug these trenches – 32 days since. Lightening very vividly in N. E. Ordered to fire upon enemy's working parties.

June 20

Enemy commenced cannonading at ½ past 3 this morning & kept it up all along our lines until ½ past _____ o'clock. It was the longest & warmest since we have been besieged. On picket tonight.

Sunday, June 21

Went to Vicksburg. Visited Miss Gibbs. Called up on Miss Williamson & cousins, with Lleut. Guion & returned to pits by 5 o'clock. Was in Col. Crow's tent when news came from left of regiment that Major Martin was just killed – it was 15 minutes of 7 – the greatest loss our regiment could have met with in one man.

Heard Pem Dazy died today. He was at upper batteries, went to be & was found dead by his comrades.

June 22

Yankees have dug up close to our works all around our lines – so close that they throw over notes & put them on wild canes & hand them to our boys. <u>Sergt. O'Brien</u> brought me a postage stamp to put on a letter to send to New Orleans. They swap knives, canteens, etc., with our men. By *agreement we do not fire upon each other unless one party commences to work. They fire <u>at night</u> at each other.*

As Sanders recorded his notes on history as it was occurring for him, Chaplain Foster continued to pen his letter depicting the ever declining conditions within the Confederate lines, contrasted by the attempts to keep morale high. Rumors of victories in the east by Robert E. Lee and the growth of Johnston's relief forces that would soon be upon Grant's rear kept spirits from flagging. The stress and exhaustion suffered in this environment are palpable.

"…Third Week. The mortar shelling this week was most terrific. Hospital No. 1 where the most of the wounded of our regiment were carried was most unfortunately located. It was in reach of the fire from the lines and was about the limit of the range of the mortar shells from the river. A negro while nursing was shot down by a Minnie ball while in the act of waiting upon the wounded. One of the wounded was also hit by the same kind of missile while lying on this bunk. Fortunately the ball was too much spent to do much damage. The house on top of the hill where were the sick and some of the wounded also, and where the cooking was done and where we all took our meals, was struck several times by cannon shot and shell from the lines. While at dinner, one struck and exploded tearing down a large portion of the brick wall. A Sick man had just risen from his bunk to look out the window. He left his watch and coat where he was lying. The coat was torn to pieces and the watch broken into a thousand fragments. Was not there a special Providence in this? Another shot passed through the house, barely missing two of the doctors while they were dressing – passed through two of the walls of the building and finally inflicted a mortal wound on a poor fellow who was just recovering from a long spell of sickness. His hip was torn to pieces and he died the next day. While we were at breakfast one morning a shell just passed over our heads, hit a few steps in front of us, buried itself in the ground and then exploded, scattering the dirt all around. We eat our meals more rapidly after this and sought the valley below. Every time we eat our meals there, shells from the lines would trouble us. Also

those monsters from the mortars. Scant as our rations were, we could not eat them in peace.

Eight mortar guns were now playing upon the town and vicinity. Two of them ranged directly at our Hospital. I don't suppose they could see the yellow flag. If they could see them (they) seemed to have aimed at it. O! how annoying to all, especially to our wounded. Day and night they keep these poor suffering men in dread. At night the firing increases. They burst above the valley and send their howling fragments in the vale below in the very midst of our wounded. Now a large piece falls in the tent and strikes in the street between this bunk, so that none are hurt but all are made uneasy. Now one hits the bunk upon which a wounded soldier lies and tears it down to the ground. Another piece falls through the tent, strikes the ground nearby and bounces upon the pillow where one is lying. They come rushing overhead, every one appearing as if they would fall right upon your head. Thus day after day our wounded, as well as others, were tormented by this missile of destruction. They could not sleep at night – were always in dread. No wonder, under such circumstances, that they did not recover fast – that many died, for sweet refreshing sleep had no sooner closed their eyelids than thundering shell would explode above their heads and drive slumber far from their weary eyes. The well and sound could not sleep with unbroken slumber but would be awakened out of a sound sleep a dozen times during the night by these unwelcome messengers. None who lie down at night had any assurance but that before the day should dawn his body would be torn in pieces by a fragment of shell.

There were two nights during this week that I can never forget. The firing from the mortars was more frequent and nearly every shot explodes above us and around us. Lieut. Owen of our regiment was wounded and had come to this hospital for treatment. We slept together on the side of a steep hill in the valley but had no care or any protection beside the position. The doctors had now left their rooms and had caves to which they would resort when not on duty. Our position was exposed also to the fire from the lines and we were on the wrong side of the hill for protection from that source; so when the firing from the mortars would slacken and that from the lines increase, we would change our position to the opposite side of the valley. Then again the mortars would become more furious and we would rather risk the firing from the lines. Solid shot from the lines would strike against the hillside above our heads and the large mortar shells burst above, throwing their fragments all about us. At night we would watch the flying meteors and when one would seem to be making the descent right on our heads we would shelter as close as possible to the side of the hill. We would lie down to sleep and by the time that sweet slumber began to close our eyelids, our nerves would be shaken by a tremendous crash near our heads, which would dissipate all sleep for a while. Then again, composing ourselves, we would again fall off into a doze, only to be disturbed again by the same unwelcome sound. At midnight when the whole world is wrapped in forgetfulness, we were scared, frightened in our dreams and disturbed in our slumbers. All we could do was to commit our souls into the hands of Him that never sleepeth and who is able to save from death. One night the firing was so hot I thought I would try a cave in the hollow beyond us; so into it I went before sunset. It had been a vacant one and I thought I would have it all to myself. I moved my blankets over and congratulated myself upon having a good night's repose. I felt more secure from danger. When night came, here comes two or three men; soon after a few more, until the cave is crowded full. I thought I could still stand it and remained quiet for some time. The shells were raging over us and would sometimes strike so near us that we would entertain some fear that our cave might be crushed in by the falling of some unexploded mortar shell. After a while the place became so hot and so crowded and the mosquitoes so bad that I determined to leave and seek my same old place where at least I could have some air and room. So I took up my bed and over the hill went my steps, increasing in length and rapidity as some howling shell would seem to pursue me. That was the only night I ever tried a cave. I was satisfied with the open air afterwards.

Near our hospital, in the same valley, was a large cave, with two or three families occupying it. They had several children and could with difficulty keep them within. Some of the little fellows would crawl out and go to playing on the green grass, until a shell would explode near by, when they would go rushing back again. An old woman, who was their grandmother, was much annoyed at the conduct of the children and would be always calling them in. She seems to have had a perfect horror of a shell. When the firing would subside, she would venture out, but as soon as a shell came in a quarter of a mile she would run back to her hiding place. They had their cooking done at their homes and their meals brought to them. They became exceedingly wearied with their cramped position and wished the siege would end in some way.

Our eating at the hospital this week has been very scant. At first we had plenty of bread and beef. Now we were allowanced to a small piece of beef and pea bread. The pea bread was made of peas and corn ground up together and mixed in about equal proportions. It presented a black, dirty appearance and was most unwholesome – as heavy as lead and most indigestible. But we did not have enough of this. We were thus kept half hungry all the time – consequently not in the best humor. But we fared better than our poor soldiers in the ditches. There were several orchards around and the apples were half grown. The trees were soon stripped of their premature fruit. Even soldiers from the line came out to share in the treat. The doctors at the hospital lived like kings. There was no famine to them. Their tables groaned with luxury and with every abundance. Though Dr. Minor, the Surgeon in charge, was a graduate of the same college and from the same State, and was acquainted with my brothers and had been at my father's home and seemed to be very friendly, yet it was never convenient for him to ask me to take a meal at his table, when he knew that my fare was miserably rough and short. Notwithstanding my position as Chaplain, he sent me to the same table with the nurses, where it was a rush to procure what little we obtained, and, when not wishing to rush like a dog for my food, I requested of him that he would allow his servant to give me my portion to myself, even this boon was denied me and for my miserable fare I paid one dollar per day. But as yet I could not help the matter; my duty was there with the wounded and there I must remain.

This hospital continued to be so much exposed that the physicians were talking about moving it to some more secure location, but it was a serious job and they dreaded it. About this time the firing was not so dangerous and they abandoned the idea but they had long since refused to receive any more wounded and they sent off a great many of the sick. About this time the mortars ceased firing altogether. What was the matter? Some said that our men had gone over at night and silenced them. Others thought that they had gone up the river to drive Gen. Price out of Helena for it was reported that he held that place. All kinds of rumors were floated amongst the garrison. We heard that Gen. Price had captured Helena and had taken several gunboats and that he had turned all the guns towards the river so that no transport could pass. This report was generally credited, so that our spirits were greatly raised and we thought that Grant would be made to feel the pangs of hunger and would suffer the fate to which he had doomed us. The silence of the mortar boats at this time confirmed our minds in such a belief. We also heard that Gen. Lee had again defeated Meade and had demolished his entire army and that he held Arlington Heights and was shelling the City of Washington, after having demanded a surrender. This intelligence was said to have been received from a Northern paper. This, however, was not generally credited, though all believed that Meade's army had met with a great defeat. These rumors, for a while, cheered the heart. We felt more confident of success. Besides couriers would come in stating that Johnson had an army of ninety thousand men; that they had organized and were coming to our relief, that he would attack the rear of the enemy in ten days at most. Some said that they could hear his cannon in the rear. Again during this week the enemy opened a grand general fire of artillery as they did before, in order to intimidate our men and annoy them as much as possible. About three hundred pieces of cannon were fired and loaded as fast as possible. The whole air was again filled with burning fuses and bursting shells. Our cannon dared not open their mouths but hid themselves behind the embankments and hills. Even there, they were sometimes dismounted and torn to pieces, their caissons exploded and their men killed. The breastworks were in places torn down and many of our brave men had seen their last day. But, compared with the fierceness of the fire, comparatively few were killed. Our hospital building was shot through and through and the hill was for awhile cleared of its occupants, for all those who were badly sick were removed and those who could walk sought shelter in the valley below. Solid shot and shell would fall in the tent amongst our wounded but they seem to have been defended by the hand of God. Thousands of these missiles would pass over and fall in the city. All who had caves sought protection. Mules, horses and cows were killed on the surrounding hills. This heavy firing lasted for more than an hour and then subsided to the usual firing, the continual sharpshooting and the occasional booming of the batteries.

Another week draws to a close and no relief from Johnson. Our men are weak from constant fasting and long continued confinement. Some become disheartened and begin to fear that Johnson will not come at all. The question with all is, how long will our rations last? Some say not more than another week – then we hear that there is enough to hold out to the Fourth of July. All hope now was from without. There was no doubt but that our rations were quite limited. The more hopeful still look for assistance as confidently as ever…." (to be continued)

McClernand Relieved

In mid-June, Grant was presented with the opportunity he had longed for to deal with a different foe. The self-aggrandizing McClernand had finally gone too far. He had a copy of his orders to his troops published in a northern paper congratulating the men for their successes on May 22nd, while casting fault on McPherson and Sherman for not adequately supporting him. He strongly implied that had they done so Vicksburg would have been theirs. Not only did this completely anger and alienate his fellow Corps commanders, but violated strict army orders not to publish any army orders in the press. On June 18 Grant summarily relieved him of command of the XIII Corps and sent him home to Illinois. He was replaced by Major General Edward O.C. Ord.

Shortly before McClernand's dismissal, Captain Young finally arrived at Chickasaw bluff as part of incoming reinforcements on June 11th. He reported home to his wife, telling her of their position and intended use to counter any advance on Vicksburg by the Confederate General Johnston.

Mississippi
Chickasaw Bluffs or Haynes Bluffs
June 12th 1863

Dear wife

> *I once more imbrace this preasant opportunity of informing you that I am well at preasant hoping if these lines comes to hand they may find you all well.*

> *I rec'd two letters from you yesterday. I was glad to hear from you, and I was sorry to hear of you being sick, although that is something beyond our controle, yet I feel very sorrowful when I hear of you being sick. I will say to you we landed here last evening after a two days run. We are on Chickasaw Bayou Haynes Bluff where there was such a battle fought last spring by Sherman – Here is the greatest natural fortifications in this whole country, we are going to ditching and making fortifications here in Order to Defeat Rebel Jonson that is supposed to be coming in the Rear and to Reinforce Vicksburg and if he passes us he will have a nice time of it, he is said to be on this side of Black River with a large force. Our officers feels confident of success if he should come as for the amount of troops that is. I am ignorant though. We run two miles further up the Bayou to where Gen Kimballs Devision is camped and the whole Bluffs was lined with troops and then we come back to the lower end of the range of bluffs where we will stay – We are in eight miles of Vicksburg, where the Cannon is Roaring day and night. We can see the flash of the guns of at night and hear the shells burst, It has been three days since they have replied to Grant from the forts in Vicksburg, the day before yesterday Grant took three whole batteries and the men that maned them. I seen the Rebs going up the river, It is rumored here that they have offered to surrender if Grant would gave them three men, it is thought that jeff Davis is here but I think that uncertain. There is know*

doubt of Grant taking the place, We will not go to that place for he has more troops than he can use at that place and all the chance for us to be in a fight is to weight for Johnson and if he comes he is sure of a thrashing for we are reinforcing beyond anything that I could think of, The River is speckled with troops coming here for to be prepared to meete Johnson if he should come. We went down on the Mississippi River with in ten miles of Vicksburg and then run up the Yazoo River some five miles and then took the Bayou so we are camped some twelve miles from the Mississippi River –

You wrote you was going home with you Father next fall. I wish you to use you own pleasure but I do not know what will become of the things, but if you can make any disposition of Our stock and Rent the place I would be glad for you to go but if you have to leave all the things I am afraid they will go to destruction, I want you to have that field below the House sowed in wheat and the field that Halder has in wheat. Have them two sowed in wheat. If you go to Illinois I would like for you to have the Clover field sowed two. I do not wish any corn tended on the place next year. If you do not go I would like for you to have them two fields below the House sowed to for Our selves if you can hire them broke up and if you rent them out I do not want my mares and plows used. Let the man furnish his own teem. If you stay at home you had better not sow the Clover field. Keep it for pasture unless you can have that fence run down the branch by taking away the fence between that little filed that Halder in wheat and the wood and run it down the branch and that would make pasture sufficien for the stock but I leave it all for you to manage for you self, thinking that you will do the best you can for us.

J. W. Young

E Young

On the 19th of June, Young again writes that he hopes Johnston will come so that they can completely defeat him and end the war. He also mentions the increased pay he is now earning as a captain telling his wife to spend what she wants to spend for "life is hard".

Snyders Bluffs Miss
June 19th 1863

Dear Wife,

I embrace the preasant opportunity of writing you a few lines to let you know that I am well at preasant hoping if these lines should come to hand they may find you and the children all well.

I rec'd 2 letters from you today. One by mail and the other by the hand of T. Butcher. I Rec'd the thing that you sent by Wm Sparks although he did not come. He sent them by T Butcher and he went to Lagrange for Both of his Boys were there sick.

I sent you Seven Photographs for the Children while I was at lagrange and I have got Six others I intend to send. One to you mother and One to John and Elizabeth and I will send the balance home. We are here at Our Old camp on the Bluffs and are fortifying and making ready for a battle but I do not have any idea when it will come and it may be that it will not come a tall and if Johnson just knew what was good for him he never would come, for he is sure of a thrashing if he comes. All the Military Men thinks if he does we will capture his whole forces. Our Army, as Gen Grants Forces combined is able to whip any forces that is likely to be brought against it. The army here is fifty thousand strong and is reinforcing all the time. General Grant says that he can take Vicksburg at any time he choses but if they will reinforce Pemberton at Vicksburg that is the thing I understand to be the desire of General Grant so as to make as large a battle of it as posable for we have the fortifications this time and Vicksburg is surrounded so that One half of the forces could be spared from there to help us, and at the same time keep General Pemberton cooped up in his hole. I feel perfectly Safe in Regard to our condition, for the Enemy will have to whip at least a hundred thousand troops that the most of them never has been whipped and in addition to that we are in fortifications that is as good as Nature and art can make. So I think that in a short time you will hear a favorable account from Vicksburg.

There has been the most wonderful display of General ship here by General Grant that the world has ever saw, Napoleon not excepted, for he just swung a large army sufficient to surround and hold the Rebels in the City at the start. There has hardly been a night but the Rebels has tried to brake out, and leave but if they was out of the City they could not escape for this wing would hold them. I will say a few words more and quit. We have our fortifications all completed and we are ready for the fight but if they stay a way three weeks yet we will keep improving for there never was fortifications so strong but what they could be improved and strengthingind.

I wish you to tell the sympathizers that they may fix for some thing else for in spite of the Rebels South and there friend North that Vicksburg and all there Army is gone up, they ought to meete up there oftener of nights. I under stand that Friday night is there time they meete to devise plans and plot there treason a gainst there Government. Tell them to meet Tuesday night and go and clothe them selves in sack cloth, and take a pan of Ashes a pon there Heads, and mourn over the defeat of there brethren. I do think that these Open harted Rebels in principle is far better than them cowardly simpathizers, they are cowards and would fight for the south if they had pluck enough, but all they can do is whine and yelp a bout the niger. I care nothing for the negroes. I am for union and that Only and if they was down there a while they would soon learn to care nothing for Slavery so they could put down the Rebillion the easiest way that would soote them best.

I think this battle if Johnson attempts to come here with such a force as is thought that he will bring that will end the war and I think we will be at home this fall. Tell all my neighbors Howdy for me especially the old ones, for I think I will see some of my young friend down here before long. I would like for them to come to our company. I will let you know how the health of the company is. Our Boy(s) (are) in good health and fine spirits. I expect that Capt Fletcher is dead. I hear from there the 13th and it was thought that he could live only a few hours. Tell all the children that I will send them a preasant before long. I will send them some money. Mary and Martha can buy there dolls and Willey and Jake can get there candy. I was *very glad of that handkerchief for I had none. We will draw our money in a few days. I will draw Forty Dollars that will Bring me up to the first of May when my Lieut pay did com. I get $100.05 per month. I will send some money when I draw. I want you to by just what you want and live well for live is hard.*

I will bring my letter to a close by subscribing myself your loving husband until Death

Joseph W. Young -

Elizabeth Young

Tell Esqr Carter that I will write him an answer to his letter in a few days.

George Deal shared with his wife Sarah that the 20th Ohio is alternating every two or three days with troops in the rifle pits at the front. While he can't imagine the rebels holding out much longer he remarks that "the balls come over pretty thick" when they are in the front. He continues to explain to his wife that there is no way for him to come home until the war is over.

Camp in the rear of Vicksburg
In a big hollow
June 16th, 1863

My Dear Wife,

I take my pen to write a few lines to let you know I am well with the exception of my feet is pretty sore and is swollen some but they feel better now then they have been. I was in the hospital one week but the reason why I was left at hospital was because they was ordered on a march and I couldn't stand marching but the regiment did not go. So I came back to the camping again. They are still a sieging here yet and I can't tell when this fight will be over but I think it won't last but a week longer. I don't know much how they are a going to hold out any longer for I have heard they are starving already. IF that be so, it won't be long before we are in Vicksburg but it may be longer than I think for I have (been) out in the rifle fights yesterday and the balls come over pretty thick but there wasn't any of the camping....that time but I don't know how soon there will be. We go in the rifle fights once or twice a week. I think we will get along alright.

You musn't think hard of me not a writing to you any sooner for I wrote just as soon as I could. Be in good heart and content yourself and I will come home just as soon as I can. Now Sary you know I can't come home now for it is impossible for me to come. I do hope the time will come when we all will come home and enjoy our families again. I think the time is near at hand when peace is declared. I hope these few lines will find you enjoying good health and doing well. Well, I hope you have your house fixed up a little better than it was.

I must draw to a close. You direct to George Deal, 20th Ohio regt, Company K, in the care of Capt. Kaga via Memphis, Tenn. They will come all right to me.
So no more at present but I remain your husband till death,

George Deal.

This is to my wife Sarah Deal.
A post script read:
Be good to my sweet little children and yourself. I will send a little book that I got in the hospital. I would like for you to send me dozen postage stamps if you have them handy and can get them handy. So write soon to me soon if you can.

Another week, the fourth of the siege, has come and gone. Chaplain Foster expresses relief and joy at a respite from the mortar boats' continuous bombardment. The streets are full of life for but a moment's time before those boats commence their deadly fire again. Another Sabbath lost to the unceasing war. Rev. Foster changes his base to a new hospital established in the town. It is from this location that he begins to pen this odyssey of the siege, looking back at first then continuing to add daily in real time until the end.

"…4th week. Owing to the silence of the mortar boats, the people of town, the wounded at the hospitals and all the attendants felt great relief. The caves were deserted in town and women and children came out with joy and entered again their pleasant rooms. The streets were filled with citizens. The whole town seemed to breathe freer. Now one could see ladies walking the streets at their leisure – not with the hurried, uneasy step that marked their gait during the bombardment. What a blessing to walk the pretty streets of this city of hills without hearing the rushing of shells or the singing of flying fragments. But, alas! This quiet did not last long. Afar off in the distance, from the same fatal spot across the peninsula, a cloud of white smoke rises up. Then the dull, heavy sound is heard – a sound too familiar to our ears – now comes the rushing shell – high up in the air it explodes and sends its whirling pieces all around. Before this unwelcome noise had died out in the distance, another cloud arises and here comes another unwelcome visitor, and then another follows in quick succession. The mortar boats, after a silence of one or two days, have again opened upon the devoted city. What a bustle among the people – what a confusion in the streets. Mothers send for their children. They prepare to leave their comfortable houses. Everyone walks with a quick and hurried step. The courier puts spurs to his horse and flies with speed upon his errand. The teamsters put their horses into a quick trot and seek refuge behind the steep hills. The streets are soon cleared. The same feeling of dread and suspense settles down upon the mind. I happened to be in the town when the firing began and was deeply impressed with the change that came over the city. All our hopes were dissipated – the mortars had not left, neither had they been silenced. They had only ceased for the want of ammunition – now they had a new supply. Farewell then quiet and peaceful moments and dear, happy hours of unbroken sleep. Ye wounded, suffering men, open now your eyes and ears in dread suspense. Sleep no longer with sweet slumbers during the long watches of the night. Again you shall be scared in your dreams and frightened in your slumbers. Your eyes shall now remain open

and wakeful and your weary limbs become doubly fatigued while you drag your burdened existence through long tiresome nights, listening to the bursting bombs and flying fragments as they fall around you, above you and near your miserable couch.

They seem to fire those mortars more rapidly than ever. One day I was standing upon the portico of the second story of the hospital building, watching the firing around the lines and enjoying the beautiful scenery that was spread out before me, for it was a high commanding point and overlooked the whole city, as well as part of our lines, and while I was thus employed, enjoying the wide extended view and the cool refreshing breeze, one of those mortar shells exploded in front of me, high up in the air, and sent one of the large fragments with singing, silvery sound right toward the building. It descended close to the porch on which I was standing and struck the ground near the steps with great force, tearing up the yard at a fearful rate and filling the second floor with dirt and sand. One of the sick men, a pale, slender fellow, was just going out to get a drink of water. He was knocked prostrate on the ground, almost covered up in dirt and we thought he was torn all to pieces. No doubt he thought the same for he lay there for some time. Feeling no pain, he at last concluded that he could rise up. He stood upon his feet, shook the earth from his clothes, surveyed his whole person and then proceeded on quietly to the well, where he had started to get a drink of water, as if nothing had happened to him. This incident disturbed my pleasant reverie and I preferred not to remain any longer on that porch – as beautiful as the scenery was and as refreshing as was the breeze.

Again, Lieut. Brock and myself were reclining on the side of the hill watching and dreading those mortar shells. Here comes one making its path directly towards us – it explodes in a dangerous position. We got as near as possible to a large apple tree near us and await the result. Here comes one of the fragments. It threatens to fall upon our defenseless heads but the shield of God warded it off and it falls to our side but two or three steps from us and throws the dirt all over us. The piece would weigh twenty pounds, tearing up a large hole and burying itself more than two feet in the earth. This shocked our nerves considerably; we felt thankful for our deliverance.

As soon as Lieut. Brock had recovered from his wound, I attended him part of the way to show him the best route to the lines. The shelling from the river was very severe and we had to cross a place that was particularly in their range. As we approached the place we discovered that the ground was torn up in several places. One would now explode to our left, some to our right. We could not avoid watching their movements. Presently one comes directly toward us and explodes at the most dangerous position. We stop – We hold our breath in dread suspense. Pieces fly and fall all around us. A large piece falls directly behind us in the very path in which we were walking. Had we stopped three steps sooner we both certainly would have been killed, but it is not in man that walketh to direct his steps. Why did we not stop sooner? The hand of God controlled our steps and spared our lives.

The Sabbath again spreads its sweet, soft light over the earth. All nature is calm and serene. The birds sing sweetly, the soft and gentle breeze rustles through the green leaves, the blooming Spring has now merged into the gay and cheerful summer. But while all nature is quiet and beautiful and refreshing, wicked man converts this paradise into a place of torment and evil. On this holy Sabbath there is no rest, but war, with all its horrors, is desecrating its peaceful hours. No church bell chimes with silver tone, inviting careworn men to the worship of the living God. The air is filled with the crashing sound of bursting shells – nor can one in the shining morning or in the dying light of the declining evening, retire to some unmolested spot to hold sweet communion with God. Everywhere the missiles of death are flying around. His devotions are disturbed – broken up – By the time he confines his mind upon some consoling passage in the word of God, a thirteen inch shell explodes so near as to divert his attention and dispel all calm reflection. That calmness and serenity of mind which is so essential for the enjoyment of religious emotion is destroyed by anxiety, suspense and confusion. Often have I opened my little Testament and tried in vain to read a chapter with proper feeling. Again and again would I reprove myself for such a confused state of thought, reasoning with myself that my life was in the hands of God and that he would protect me at all times. Then I would resolve not to regard the danger but soon a singing fragment of shell, striking on the hillside near-by, would dispel my good resolutions and disturb my thoughts. A time of danger is not favorable for religious emotions, though one is most solemnly impressed with the fragility of man and his dependence on God.

Since our hospital had now ceased to receive any more wounded and had sent the sick to the Washington Hotel, a new hospital opened in town near the river, and since the most of our wounded at Hospital No. 1 had either recovered almost, or had died, I concluded that I would be more convenient to our wounded at other hospitals if I could get lodging in town. Besides the doctors were talking continually of moving this hospital to a more secure place. In addition to this I did not think I was rightly treated here. Under these circumstances, I went in search of a new location. I had ascertained that Dr. R. H. Whitfield had charge of the newly opened hospital in the Washington Hotel. There I went. Dr. W. kindly offered me a place in his own room and a seat at his own table. To me this change was delightful. Here we had a plenty to eat and I was compelled to watch my appetite closely, not satisfying it fully for two or three days. I eat about what I thought a decent man ought to. I often ceased with as keen an appetite as when I began. In a few days all was right, the change of board restored my system, I recovered from my puny spell and began to strengthen every day. Here I could have retirement, was more convenient to the wounded and sick of our regiment. Besides it was comparatively secure from those troublesome mortar shells, for the most of these passed over and it was too far from our lines to be disturbed by firing from that direction. I had a good bed, a chair to sit in a table to write on. Had it not now been for these conveniences I would not now have the pleasure of writing you this letter. This hospital contained the sick from the whole army. Besides the large hotel it comprised three other large buildings. Dr. W. with several assistants attended to the invalids. All the rooms were soon crowded with the sick and the dying.

Everything was conducted as well as possible but O! The horrors of a hospital.

On the lines there is no change. The firing continues incessant. Their sharpshooters approach nearer, until they entrench themselves under our very works. They continue to pour a perfect stream of Minnie balls on the heads of our men. One cannot rise above the parapet without endangering his life. A hat is placed on a gun stick and raised up. In a few minutes it is pierced by half a dozen balls. One cannot rise to adjust his blankets or to relieve his cramped limbs without great risk. Our men, for a pastime, dig small excavations in the ditches, which affords protection from an enfilading fire. Some cut portholes through the breastworks and through these small holes fire upon the enemy. About this time we planted a mortar in one of the valleys behind our works. Now we open a fire upon the enemy from this retired position. What a terrible fuss this mortar produces amongst the enemy. It does not more than two or three shots before it draws down upon its devoted head the concentrated fire of all the enemy's available guns. The 40th Miss. Was in front of this ill-fated mortar of ours. So severe was the fire that our breastworks were leveled to the ground in places and this regiment forced to retire for a while from the ditches. Stop that old mortar was the command! The impudent thing was commanded to close its mouth and to remain as meek as a lamb. When this had ceased, the enemy, after inflicting what they thought was sufficient chastisement for such presumption, relaxed their fire and our retiring regiment again took their places in the ditches. During the night the works were repaired. Only now and then, at long intervals, and very slyly, would our old mortar dare to open her mouth – though concealed deep in the valley below. How long shall the endurance of our men be tested? Who ever heard of men lying in ditches day and night, exposed to the burning sun and drenching rains for a period of thirty days, and that too under continual fire and on quarter rations? Their limbs become stiff – their strength is frittered away – their flesh leaves their limbs and their muscles relax and their eyes become hollow and their cheeks sunken. Their clothes are covered with dirt and O, horrible! Their bodies are occupied by filthy vermin. The detestable body guards. Thus were men of refinement and polish, in the habits of preserving great external decency, subjected to this deep and severe humiliation. Nor could this be avoided for the ditches were alive with these crawling pests and to escape was impossible. This was not the least of the many vexations with which the brave defenders of our country were afflicted. Our men begin to show signs of discouragement. They have waited for Johnson so long, that hope deferred makes the heart sick. Often they imagine that they hear his cannon in the rear. News is brought in that he has crossed the Big Black; that they had an engagement with the enemy and defeated them. But so many false reports have been circulated that our men are slow to credit any. It is now near the middle of June and no relief. The sanguine still hope, while the desponding give up all hope...." (To be Continued)

The Final Stages of the Siege

Toward the end of June, the Federals attempted to overrun the Confederate Redan close to the Jackson Road. Twenty-two hundred pounds of black powder were exploded in a tunnel dug beneath the fort on June 25th followed by a rapid assault. The explosion did significant damage to the redoubt and men of Logan's division poured into the resulting crater. The Confederates were not caught completely by surprise though. They had heard digging beneath them and in preparation for an explosion had pulled back from the edge of the parapet as to minimize losses to the defenders. The resulting fight was desperate, and while the Union men gained a toehold that they held for three days, they were eventually compelled to withdraw.

Major General John Logan's Headquarters before Vicksburg. The 20th Ohio was one of Logan's units. (Library of Congress)

While the attempt to reduce the Confederate Redan was taking place, Osborn Oldroyd and the 20th Ohio had been repositioned to the bank of the Big Black as additional strength against any attempt by Johnston to relieve Vicksburg. He recorded the following in his diary from the 25th and 26th of June, 1863. He foresees the soldiers from opposite sides being the first to break bread together when the war is over.

June 25th 1863

We have orders to stay in camp, ready to move at a moment's notice. Our marching orders are still delayed, so we have enjoyed a good rest. We are now out of hearing of the guns at Vicksburg, and it seems very still around us, indeed.

The term of the enlistment of some members of our regiment has now expired, and they seem to want to get home again to see their mamas; but go they cannot until our "Rabbit is caught" shame on them for wanting to leave before the flag flies over Vicksburg. Many of them have had letters from friends at the North, urging them not to stay after their time is out. But they may as well make up their minds that Grant will hold them till Vicksburg is taken.

June 26th

We have heard that Port Hudson is ours, and I hope this is true, for it will tend to hasten the surrender of Vicksburg.

A little dirt has been thrown up ahead of us, as a shield, in case we have to fight the enemy. We hear all sorts of reports about the strength of Johnston's army, but the truth will only appear when we meet it. One captive said the report in Vicksburg was that Pemberton despaired of getting help from the outside, and was ready to surrender when the last meal rations have been eaten. He probably understands the resources of our commissary, as well as the magnanimous disposition of Grant to issue provisions to a starving foe. Well, why not? The first square meal received from Uncle Sam will be an occasion to them of thanksgiving. They will get the best that we can issue. And when the war is over, true soldiers of both armies will be among the first to break the bread of reunion and quaff the cup of restored peace and good will."

Within the Confederate defenses, Jared Sanders recorded the explosion and fighting at the Confederate Redan as heavy cannonading and "angry sharpshooting" on the 25th. He reports the loss of another soldier as well as the wounding of a young lieutenant from the regiment. On the 29th he records the blowing up of another Yankee tunnel and his entries late in the month include misinformed "news" of Confederate victories outside of Vicksburg.

June 23

  Cloudy day. Enemy tried to charge our right at 1 o'clock last night. Heard very heavy firing in that quarter – some prisoners taken. Read Vicksburg paper of 23rd. Rations are short & we eat <u>two</u> meals per day – at 9 in morning & at 3 in evening – <u>stylish</u> <u>in a ditch!</u>

June 24

  Sprinkled during last night. Cloudy today – but no rain. Wrote letter to <u>Cousin J. W. Sanders</u> in New Orleans. Sent it to Provost Marshal with request to send it out of our lines by prisoners. Three men of the 16th wounded to to-day. Heard Yankees attempted to charge on right again last night.

June 25

  As usual, in pits all day. Men make peach preserves & purslane greens in order to enlarge their rations – poor fellows, they suffer a good deal – but <u>we</u> get enough to "live on". All were roused at ¼ of 5 this evening by tremendous cannonading on right. All of opinion that it is Johnston coming in. May it be so! Sat up till late, 12 o'clock. Angry sharpshooting where the charge was made this evening on the right. Saw Vicksburg paper of the 25th which says Lee is in Pennsylvania.

  Young Austin killed by explosion of shell which he was <u>fooling</u> with.

June 26

  Cloudy. The most tedious day to me since the siege. In evening heavy firing in front of town. Rations cut down from 8 small biscuits, enough peas for one meal, & a quarter <u>pound</u> bacon, to 4 biscuits – rice, about 2 inches square boiled, small amount of peas & bacon.

June 27

  Was ready to go to town when I heard Lieut. D. Dubois had been hit in the heel by an 8 inch shell while walking in the road on our left. Went immediately to see him, but he had been taken to our hospital. I went to see him – poor afflicted boy - & found him very sad, the doctor having declared amputation was necessary. He received the wound in right heel at ½ past 7 & his foot was taken off before 10.

I went to Vicksburg & prepared his room. In evening Lieut. Buckner & I went on Sky-parlor hill – had a magnificent view. Saw two gunboats below with awning stretched & their decks lined with men – also (some or many) transports were below. _____the 100 pound parrot gun ____ is on a boat close under the banks like the mortar boats. The mortars were shelling at the time & their peculiar roar was heard over our heads as they sought the earth to burst or bury themselves.

Sunday, June 28

Remained in town last night to assist Dubois to his room. Was unable to sleep soundly on account of the mortar shell. One burst so near my window that smoke of powder woke me up. Went to Episcopal church with Lieut. Guion. Saw paper, Mobile *Evening News,* of 17 June. Ewell had taken Warrenton, Va. Nine thousand prisoners taken. In this department, Yankees repulsed 25 times by garrisons at Port Hudson. In the Trans-Mississippi department, Louisiana had been evacuated by Banks. Gen. Mouton was in Franklin with 7,000 men. All of Kirby Smith's army was moving to Mississippi river in order to attack Federals at Young's Point, Milliken' Bend & Helena to lessen Grant's army. No one can appreciate news until they have been 40 odd days besieged in times as wild and unsettled as these. A late paper would command hundreds of dollars. Went to pits at 5 in evening.

June 29

No charge around our lines except the Yankee sappers & miners are coming close to our left – up a (trench?) digging behind a (probably sap-roller), a large cylinder affair filled with dirt & etc., to keep off our shots while they work behind it. The long drought has dried up most of our springs – we haul water from the Mississippi river. The Yankees now shoot across the Mississippi into Vicksburg with <u>rifles.</u> They shoot at anything they can see, man, woman, or child. Went to stockade on right of brigade with fatigue party. Yankees were within 20 feet of our lines trying to work under us. We had blown them up the night before – filling their mine.

June 30

Very warm day. Our brigade <u>administered</u> by Lewis Guion _____. Saw Vicksburg paper. Gen. Smith was "<u>over</u> the river" threatening the enemy. This is last day of June – <u>43 days</u> since the siege began. With sufficient provision we could hold the city long against the cowardly enemy – for their attempts to charge us have not been as bold as Hector's attach upon the Grecian walls with his brave <u>Trojans.</u> Many of our brave boys have lost life or limbs during this month.   The <u>dead</u> will be remembered by a grateful people. The <u>maimed</u> have a badge of honor & a standing claim upon the generosity of their fellow citizens. I hope the girls of their choice will not be like "Hood's <u>faithful</u> Nelly Gray" who said to her lover who had returned with one leg from the wars –

Before you had these <u>timber </u>toes
Your love I did allow,
But then, you know, you stand upon
Another <u>footing now.</u>

Johnston's Tentative Advance

In Jackson, realizing that Pemberton was finished if he didn't get some sort of support immediately, Johnston finally began moving his troops toward Vicksburg in an attempt to save Pemberton's valiant and suffering force. He planned to attack Grant's rear on July 7.

As for Johnston's advance, Charlie Moore wrote to his parents that as a staff member of the Burnets Battalion Sharp Shooters they were in position east of the Big Black awaiting Johnston's order to advance. It is clear from his letter that the rank and file of Johnston's army were still uninformed of his true intentions. Moore's previous commander from the 9th Texas Infantry had asked him to return as sergeant major of the regiment. Having accepted and awaiting final approval from Johnston himself, he signs off as being in that role.

Head Quarters
Burnets Battalion Sharp Shooters
Maxeys Brigade
Mississippit, June 26, 1863

Dear Pa & Ma,

I have a very good opportunity of writing you at this time, as a matter of course I will take advantage of it and write you a few lines. Mr. Weass, from my old Company, having received his discharge caused from loosing his left arm at the fight of Murfreesboro, starts for Old Graysero in a day or two. And for news, there is nothing very important on this side of the river. Every eye and mind is turned towards Vicksburg, that manorable, noble and gallant stronghold still holds out. She is almost completely hemmed in by the Abolitionists. They have entrenched up to about 10 yards in one point of our forts, shelling as they come but our boys are not idle, they are enfilading inside so that if they are successful in taking that point we will flank them completely and it will be of no benefit to them. Some say they (The Yanks) are tunneling, but we hear thousands of reports that are not true. Everybody is in good spirits and all have the utmost confidence in its holding out unless they get short of provisions or Ammunition, which reports say are plenty for some time yet. General Pemberton says he will hold out as long as there is a horse or mule or even a dog to eat, and whenever Old Joe finds that it can't hold out any longer he is not going to stay here in the rear with the army he has. I don't know but I think (if reports are true or even if half true) the Yanks are whipping themselves. It is bound to be very sickly and no doubt they have lost 25,000 men in their unsuccessful assaults on the place (reports say 1,000 but they still hang on.) We can hear the guns all the time. Nobody knows the next move, "Old Joe" has everything wound up in mystery but when he does move, woe be unto the Yanks or Rebels (or both). The battle is imminent and it is going to be bloody, but all are confident of success.

No doubt before this reaches you the tale will be told but don't feel uneasy about me. If I am well I will be in it and if it should become my fate to fall it will be a consolation to you all to know that I fall at my post of duty. I entend to fight them until this war is over, if nothing happens, my presentiment if that I will come through safe, but enough of that, now, for something that will surprise you. I met up with the Old 9 and it was so tempting. Col. Young said he could not do without me and the boys were ever so anxious to get me back. I studied about it and came to the conclusion that it would be to my interest to do it, consequently I exchange with the Serg. Major and all that prevents me from being Sergeant Major of the old "9" is getting the approval of Genl. Johnson. The papers are all fixed up and signed up to him. I consulted John Cother and told him if it was not aggregable to him I would not go but it was to my interest and he could not refuse, and another thing, I am satisfied John has a friend in Cap. Hurt and will fair well, and if we were in an engagement together it would be a double dread on my mind. Col. Young is a friend of mine and will do better by me than Burnet "can" do. The boys are all well in the command and the 9th. C. Douglass, John Miller, J. Daffy in fact all are in fine health. The soldiers in general are in good health and good spirits. To give you a correct letter about the situation of the army and the country, I would have to be better acquainted with the geography of the country, which I am not, but we are on the east side of Big Black. I saw all the Stones Regiment. John Stewart was killed at Thompsons Stations. John Simmons was thrown from his horse and his arm broken and Bene stayed with him to take care of him. __ is with them – If you can get to see Mr. Weass he can tell you a good deal about them that I cannot think of. I must quit for this time. Give my respects to inquiring friends – My prediction is that this battalion will run the first fight it gets into, that is, enough of it to disgrace it. The biggest portion of it is mighty rotten. Some of them wouldn't care if the Confederacy was in the bottomless pits of hell. So peace was made but I hope they will not disgrace the name of the Texas soldier. As for my part, I think I have a brave heart if *my eyes don't get cowardly. Well, I must quit. Give my love to all neighbors and friends. Patterson is at Post Hudson yet.*

> *Good bye, Charlie W. Moore*
> *Sergeant Major of the Old 9th*

As a post script Moore added the following.

These rings, John sends one to Bell, and one to Johnny. The one with the star in it was sent to Bell, the other is the largest and will probably suit her best.

> *Keep them.*
> *Charlie.*

Camp on Big Black
15 miles from Canton
On Vicksburg Rd.

By the 29th Johnston was no nearer the Big Black, for the 97th Indiana and Joseph Young were part of a large reconnaissance in force seeking to find him and bring him to battle.

> ***Near Black River Mississippi***
> ***June 29th 1863***

Dear Wife

Once more I am permitted to seat my self to inform you that I am well at preasant hoping if these lines should come to hand they may find you in good health. I make know doubt but you are uneasy about me for it has been so long since I have wrote and the reason is we left the Yazoo River at the time I was going to write to you, and this is the seventh day since we left, and we left on a scout for the purpass of finding the Rebel Johnson and giving him battle, there was a bout Thirty thousand infantry beside the cavalry and artillery that left the Bluffs at same time with us for the purpas of making a reconoicance, but all our scouting and hunting has been in vain. We are cutting down the time here to prevent a cavalry dash, but I do not thing that there is any Rebels in this country only what is in Vicksburg, and I do not think that they can get out to do us any harm for they appear to stick close to there holes and if they could they would pull there holes in after them – We left all Our Camp equipage and every thing and it is there yet and when we will Return I do not know. We went in A F Phillips this morning for to get paper for the boys to write and to get Muster and pay Rools (roles) for they have to be made Out and we be mustered the last day of this month so tomorrow I will be very busy for I guess I will have to do it by my self for Jerauld is sick.

As for the prospect of a battle I think with Our troops at this place, I think is slim for I think the Rebels is moving in an other direction and I think we will leave heare shortly but where I do not know, but there is so many troops here that I think they will be dispersed to Other points. I think we go to Mobile or to East Tenn and this is nothing but guess work with me. Our Army is in excellent health and in fine spirits. My mouth has been sore a long time but I think it is some better at the preasant but my general health is excellent at this time. I received a letter from you of the 15th this month. I am glad to hear from you at any time. Be sure and write every week as I am anxious to hear from you every day. You wrote Johns Sparks had come in and he was union. I tell you that made me feel proud for I am glad to hear of all my connexion being union. Tell him to write to me and give me all the information he can.

I rec'd a letter from John and they was all well and in peace in Iowa. You wrote that you wished me to send them potographs. I will send them to you as soon as I got to camp. Give the children one a peace and the rest you can give to others or do as you please with thim. If Frank wants One gave it to him. Distribute them as you please. I must close for the preasant by subscribing my self Your Affectionate husband till death.

Joseph W. Young

Elizabeth Young

Chaplain Foster recorded another week's worth of experiences and impressions for Mildred to read, so that she could understand what the siege had been like and his part in it.

"...5th week. This week passes away without any particular variation. My duty calls me to visit every day the wounded at the different hospitals. The mortar shells fall in every part of town; in many places depriving the suffering of what little repose they might otherwise enjoy. At Hospital No. 1, my old home, the firing continues very dangerous. Well would it have been for some had they have moved all the wounded to some more secure place when they were speaking of it. Surely they had sufficient warning. There are one or two cases which I must here mention. At this hospital there was a young man from some Louisiana Regiment that was dreadfully wounded upon his shoulder by a shell. Nearly all of the flesh from one of his shoulders, down towards his back was removed. By the closest attention his life may be saved. The Captain of the Company to which this young man belonged, happened to have his wife with him at the time and she was a particular friend to the wounded boy. She attended him to the hospital and for several days did not leave him, day or night. Then she made arrangements to stay in town at night and returned every morning. No matter how severe the shelling was she came as regular as the rising of the sun, always bringing some good nourishment for her friend. The wounded man improved under this kind treatment. Often have I noticed this brave woman make her visits at the peril of her life. She would go when the shells were falling all around, when the road to town was literally torn up by them, when even brave men would shrink from the danger. Thus week after week, with untiring diligence, would she nurse and feed this young man. Now her cheek becomes pale from constant labor and her strength evidently begins to fail. About four weeks after the wound was inflicted, a young man of the same company attends upon his wounded friends at night. He remains in the ditches during the day and at night he watches at the bedside of his wounded friend. On a certain night the firing from the mortar shells was furious. One bursts overhead; a large fragment passes through the tent and takes off this young man's head, while he was sitting up with his wounded friend.

You remember the case of that young man who was wounded through the mouth and who bore his sufferings so patiently. When he was just beginning to recover, he changed his bed and one night in the fourth week of the siege, he was struck by a piece of shell on the thigh and a most dangerous if not mortal wound inflicted. How depressed he seemed; how hard he thought his lot was. (page 41 missing)

Page 42: ...in the cool refreshing waters of the mighty river, a tremendous cannonading opened along the whole line. It was certainly the heaviest that occurred during the siege, for the enemy had been mounting new guns all the time. They had received and planted some heavy pieces and they opened upon us with all their might this morning as soon as they could see how to shoot. Some of their shot came clear across the whole town and fell half way across the river. They make a peculiar sound when they strike the water, sounding more like they came in contact with a rock than with a yielding element. For two long hours they continued this awful fire. The gunboats below also joined the revelry. Surely they must be demolishing our works and killing our men at a fearful rate. Some thought they intended another charge, but they had enough of charging and were content now to annoy our men by their artillery. As severe as this firing was and of as long continuance as it was, but few of our men were hurt and but little damage was done to our works. If such a shelling as this could not drive our men from the trenches, they need not try any more. But some of our brave boys were sent to their long home, where they will never hear the cannon roar.

Sunday again comes. Every morning I visit our sick and wounded. At Lee's Brigade Convalescent Hospital there is preaching every Sunday. The place was tolerably secure. This Sabbath I attend there and preach them in the evening. There I went with seven Chaplains, three of whom were Baptists.

This week the enemy began to plant guns on the other side of the river. At first they fire a small movable cannon and change their position at every fire. Our old Columbiads thunder at the little impudent thing. Here comes another shot from this small cannon and strikes on the street before you hear the sound. Our guns fire at the smoke but no doubt the active thing is far away from this, for it seems to be drawn by horses. Thus they were trying our strength. After awhile they plant a heavier gun on the opposite bank behind a mound. They open fire upon the town and make it dangerous to walk the streets. Our large guns open a furious fire upon this small gun. Old Whistling Dick tries his skill also, but in vain. They cannot dismount it. Sometimes the shell would burst exactly over the spot and we would think that it was silenced but after awhile...

Page missing

....pretty early in the morning for we will eat it all up pretty soon." They would talk and joke every evening.

In town was a high hill on which a house was built and where our men were accustomed to watch the movements of the enemy's hats in past days. It was now occupied by a company of Engineers. There I would frequently go at sunset and take a view of the great river and the surrounding scenery. Often on Sunday evening would I wonder – What shall be the fate of this city and our army by the next coming Sabbath. One day the enemy opened fire upon the Sky Parlor as it was called, for they had observed our men upon this point. Two were killed and three or four wounded. This made us a little shy of this parlor of nature's.

As I was walking down the river on a visit to the Marine Hospital, I saw several men cutting up and dressing what I at first thought was beef. But near-by I discovered a head with long ears, a veritable mule's head. It was mule beef! This told a sad tale. Our provisions were running low. The sixth week has now closed and nothing from Johnson. Our fate seems to stare us in the face. Still we hear rumors that he is coming with a mighty army. O, that we could hear his cannon thundering in the rear! What a welcome sound. Can't our government send us relief? Shall Vicksburg fall for the want of energy on the part of our government? Will all the blood shed be spilled in vain? For the first time, dark doubts would cross my

*mind. Maybe Johnson cannot get sufficient troops to come to our relief.
Ever of a hopeful disposition, I would not listen to such fears, but would still
believe that at the last hour, the long expected help would come. Visiting the
lines frequently, I discovered that the men generally had almost given up
hope of relief from without. They considered the place as lost, though they
were willing to lie in the trenches another month if it would save the
place..."* (to be continued)

Confederate Canon Whistling Dick was forged at the Tredegar Iron
Works in Richmond. Due to the rifling of the barrel each round made
a whistling sound as it shrieked toward its target. (Library of
Congress)

The Closing Days of the Siege and Surrender

On June 28th another charge was exploded under the redan, but after
the dust had settled the northern officers suspected that not enough
damage had been done to warrant yet another costly assault. They
also realized that Vicksburg could not possibly hold out for more
than a few more days. These two factors convinced them not to send
in the assaulting troops.

On July 2nd, Joseph Young wrote to Elizabeth that Vicksburg would be taken within a few days for Grant was planning on a final storming of the defenders and ending the siege.

Oak Ridge Miss
July 2nd 1863

Dear Wife,

 I seat my self to write you a few lines to let you know that I am well at this time and I hope if these lines should come to hand they may find you all well. I have nothing of importance to write at this time, we have drawn our pay up to the first of May. I drew $40.00 that made me up to the time I rec'd my commition. We will be paid in a few days a gain and I will send you money enough to pay of(f) that mortgage and to buy what necessaries you want. If I can I will try to come home this fall and see you all but if I do come I do not wish to stay there for I would be subject to insult and here all is for the union no dissenting Voice. I understand that there (is) a good deal of trouble up there. I expect more than we have down here for we have been in no battle and there is no probability of being One. Vicksburg will be taken in a few days for Grant is going to storm the place. I have wrote 2 letters to you lately and One to Mr. Carter so I have nothing new to write at this time. I wish you to write often and I will write every Opportunity. It may be that I will not write as regular as I have been writing for I may not have the chance.

 Tell the children to not forget me. I will Send them some money that they may by there dolls and candy. Elizabeth you have know Idear how bad I want to see you. It seems to me like if I could just see you Once more I could be satisfied. You and the children is all my care at the preasant it is the last thing at night and the first thing of a morning. we must live in hopes that there is a better time coming. I will close for the preasant by subscribing my self Your affectionate Husband till Death.

Joseph W. Young

Elizabeth Young

John M. Lemmon of the 72nd Ohio Volunteer Infantry arranged to send routine letters to the *Fremont Journal* chronicling the exploits of the regiment. His letters covered the entire period of the war and have been recently republished in Daniel A Master's book, *Sherman's Praetorian Guard*. The 72nd Ohio was brigaded with the 93rd Indiana, the regiment Brad Quinlin's great great grandfather served in until his death during the Vicksburg campaign. On July 2nd and 4th Lemmon sent two letters to the *Journal* from Markham's Plantation, the site of Quinlin's ancestor's death.

Markham's Plantation, Hayne's Bluff, Mississippi
July 2, 1863

Have the Journal readers expected a letter from "Seventy-Six" each week and felt any loss at the absence of such letters? Then hear his reasons for failing to gratify them: want of time, want of wherewith to write, and indisposition. Since my last this division has about faced, made a march of 18 miles and now faces the supposed enemy in our rear. We occupy a position not far from Black River and nine miles from Hayne's Bluff along what is known as Bear Creek. Maj. Gen. Sherman has command of a large force composed of the 13th, 15th and 17th corps. He is entrusted with the protection of Gen. Grant's besieging force from attack in the rear. His force is amply sufficient for any emergency.

The 72nd is pushed well in advance for picket duty, having been specially selected by Gen. Sherman for this honorable position. Although we have a great amount of picket duty to perform, the regiment has greatly improved in health since leaving the rifle pits at Vicksburg. Col. Crockett left very sick at our Walnut Hill camp and is now no better. Doubts are entertained of his recovery, yet the cances are he will get well. His disease is congestive fever. Gen. Buckland has also been sick for two weeks with remittent fever and is very bad. His recovery is not doubtful, however. Joshua W. Watterson, quartermaster of the 72nd, is also seriously ill. Maj. Charles G. Eaton is commanding the 72nd and Col. William L. McMillen of the 95th Ohio commands the brigade in the absence of Gen. Buckland.

The weather is now very hot. I do not know the degree of heat but should judge it equal to our hottest days in Ohio. The men endure the heat very well, in fact seem to be little effected by it. The only deaths since my last are Private Martin Engler of Co. H killed and Private Edward C. Owens Co. D killed, both on picket duty at Vicksburg. Private James F. Burroughs of Co. A died of fever, Private Thomas Nevil of Co. K died and Private Amos Krotzer of Co. D died of congestive fever.

Of news at Vicksburg, I know nothing more than would be old to your readers. Matters are going well, and our forces continually gain ground. Before this reaches you, Vicksburg will, I prophecy, be under national control. We are to be paid tomorrow for March and April.

For his part, Grant had indeed determined to make a final all-out assault on the Vicksburg defenders on July 6th.

On July 3rd, however, Pemberton sent General Bowen under a flag of truce to propose terms of surrender with Grant. Pemberton and Grant consequently met at 3:00 that afternoon beneath a small tree 200 feet from the Confederate works while soldiers from both sides watched in anticipation. In the end, Grant agreed to parole Pemberton's men rather than take them all as prisoners of war, thus finalizing agreement to the terms of surrender later that night. The 48 day siege was over. The city was officially turned over to the victorious Union army on July 4th, 1863.

Lucy Bell, interviewed by Gordon Cotton in 1906 shared her memory of the surrender and Grant occupying the city on July 4th.

"our house was occupied by Colonel Allen Thomas of the Twenty sixth Louisiana Regiment, a few staff officers with him, and father had opportunity to know what was going on in Military ranks. On the evening of the 3rd of July all was quiet: people could be seen walking around, concluding that the silence meant dreadful things on the morrow. We were all sitting outside the cave, twilight approaching when father came in sight. Mother thought father had decided to die with his family the next day for

everybody thought that General Grant would make the effort of his life to take the city on the 4th. Father came to mother, looking sad, with tears in his eyes, and said "You can all come home for a night's rest. General Pemberton has surrendered, and General Grant will enter the city in the morning.

We went home. Men felt very bitterly toward General Pemberton because they were so determined that the place should not be taken on the 4th, and never dreamed that a surrender was ever thought of. The morning of the 4th, how sad was the spectacle that met our gaze; arms stacked in the center of the streets, men with tearful eyes and downcast faces walking here and there; men sitting in groups feeling that they would have given their life-blood on the battlefield rather than hand over the guns and sabers so dear to them! The drummer-boy of a Tennessee regiment, rather than give up his drum, gave it to my brother, but it was very soon taken away from him. One poor fellow gave me his horse, which was branded with the letters C.S., and my two brothers hid him in the yard; but it was only a little while before a Federal Soldier came and took him. The instruments of the band of the Tennessee Regiment were stacked on the corner in front of our house while the guns were stacked in the middle of the street. Men looked so forlorn; some without any shoes, some with tattered garments, yet they would have fought on.

While this gloom hung over the Confederate forces a glance over the hills to the north and east of the city brought into view the bright-shining bayonets and sabers of a mighty host approaching the city by way of Glass Bayou bridge and Jackson Road. General Grant led that part of the army that came by way of Jackson Road. — While the army was entering the city from the rear, the river-front presented a scene of unsurpassed grandeur. To say that the scene looking from the upper porch of our residence, where we commanded a fine view, was superb in its magnificence is to say little. The inspiring grandeur of gunboat after gunboat, transport after transport, with flags flying to the breeze, broadside

*after broadside belching forth in honor of a victory dearly won, bands
playing made a picture that can never fade from Memory"*

Chaplain Foster completed his epistle to his wife upon the surrender
of Vicksburg. His words express his deep sadness at the outcome,
willingness to have continued the fight, but also his gratefulness to
God for having spared him through the ordeal.

*"...On the 3rd of July the firing begins to cease upon the lines. What can be
the matter? A flag of truce is sent in from our General to the enemy. What
is the meaning of this? Great excitement prevails throughout the garrison.
Some suspect that a surrender of the town is in contemplation. At such a
thought the indignation is universal and almost beyond control. Our brave
men, who had endured so much from hunger, danger, exposure and fatigue,
could not endure the thought of losing all their labor. The thought of
yielding up their arms into the hands of a hated foe and becoming prisoners
of war was beyond endurance. To calm this excitement and give the men
time for sober second thought, so that mutiny and rebellion might be
avoided, the rumor was circulated that the flag of truce was only to request
permission for the removing of some citizens out of the enemy's lines. Now
the ceasing of firing extends around the whole lines. Silence reigns where
but a few hours before the terrors of war were furiously raging. The streams
of Minnie balls now cease, the bursting shell is no longer heard. On the
extreme left, firing still goes on, for the intelligence has not reached to that
point. All now has stopped except the mortar guns and the Parrot guns that
play upon the city. There is peace on the lines but war in the city. In fact,
the firing upon the town seems to increase in fury. New guns have been
planted on the opposite side of the river. In the afternoon, when the firing
was somewhat subsided, I started down to the Marine Hospital, which was
down the river more than half a mile. Just before I reach the place a powerful
battery of Parrot guns open upon the town and the range of their shot was
between my position and the hospital. O, with what power would those
furious missiles come and strike the hills and rocks and the walls of
buildings. I watched the range of the shot for awhile and came to the*

conclusion that it would be risking too much to proceed, so I concluded to return and await a more favorable opportunity for my visit. As I was about to return, other batteries opened upon the town, the mortars shortening their fuses and shelling the streets next to the river. But the street on the river's edge seemed to be safe enough for one to walk without much danger, for the shot and shell passed over, so I went down near the river and with pretty quick step was making my way back. Our large siege guns were replying most furiously. Gen. Pemberton, looking upon matters as desperate, had given the order to return shot for shot with the enemy, so all our guns on the river replied rapidly. The firing was by far the heaviest that had taken place on the river during the siege. Our large Columbiads poured their rushing shell over my head – the enemy's shot in reply passed over. The mighty river rolled the resounding thunder along. It was fearfully sublime. With quick step I was making my way up the river, on the lower street, endeavoring as soon as possible to pass this dreadful crossfire. The mortar shells and shot generally passed over my head. Now one explodes over the river's edge just in front of me in a most dangerous position for myself. I was aware of my imminent peril. At the moment of the explosion I stopped – held my breath – and waited in awful suspense the result. Fragments fell all around me. One piece came down near me and struck the ground in a few feet and rebounded and struck me in the side. It was a fragment from a large mortar shell, weighing more than one pound. It came down in a line so perpendicular to the earth that it spent most of its force on the ground. I could see the piece as it rebounded and endeavored to evade it. It only stung my side without breaking the skin or even bruising the place. I picked up the fragment and went on my way rejoicing for this narrow escape; thanking God that he had let me off with such a gentle stroke. Others had been mangled and torn to pieces; some sent to the grave, others disabled and maimed for life, but he strikes me so gently with his kind hand as to teach me my great danger and to show me his protecting hand. Just before I reached the hospital where I was residing, after having arrived safely out of the range of the firing, I heard the shrill note of the artilleryman's bugle. It was the first time I had heard the blast of the bugle during the siege. In a moment our cannon ceased firing; the enemy beyond the river also ceased and stillness again rested upon the peaceful bosom of the Father of Waters. Now for the first time for many long weeks the sound of cannon is not heard. AT three o'clock in the evening, Gen. Pemberton, in person, seeks an interview with Gen. Grant. This looks very suspicious. I visit the lines. The impression there prevails that a surrender will be made. Night approaches. All is still. The morning dawns. I arise by the dawn of day. I listen for the usual sharpshooting. The crack of the rifle is not heard. How glad would I have been to have heard once more the booming of the cannon. A sound once so annoying, yet now so welcome, for it would have told the glad news that our devoted city had not yet been surrendered. But a painful silence, foreboding evil, reigns over the doomed city. The bright sun rises. The sound of firearms is no more heard. Has a surrender been made? Hope that had so long lingered in my heart begins to take its flight. Darkness settles over my mind. As yet we in the city had not received any certain intelligence of the result, though it was known on the lines and our noble men had already stacked their arms. They begin now to distribute clothing at the hospitals. In a short time I hear the sound of horses feet clattering on the pavement. On looking up the street I beheld a sight that I fondly hoped never to see – a Yankee officer, in blue uniform, galloping down the streets of Vicksburg; this too on the 4th of July. Here comes those hateful gunboats. They can now pass our batteries with impunity. Poor Whistling Dick, he will never have the pleasure again of sinking any of these monsters. As these gunboats come, moving slowly up the river, they fire the national salute. This sound fell unwelcomely upon our sad ears. They now rejoice, while wee weep and lament. At twelve o'clock the sound of music greets our ears. Here comes the victorious array with flying banners and joyful music. They are covered with dust for clouds of it rise as they march. They did not seem to exult much over our fall, for they knew that wee surrendered to famine, not to them. The streets are now filled with their soldiers. They break open stores and closed houses and pillage and destroy the contents. Confederate writing paper is thrown into the streets and trodden underfoot as utterly worthless. Sugar, whiskey, fresh fruit in air-tight cans, are enjoyed in great abundance. They invite our men to share in the booty and they feel no reluctance in participating. Now the steamers come pouring down the river as by magic. Ten or twelve can be seen landing at the same time. In a short time these line the levee up and down the river for nearly a mile in distance. They are loaded down with provision of every kind.

At the close of the day, I visit once more "Sky Parlor". How changed now the scene. Spread out before me are the splendid steamers of the enemy, exhibiting the riches and power of our strong and wealthy foe. As I looked upon the scene and reflected upon the mighty blow we had just received – upon a long protracted war that now awaited us – upon the streams of blood yet to be shed – upon the future strength of our young men and the carnage and desolation and destruction which should sweep over our beloved South, as I thought upon these things, tears of bitter anguish fell from my eyes and a cloud of darkness and gloom settled upon my mind. Farewell ye mighty hills, upon whose rugged peaks I have often stood and with solemn awe admired and adored the power of the Almighty, to whom belongs the strength of the hills. No more shall I roam over those lovely hills and deep valleys, for they are now in the possession of a hateful foe, desecrated by the vile footsteps of a heartless, cruel and unprincipled enemy who comes with the felonious purpose of desolating our homes, of spreading the shadow of death over our firesides and of enslaving a free and noble people. And thou great Father of Waters upon whose lovely banks I have stood as sentinel in the lonely watches of the night, looking with covert eyes across the dim and dark waters for the approach of the enemy's boats, no more shall I guard thy tolling waves nor walk up and down they friendly banks. Thy proud waves, unguarded by Southerners, shall now roll on to the might ocean upon no friendly errand for us but beating upon thy placid bosom the power and wrath of our deadly foes.

Now, dearest one, I must close this long letter, the longest one, no doubt, which you will ever receive from my pen. I have written it at broken intervals of time in the midst of other duties and many interruptions. It has been composed in the midst of danger, when I knew not but every page would be the last – while the large shells were passing overhead and the missiles of death were flying around. During our investment I have attempted to send you a letter by a courier going – in order that your mind *might not be disturbed with fears in regard to my safety. I have written only what happened under my observation and what I could gather from reliable sources. Since it was intended only for your eye, I have not been backward in mentioning incidents in which I was principally concerned. I have recorded the dangers to which I was exposed so that you might unite with me in gratitude to the great God who has been a shield to me during this remarkable period of my life.*

As a testimony of esteem and affection and tender conjugal love to the wife of my youth, with whom I have spent many glad and joyful days, I have written this hasty epistle. Now unto Him that loved us and washed us from our sins in His own blood, be glory and honor for ever and ever."

Your most affectionate

husband,

W. L. Foster

John Lemmon's short report to the *Fremont Journal* on the 4th portrays the confident truth of the beginning of the end for the Confederacy.

Markham's Plantation, Hayne's Bluff, Mississippi

July 4, 1863

We have glorious news! An official dispatch just received by Maj. Eaton says Vicksburg has surrendered unconditionally. The men are wild with enthusiasm. I have learned no particulars. You will get them sooner than you will this. We have orders to move today. Glory enough for one day and all honor to the gallant Army of the Tennessee. And forever remembered be the 4th of July 1863 for from this day dates the decline and death of the rebellion.

Respect for a Beaten Foe

Upon occupying the city that day there were no cheers of victory or taunting of the beaten foe. Instead the Yankee troops brought haversacks full of rations for the rebel soldiers and civilians alike, treating them with great respect for the brave stand they had made. After a number of days of completing parole documents, the southern soldiers left the city and headed towards their homes to await the day they would be exchanged for Union prisoners being released from Southern prisoner of war camps. While Grant's decision to grant paroles was questioned by many in the north, he realized that trying to get 30,000 captured soldiers north to POW camps would be a monumental task that detracted from his continuing efforts in the department. He also believed, after the sacrifices these men had endured during this campaign and siege, many of them had seen their fill of the war and would simply return home and not return to the fight.

In filing his report on the surrender, Colonel Ashbel Smith, 2nd Texas Volunteer Infantry stated, without doubt in his mind, that the Union soldiers had gained a high degree of regard for his Texas soldiers based on his brave mens' performance throughout the campaign and siege.

" We laid down our arms (for) want of subsistence and want of ammunition. Laying down of our arms, the surrender of nearly 30,000 men, is a misfortune which works cannot extenuate, but it was not (a) wholly unredeemed disaster. The second Texas Infantry achieved one victory- they utterly destroyed any prestige which the enemy might have heretofore felt when the soldiers they should encounter should be Texans, And this was evinced in the marked and special respect with which the enemy officers and men, after the surrender, during our stay in Vicksburg. We want to treat and speak of the members of the Second Texas Infantry. When the Second Texas Infantry marched through the chain of the enemy's sentinels, the spirits of most of the men were even then at the highest pith of fighting

valor. Released from the obligation of their parole, and arms placed in their hands, they would have wheeled about, ready and confident.

> *Very Respectfully,*
> > *your most obedient servant,*
> > > *Ashbel Smith*
> > > *Colonel Second Texas Infantry*

(In the siege of Vickburg the Second Texas began with a roster of 408 men on May 17 1863. During their time on the line of Vicksburg their casualties were: 38 killed, 73 wounded, 17 missing, died of Illness 11. Final number of dead totaled 74.)

Jared Sanders wrote the following for the dates of July 1 – July 11 in his Vicksburg diary, describing the last few days leading up to the surrender, continuing through the 11th of July when the 26th Louisiana and many of the parolees left the city behind.

July 1, 1863

Things as usual. Yankees in many places are very near <u>under</u> us. Heard Yankee band playing. Col. Thomas, 26 Louisiana Volunteers, thinks we will be charged on 4th July.

July 2

Extremely warm. Yankees place two loaves of bread on a pole in front of our liens to tempt or tantalize hungry eyes.

July 3

Beautiful morning. Flag of truce at 8 in morning. At dark were still under flag of truce. Everyone is <u>suspicious</u> – for we have been half starving for some three weeks.

July 4

The glorious fourth! God grant that we be not surrendered on this day. At 10 o'clock was astounded to hear the city was surrendered to Grant & we had to stack arms outside of works. Pemberton, commander of this department, had two weeks full rations when we came in the city. He should be stricken from the rolls of our army.

At ½ past 10 enemy saw their flag as it is put over our works – bitter humiliation to us who have suffered for 47 days in defending them. At 11 was marched into town to our own barracks. Gunboats came down in front of city immediately. Then brigades of enemy marched in under their flags & to foreign music. Their arms stacked, they commenced plundering every house. They came in my room, stole my pistol in presence of officers & men – stole Lieut. Dubois hat. Such a people! Such a people! Walked down to river bank & saw over 60 steamers already at our _____wharves & a great many gunboats. Oh, my heart sickens at the sight!

July 5

We <u>are still inside & prisoners.</u> All anxious to get out of the Yankee lines again. Wrote to <u>Cousin Jared W. Sanders</u> in New Orleans & gave the letter to a Yankee officer whose name was J. W. Sanders – quite a coincidence! Enemy are forming negro companies in the city. They got into town July 4 about 12 o'clock and at 4 <u>Captain </u>Bateman and I saw negroes standing up in two ranks & Yankees taking down their names. They pressed all the negroes of our army into their service today. _____, <u>Capt. Bateman's boy,</u> not gone yet; Oliver left on winning _____ 4ᵗʰ of July & is on a steamer.

July 6

Awaiting our paroles – which we will get tomorrow. Our army very much demoralized with wish to go home instead of going into parole camp.

Vicksburg after surrendering was sacked by the enemy's lawless soldiery contrary to the terms of surrender. Soldiers could be seen jumping out of every window in town – what a shame!

July 7

Heard of fights at Helena, Ark., Big black & other points. Can see negro gunboat. Men going around town with large full blue pants, white shirt with blue cuffs & collars. On their head is a round blue cap with white covering. _____marine brigade is uniformed with white trousers, blue coats & white sashes going over right shoulders to left side & around their waists. Our company was paroled at 5 o'clock this evening. Each man was given a parole, & then the company stood up in line & with right hand raised, swore to the terms & article stated in the parole.

July 8

Heard that Washington City was captured by Lee. Yankees treat us very well but will not sell us anything. Confederate money selling from 3 to 10 for one greenback U. S. money. Had chicken, oysters & sardines tonight – quire a rarity.

July 9

Our brigade ordered to march but from some cause the order was countermanded. The Federals set our men over the river in violation of the terms of surrender.

July 10

Still in Vicksburg – bored by sight of blue legs. Called upon Miss Gibbs at 10 o'clock. Soda water is not allowed to be sold to us – all the founts are closed today. Understand that the army will march out tomorrow.

July 11

Understand we are to leave this place today. Heard from Yankees that Genl. Lee had been defeated in Pennsylvania by Meade. AT ½ past 3 "fell in" to leave Vicksburg. Oh, With what reflections - ! Such a soldier's life – his friends & comrades fall & bleed in defense of some spot which in time is lost by some incompetency among their commanders. Marched out to fortifications – halted & shortly were searched by Yankee officers for Knives & etc. A negro regiment passed us under white officers. All equally man looking – negores & commanders.

Our servants not allowed to come out with us. They were pulled out of the ranks if they attempted to pass out among our soldiers. At 6 o'clock got outside. Marched 3 miles & bivouacked for the night. Thus has ended one of the most gallant defenses of a besieged city recorded in history!

The following is the wording of the parole papers for Private I. T. Tunnell, Co B, 43rd Mississippi Volunteer Infantry.

VICKSBURG, MISSISSPPI, JULY 6 A.D. 1863

To All Whom It May Concern, Know Ye that:

I T Tunnell a Private of Co B of Reg't 43 Miss Vols. C.S.A, being a Prisoner of War, in the hands of the United States Forces, in virtue of the capitulation of the City of Vicksburg and its garrison, by Lieut. Gen John C. Pemberton, C.S.A.. Commanding, on the 4th day of July, 1863, do in pursuance of the terms of said capitulation; give this my solemn parole under oath----

That I will not take up arms again against the United States, nor serve in any military, police, or constabulary force in any Fort, Garrison or field work, held by the Confederate States of America, against the United States of America, nor as guard of prisons, depots or stores, nor discharge any duties usually performed by Officers or soldiers against the United States of America, until duly exchanged by the proper authorities.

George Deal was part of the rear guard troops awaiting/looking for Johnston's army and was encamped 15 miles behind the Vicksburg lines at the time of the surrender. He wrote home on the 4th not knowing that the city was in his army's hands. His follow up letter two days later rejoiced at the news.

Camp in the rear of Vicksburg, Mississippi
About 15 miles from Vicksburg
July the 4th, 1863
My Dear Wife,

I take my pen to write a few lines to answer your kind letters you sent me. I received two letters in a day or two from you and was glad to hear from you but I am sorrow to hear you heard such bad news about me that hain't so. Babcock is dead. He was shot at Vicksburg but Blakeley is not wounded nor the Captain hain't dead, he is only wounded and is gone home. most to anyone can hear battles report. So you don't believe that I am sick or dead till I am or you know it for certain. I am in tolerable good health. My feet is not well yet. My ankles is swollen but I am well enough to do duty. I went and picked (on picket) yesterday and we walked a quarter of it to camp for the mess. We had a good mess for dinner today.

You wrote something to me about that wheat. You are to get one third in the bushel. I want George Fowler to see to dividing it if he will. I am sorrow to hear you hain't got letters from me any sooner. I have wrote to you oftener I know but you don't get my letters. I know or if you would get more letters from me then you do. I will try and write once a week to you if I can.

I am glad to hear you had good luck with your colt as you had. So you take good care of it is all I want or care for give that baby. You can tell her to name it Peater. Dick and I want to know if it is a young… or not.

I am sorrow to here Davenport but if I was at Cincinnati hospital or Camp Denison, I would come home soon. The guards wouldn't hold me much longer but the way it is it is impossible to get home but it is alright if I get home safe but if I don't I can't help it. So don't fret for me, I will try and take as good care of myself as I can. So you take good care of yourself and my poor children and try and take good care of yourself as you can.

We are got paid up again. I got ...dollars. I hope you won't fret so about me as you did. I am sorrow to hear that. So I must close. You must write soon and I will do the same. Direct you letters 20th Ohio regiment OVI via Memphis, Tenn in care of Capt. Kaga in the …. Of Vicksburg.

So you are my love and still will be. No more at present but I remain your husband till death. This is from your husband George Deal to his wife Sarah Deal so good by Sarry.

I hope that couple that go married had good time of it, do well and get well of it. So no more. George Deal.

This is the fourth of July but it don't look like the fourth to me now like it did when I was at home. So no more at present. George Deal.

Camp Vicksburg, Mississippi

Oh happy day to us all
July the 6th, 1863
My Dear Wife,

I take my pen to answer your kind letter I received the other day from you and I was glad to hear that you was well and to hear my children was well. I hope they will keep well. I am tolerable well. My feet is getting better and I have a good appetite to eat. This letter I got had had a piece of calico in it. It was a piece of some of my children's dresses I guess and you sent a few verses pasted on a heart. I am a going to send it back so you can see I got it and I was glad to get them or see them.

We have gained the great victory at last. Vicksburg was surrendered up on the fourth of July. Happy fourth! It was surrendered up with 35,400 prisoners besides what was killed and wounded. For further particulars I can't write. I will write it or more the next time I write to you.

I expect we will stay here for awhile to guard the place. It is impossible for me to come home. I know I would like to come home as well as you want me to come but I can't come.

I have drawed twenty six dollars more of my money then I did and they say we will draw some again in a week or two. I am a going to send you some money just as soon as I can get a good chance to send to you.

So know more at present but I remain your husband. To Sarah Deal, George Deal

To Sarah Deal by Henry Souder

Sherman Pursues Johnston

Meanwhile, Sherman, who had been waiting for Johnston on the Big Black, was spoiling to get at him. As Sherman was preparing to march out to meet the latter in battle, Johnston was informed on July 5th of the surrender. With nothing left to be gained at this point, Johnston and his 30,000 men retreated toward Jackson with Sherman's 40,000 close behind. By July 16th Johnston had abandoned Jackson. Sherman occupied the city yet again, and the last threat to the Federals in Vicksburg was gone.

On the 15th of July, Captain Joseph Young was in a hospital outside of Jackson. He described the situation as Sherman's approach was soon to occupy the town upon Johnston's withdrawal. The siege he references is not Vicksburg but a possible plan for Jackson that never materialized.

Jackson Mississippi
July 15th 1863

Dear Wife and Children

I Once moere take My pen in hand to inform you that I am not well yet. I am so as to be a bout. I think I have give down under the hot weather and fatiguing marches. I was taken on the 7th this month when we crossed Black River and I have been feeble every since.

I am here in a hospital 1 ½ miles from Jackson. I am Recruting some —

Give your self no uneasiness a bout me for I wll get a long well.

I hope you are all well.

I rec'd a letter from You and Mr. Carter. Yours of the 25th June and his 28th June. I was truly glad to hear from you all. Take care of my wheat the best you can. I know it is hard for you to do any thing but Mr. Carter said he would cut the wheat and I think I have friends enough to Bind and shock it.

I will give you some of Our travails. We left Oak Ridge 4th this month and landed here 12 and Skirmishing has been going on ever since. There has been no casuality in Our Company. Only Lieut Jerauld Yesteray had his left Arm shot off with a cannon ball so that leaves the company with Out any Commisioned Officer. But I will go to the Company to morrow if they are going to go in action and if not I will stay here longer —

I do not know the forces that the Rebels has here, but we have not Made any demonstration a gainst them. Our Infantry and theres has done very heavy skirmishing. Our artillery is all still all Round the lines —

We have the place completely surrounded and Grant says he will make a seege for he intends taking it with as little loss as posable. I think we might take it. 2 days we will make a clean sweep.

I am powerful anxious to hear from You Often but it seems to me that Id not now. it has been Two weeks since I have hear(d) (from) you. Be certain not to be uneasy a bout me. I will take good care of my self and you and the Children do the same. If I should get bad sick I would be set to Ind. Content your self the best you can. I would like to be with you the best kind but I can not come at the preasant and it is impossible for You to come and if You could get here you would be by your self for I have seen but One white *woman since I left Lagrange. There is not a woman in the army. It is getting late and I will close for the present. Write often.*

      Give My Respects to Mr. and Mrs Carter and tell him I will answer his as soon as this battle goes off. I Remain Your loving Husband Till Death.

      Joseph W. Young

Elizabeth Young

On July 12th Jared Sanders continued posting in his diary while on a long march and transport, following his departure from Vicksburg. Ultimately, his sojourn ended in Richmond, Virginia on August 3rd describing the declining value of Confederate money the closer one gets to the capital.

      July 12

      Up and marching by 4 o'clock – passing over a desolated country. Arrived at Big Black late in day – about 1 o'clock. Were halted at old <u>Camp Hall.</u> Saw Mrs. George Marshal's place – in ruins. Lay down to rest by her house & reflected how (it had) changed. The last time I was there, I met a crowd of happy girls at a wedding party. Gen. Green of _____ was there, who no(w) lies at Vicksburg – killed during the awful siege. Bathed in Big Black. Bought a horse off Yank for $5 in <u>Green Backs.</u>

      July 13

      Yesterday marched 15 miles. Moved early to Edward's Depot. Here Frost, Lanterman, etc., left for Louisiana. Rained on us before arriving at Raymond, ___miles from where we camped.

      July 14

      Men & officers broken down feet blistered, etc. Passed Cooper's well at _o'clock. I riding on old <u>Jolly.</u> Saw Mrs. Lathrope. We arrived at <u>Biram</u> station on New Orleans & Jackson Rail Road. Crossed Pearl river & camped for the night. ____ miles from Raymond. Saw _____of

Louisiana here. Enemy has burnt depot here. Can hear cannon at Jackson – 10 miles distant.

July 15

Most of regiment have left for Louisiana without going to camp to be furloughed. Thirty-seven in our regiment & in our company all are gone but one more commissioned officer & one or two privates. Ordered to Brandon – <u>20 miles off.</u> Before we got to Brandon we were turned off the road to Enterprise, 90 miles further, for Gen. Joe Johnston is about to evacuate Jackson, Miss. & does not wish us to be in his path at Brandon. We are marching <u>too far</u> in one day as our men are feeble from effects of the siege.

July 16

Now 5 miles on Enterprise road. Halted to wait furloughs. Played cards to pass off the time. Men foraged on the neighborhood – corn, cattle & hogs suffered all day.

July 17

Heard Johnston was evacuating Jackson. Sent to Brandon for rations. Young soldier died close to us on the road side. He had marched until 12 o'clock & at four he died. It is common to see the dead & sick laying in woods on the road side.

July 18

We are ordered on to Enterprise. Left ahead of regiment to get some biscuits baked. Found a Mrs. Martin willing to "make-up" my flour. Saw planters driving off their negroes & stock from the country so very soon to be overrun by the enemy as they suppose. I think Gen. Grant will not follow Johnson <u>20</u> miles beyond Jackson, Miss. – on the principle that the enemy cannot go over 60 miles into the interior unless following a water course.

Got Lost. Stopped at Antioch church 18 miles distant from our camp of last night. I came by <u>Cato</u> & found a miserable country everywhere enemy went. Was riding <u>Jolly</u> in company with Lieut. Guion.

July 19

Marched in direction of (Parkville or Porkville). Found nothing in the country but "poor people & red bugs." Passed through Trenton, & encamped near Ocoha Creek, 18 miles from Antioch.

I stayed all night at a Mr. Turnipseed's & bought mule for $150. Worth 50 dollars <u>perhaps.</u> Bateman fixed up our ambulance.

July 20

Stansbury, O'Brien, etc. left us here to return to Louisiana with our consent & the Colonel's. Enterprise is 30 miles from here.

Marched 20 miles & encamped.

July 22

Arrived at Enterprise at 12. We are all furloghted here for 30 days, to report at Demopolic. Bateman went to Mobile.

July 23

Bought shafts for ambulance from Government at $10. On my return to camp in our pine grove found my valise in rain. Everyone for himself in these war-times!

July 24

The regiment got off for Louisiana this morning with our regimental wagon to carry baggage. Bateman, Dr. Lashbrook & I remain to go in our ambulance. Lieut. Denisson is not going to Louisiana.

July 25

Concluded not to go to Louisiana. Sold out my part in our horse to the Doctor & the mule to Mr. Randolph for $75.

July 26

Left Enterprise, which is on the Chichasaha River, Mobile, Ala., at 12 at night.

July 27

Found Mobile this evening full of soldiers idel, ragged, curious – looking into every shop – asking prices with no intention, & no money, to buy. Met Nee of 26 Louisiana; also Lieuts. Riely & McIntosh of 27 Louisiana. At 11 took Bay steamer for Tensaw river to go by way of Poland to Montgomery, Ala. – 170 miles.

July 28

Arrived at Montgomery at 12 & left for West Point at 5 o'clock, 86 miles distant. Had to stand up on cars to West Point – where we arrived at 3 at night & left for Atlanta, Ga., 87 miles distant. Checked my valise to Atlanta.

July 29

Arrived at Atlanta at 10 o'clock, & found cars off track in our front. Detained 3 hours here & forgot to check my trunk on for Augusta. Started on & made up time, arriving in Augusta in time for Charleston train before 6 P.M. – 181 miles from Atlanta.

Met Judge Longstreet, uncle & guardian of Gen. Longstreet of Confederate States Army & author of <u>Georgia Scenes</u> & etc.

July 30

Sent my check by express, back to Atlanta for my trunk. Got to Charleston at 6 A. M. & went to Charleston Hotel. Charleston is _____ miles from Augusta, GA. Walked down to the Battery. Saw James Island on the right; upon which are Ft. Johnson & Shell Point battery. Morris

Island beyond & running out from behind it into our view, upon which are batteries Wagner & Gregg, & a part of which is now held by the Yankees. Fort Sumter is a mile to the left of Morris Island. Castle Pinckney is close in to Charleston City. To left of Sumter is Sullivan's Island, upon which is Ft. Moultrie. Could see the enemy firing upon battery Wagner. Saw shells bursting high in the air.

Aug 1, 1863

Met Capt. Rickenbaker & Mallard. Was invited to Ft. Sumter but could not go as I am to leave town today for Richmond, Va. Got transportation to Richmond & left Charleston at 2 for Florence, 103 miles distant, & by the N.E.R.R. from Florence to Wilmington, on Cape Fear river, is 106 miles. From Wilmington to Weldon, 162 miles.

Aug 2

Arrived at Wilmington at 7 this morning. This is quite a <u>large</u> place. Saw in the river many blockade runners – steamers painted <u>mist</u> colour in order to pass early in the morning by the Yankee boats. Passed on through Wilmington for Weldon, where we arrived at 7 at night. This is a very small place. Left for Petersburg, Va. At 9 o'clock – 63 miles distant. Arrived there at 3 & left for Richmond at 5 in morning, where we arrived at ½ past 7.

Aug 3

In crossing James river could see Belle Island, where we have Yankees confined, Hollywood Cemetery to our left & the important city of Richmond in our front. Found the Capital of our Confederacy thronged with men of all classes & the business houses asking prices 1/3 higher than any other city South. It seems the closer one gets to the seat of government, the greater lack of confidence in our currency seems to have seized upon our people. Saw Mr. William Sickles of Berwick, also Lieut. Elliot of Gen. Lawton's staff.

Seth Hall wrote home in August giving a brief overview of the 8th Iowa's marches and combat during the campaign and siege. He had high praise for General Grant's performance throughout.

Sunday Aug 16th

I have just received a leter from Sarah giving me a detal account of your Coperhead riot at South Englis which we had got a slight account in a St Louis paper. it rais(ed) great excitement through out the Regiment. they all declare who I have...

(missing content)

...with the thought of such preservation and to whom such blessings come I would like very much to see you all again. I can't give you hardly an idea of what we are doing or what we have gon through by writing. it would be vain to attempt to give you a detale account of our marches & our engagements with the enemy. in short would say that from the 2nd of May to the 25 of July we were on a rapid march except the time occupied in fighting which was 23 days at Vicksburg 6 at Jackson making 30 days a <u>dry months</u> fighting in the above mentioned time besides at 3 other times we had skirmishing with the Butternuts as we were on our marches which in view of our other fighting is hardly worth making mention of. besides we wer scarecely out of the Rebbels shot one hour from the time we left Duck Point May the 2nd until we crossed black water on the 25 of July to our present camp. they wer in our front in our (rear) and on each side of us all the time but <u>Gen</u> Grant timed his troops to & required the different commands to be at the various points at surten hours which was don as accurately and all seamed to work just like clock works. the Result was we achieved a victory at every point. Grant has redeemed his former indifference and to day we are proud of him & he of us. I last seen James <u>Mc</u> on the 21 of July as we wer on our way from Jackson to our present camp. he looked well and was very hearty & cheerful you need not give your self aney uneasiness about

him he is a soldier & not only a soldier he is a good soldier and has that name throughout his entire regiment and company…

(Remainder is missing)

Colonel William L. McMillen was in command of Buckland's Brigade (First Brigade, Third Division, 15th Army Corps) while Buckland recovered from remittent fever. The following is his After Action Report for the brigade covering their expedition to Jackson in pursuit of Johnston's force.

Near Markham's Plantation, Hayne's Bluff, Mississippi
July 28, 1863

Captain: I have the honor to submit the following report of the part taken by the brigade under my command in the recent expedition to Jackson, Mississippi. The First Brigade, consisting of the 72nd and 95th Ohio regiments, the 114th Illinois, 93rd Indiana, and Battery E, 1st Illinois Light Artillery, took up the line of march on the 4th of July at 4 P.M., encamping that night near Messinger's. The next morning it moved to Messinger's Ford, and in connection with the division pioneer corps under Capt. Young, built a bridge over the Big Black. On the morning of the 6th, four companies were thrown across the river with instructions to advance as skirmishers to the foot of the hill beyond. About 3 P.M., by direction of the general commanding the division, one regiment (93rd Indiana) was ordered over to support the skirmishers with orders to advance and occupy the crest of the hill, the remainder of the brigade following almost immediately. Some opposition was made by the enemy's pickets but the point was gained without difficulty. I then marched the brigade by the flank, the 72nd Ohio in advance, to the main (Bolton) road, and great credit is due to the companies and regiments engaged. Several prisoners were taken by my advance.

From this point, it marched with the army via Bolton and Clinton to Jackson, Mississippi, arriving at the position assigned it on the morning of the 10th. It remained in reserve until the morning of the 15th when it marched to the front and with an order from the division commander, I ordered my line of skirmishers to feel the enemy's work. It soon became hotly engaged and was obliged to halt, fully demonstrating the fact that the enemy was still in force. In this attack, the brigade suffered a loss of one man killed and 11 wounded. Early on the morning of the 17th I received information that Jackson had been evacuated and occupied the enemy's works in my front, being among the first to reach the city.

On the 18th, the 114th and 72nd Ohio with Waterhouse's battery marched in the expedition to Brandon, under command of Col. Geddes of the 8th Iowa who, I suppose, will report the part taken by them in the engagement at that place. In the meantive the 95th Ohio was used as rear guard on the main Clinton road and the 93rd Indiana were destroying the railroad in the city. On the 23rd, the brigade marched with the corps to which it is attached for its present camp, reaching this this vicinity on the evening of the 25th. I cannot speak too highly of the endurance, spirit and courage of the troops comprising my command; officers and men having acquitted themselves nobly.

W.L. McMillen, Colonel, commanding First Brigade

Vicksburg in Union Hands

The Immediate Months after the Surrender

For the balance of the war it would be the northerners' turn to work on defenses, making Vicksburg a key port for the Union cause. Port Hudson surrendered shortly after hearing that Vicksburg had fallen and the Mississippi River was completely in the hands of the Union for the rest of the war. During the initial months following the occupation of Vicksburg, there were many requests from families at home trying to answer questions about those who were dead or missing.

A series of three letters were written to the parents of Henry A. Ellsworth, 4th Illinois Cavalry. The first is written by George Warren on June 26th to Mr. Elsworth, describing how Henry was wounded on the 25th of June. The second was written on the day of the surrender by Ellsworth's captain informing Mr. Elsworth of his son's death. The third was a follow up letter from Warren to Ellsworth's mother answering her request for details about her son's death. It was penned on July 21st, 1863.

In the rear of Vicksburg
June 26th 1863

Mr. Ellsworth

> *On yesterday the attack upon the enemy's works was again renewed and in the afternoon a number of orderlies were called for, to accompany different members of the staff along the lines and Henry among the rest. While returning to camp a spent ball struck him in the side inflicting a painful but not dangerous wound. We have an excellent Physician to attend him who says he is not seriously hurt. He will have the best of care and some one will accompany him home as soon as he is able to be moved. He asked me to write to you which I accordingly do. Any information I can furnish you I shall be glad to do and if any unfavorable change takes place I will notify you by the earliest mail.*

We have gained a foothold upon the enemy works and I think we have the
key of Vicksburg . The fighting has continued all night and is still
progressing –

Yours Respectfully,
George F. Warren

In camp Near Vicksburg July 4th 1863

Philander Ellsworth
        Ottawa Illinois
                Dear Sir

It is with feeling of the deepest sorrow that I am called upon to
announce to you that your noble son Henry A. Ellsworth died from the
effects of a wound on the evening of the 27th June 1863. While in the
performance of his duties on the 25th of June he received a wound in the side
& hip running up into the abdomen, was able to ride home and was not
considered in a dangerous condition.

He received immediate surgical aid and all the attentions a company
of men devoted to him could render. He seemed calm and composed the next
day and spoke of going home when he might partially recover. The next day
inflammation produced mortification and at 10 minutes before one P.M. of
the 27th he breathed his last. The simple rights of a soldiers burial took place
that evening at 8 PM. He lies high and alone on one of the peculiar peaks
that surround Vicksburg where no strangers eye would ever view his simple
pine head board, or any but the feet of friends tread on his grave.

During the interval between the night of the wound and death he suffered
little pain and died as a soldier should die – bravely.

Immediately upon his discease we forwarded to Memphis $100 one hundred
dollars for a burial case upon the arrival of which we shall send his remains
to you.

$122.20 One Hundred & twenty two & 20/100 dollars with some of his trinkets all that was not buried with him I send you today by Adams Express together with Parcel statement.

In conclusion I cannot refrain from saying that

Henry A Ellsworth Has endeared himself to each member of the company in an especial manner and erected to himself in the hearts of each member of this company a monument of kind remembrances that can never be destroyed until such time as they to may offer their lives a sacrifice to the shrine of "Constitutional Liberty". To me personally his memory is dear in an unusual sense of the term and through life I shall remember the character of him you now mourn as on almost faultless.

My… into Company log to subscribe themselves Your ardent sympathizers in this your hour of affliction.

I beg to subscribe myself

Yours Very Truly

> *E D Osland Capt.*
> *Co A 4th Ill Cavalry*

Vicksburg July 21st 1863

Mrs. Ellsworth

Yours of July 11th came this morning and I suppose from its contents that neither Henry's money or body had reached you.

He was struck with a stray musket ball while returning to camp on the 25th June about the middle of the afternoon. He gave his Sabre and Revolver to the officers riding with him and rode into camp. A bed was made for him in Captain's tent and his wound was immediately dressed by a surgeon who said it was a sever but not dangerous wound. Henry sit up part of the time until dark and said he was not in much pain, laughed about his being the first man hit in the camp and said, "He guessed it was because he was the biggest." The ball struck him in the side just in front of the <u>left hip bone</u> passed through and came out about three inches from his right hip bone in front in a line from where it entered. On the morning of the 26th he was quite feverish, said he was in <u>some</u> <u>pain</u> and I asked him if I should write to you of his being wounded. He said, "<u>yes, but don't tell them I am hurt much</u>". I read the letter to him before sending he said "<u>that is right.</u>" Towards night he said his wound pained him severely and he began to be insane. It became evident that inflammation was working and no hope of his life. In the night the only rational word he spoke was once about 12 o'clock. He rolled over and said <u>Mother.</u> On the morning of the 27th the surgeon said that it was evident that the bullet had passed through his bladder and water was running from his wound considerable – Surgeon came again after breakfast – said he could not live many hours – as mortification had begun. Nearly the whole of his Bowells was black when he died. He lived until about one in the afternoon and gradually stopped breathing –

We immediately telegraphed to you and also sent a man to the river for a metallic coffin but none could be had short of Memphis – A man went up there in the afternoon and as soon as the coffin came his body was taken up and shipped to Ottawa.

His money $122.20 was forwarded by Adams Express with a small bundle of his things – to Mr. Ellsworth –

The company paid for his coffin by subscription $84.00.

His descriptive Roll was forwarded with his money upon which you can draw the balance of his pay

(Editor's note: The fact that the company collected money for his coffin says a great deal about how well liked and respected young Ellsworth was.)

In September, B. M. Tilley could do little to allay the fears of Martha Douthit regarding the fate of her husband John. In the confusion following the parole of so many soldiers headed in various directions it was difficult to know the circumstances of anyone not in close proximity.

Fannin Ga, Sept the 29th 1863

Mrs Martha E Douthit

Yours of September 19th was received the 26th. I have not saw Mr. Douthit since about the 20th of July; I went an saw him. He was on a boat and started home that evening; by the way of New Orleans. W. D. Douthit was with him; but very unwell. We all thought he was on the mend; but I think he was about like he was the 10th. He was in good heart of getting home.

I cannot say why it is that Davis did not rite if he reached the Confederate lines; Some accident must have occurred for he was a waiting on John; and able to go where he pleased.

Of the Boys died in Federaldom you may be well assured that they were well cared for; if they are not dead they are in the Hospital at Mobile or they side but they would have wrote. it seems like the Federals would allow any to stop the other side of Mo after starting.

This is all I can tell about the Boys as I remained at Vicksburg until the 30th of July, A. P.

Yours respectively

B. M. Tilley

I was left there to wait on four of our Co. to wit W. F. Balliard J. P. Free S. P. Bradley and J. W. Marshall. Marshall only lived to get home July 1863. I have rote them for the boys of Captain Browns Co to see if they are not going back. I have been sick ever since I came home and am just able to get up to rite this with chills and fever.

B. M. Tilley

In November, another loss was confirmed in a brief report by the captain of Co C, 29th Illinois.

Vicksburg Nov 5 1863

I herby certify that corporal Joseph P Phrophater of "C" company 10th Illinois Infantry Vols was killed in front of Vicksburg on Jun 29 1863 while in the line of his duty.

J.O. Pullen, Capt

"C" Co 20th Ill infty

As the days turned into weeks, then months after the battles for Vicksburg, the men there settled into their routines.

Joseph Young sent details home to Elizabeth regarding what he would like seen done with the fields and crops before he gets home. His expectation was that the war would end by the fall.

August 1st 1863

Dear Wife

I will inform you my health is gradually improving. I hope these lines may find you all well. I have written a long letter to 29 last month and I have for got whether I rote to you to have the Clover Field sowed in wheat or not. I wish you to higher it sowed and I will send you money to pay for the work when I draw my pay. There Three Hundred and Ten Dollars due me now and I think the war will end this fall and I would like to have some Wheat growing. sow the Clover field and that corn ground that Halder has in corn on the hill. Take the seed wheat to Mr. Carters and Clean it well so the wheat will be clean. I want to see you very bad for there is many things I could tell you that I have seen and experienced since I saw (you). Tell the children howdy for me for I have not for got them yet. I got Mamis letter. Did she Rite it? Tell them to send me some word for I like to hear from them. God Bless You all. Good by for this time. Your husband until death

Joseph W. Young

Elizabeth Young

Ten days later Captain Young writes that he will be coming home on furlough in September.

Camp Sherman Miss
August 11th 1863

Dear Wife

> *I take the preasant opportunity of writing you a few lines to let you know that I am well, at preasant hoping if these lines comes to hand they may find you all well.*

> *I Rec'd your letter and few lines (from) Mrs. Woodard which gave me satisfaction to hear from you, and to hear that you was all well. I have nothing strange to write at the preasant time.*

> *I will in form you that Our Officers is gone home and I will be at home if nothing takes place by the 10th of Sept. It will be only 20 days from here which will make Six or Seven days to stay at home and that will be at the time your pap will be there. It will be more Satisfaction. It will cost me a Hundred Dollars or more but I want to see you and the Children so bad that Money is nothing. I will close for the preasant as I will be at home soon and then I will tell you all my ups and downs in the land of Dixey. Write soon.*

> *Your Husband until Death*

Joseph W. Young

Elizabeth Young

A few lines to Mrs. Woodard

> *I am well, I hope you and your family is enjoying good health. I was much pleased to Receive a few lines from one of my Old Neighbours, and was pleased too to learn that there was Women in that Country with hearts full of Patriotism although from accounts they may be surrounded*

261

with Sympathizers yet. I see you know how to Sympathize with those that is deprived of the society of loved Ones at home –

I have seen many hardships since I left that Country. Yet if I can see this Govermt Restored it will pay me for all my toils. I have lived hard slept wet and cold and on a hard bed, yet these things are incidents that was common to Soldiers in all ages of the world –

I will be at home on a leave of absence a bout the 10ᵗʰ Sept. I wish you to save me a Great Big Water Mellon as well as a nice chicken for Supper for all these nice things never gits out in the Army. I will close for preasant. Give my Respects to the Dr. and all the Children and except the same your self. Your friend VC J. W. Young

L A Woodard

By the 28ᵗʰ of the month Captain Young had to let Elizabeth know the leave would be pushed back until at least the 20ᵗʰ of September. Still, he continued to instruct her on the handling of the fields and crops.

Camp Sherman Miss
Aug 28ᵗʰ 1863

Dear Wife

I embrace the preasant Opportunity of writing you a (few) lines to let you know that I am well at preasant hoping if these lines should come to hand they may find you all well. I have nothing strange to write at this time, health is very bad at this time here. There is quite a number sick at preasant. James Sparks is the worst off of any man in Our company. I think he is dangeriously bad with Typhoid Fever. Calvin is better.

You wrote to me that you was Out of Money and if you had the money you could Buy Corn Close home. I will Draw my money to morrow. I will Draw and send you One Hundred and Seventy five Dollars. It (looks like) I should not get to come home by the 10ᵗʰ of Sept which I will not get to come before the 20ᵗʰ for we can not get our leave of absence until the Rest of the Officers comes home which will be the last of this month and if I should *not get to come a tall if you Can sell Nell for One Hundred Dollars in money down you can pay for the land and Fifty Five Dollars left and every Two months I can send you $175.00 and have plenty to support on. I want you to buy 3 good hay stacks and plenty of corn to do you. I do not wish for you to sell any wheat if you can do with out it for wheat will be a good price next spring.*

There is a talk of us Moving up the River to Fort Pillow in Tenn on the Miss River and if we do it will not be very far from home so I can come home in 3 days. I want you all to do the best you can and I will try and take good care of My self and save all the money I can and send to you for if I live to come home I would like to live comfortable the balance of my days. I wish you to dispose of the place the best you can. I want you to get Timothy seed and sow that corn ground above the well and can hatch for I do not want that tended any more so you can have that for pasture next year. I want you to buy the corn for I will send you the money to pay for it.

Take good care of the stack for this war will soon be over and then every thing will be a high price. Write to me if you have seen uncle Peter Storm and what he is doing and all about him and Washington as I never hear any thing from them. Write every chance and I will do the same. I will conclude for the preasant. Give my Respects to all my friends.

VC

I Remain Your Husband until Death

Joseph W. Young

Elizabeth Young

In the final letter available from this period, Young writes home on October 9th to let Elizabeth know that he made it back to the regiment, now in Memphis, just in time to avoid being listed as a deserter. Obviously his leave had come through and he had been able to spend a few precious days with his family. He speaks of moving east. He was to have an active role in the relief of

Chattanooga and his regiment would go on to participate in the Atlanta Campaign and Sherman's march to the sea.

> *Memphis Tenn*
> *Oct 9th 1863*

Dear Wife

> *I take the preasant Opportunity Of writing you a few lines to let you know that I am well at this time and I hope if these lines comes to hand they may find you and all the connection well. I landed here last night and the Regt came this morning so I Reported my self and I was Just on time. My time was out to day, so I had first Rate luck. The health of the Boys is not good. A good many sick. There has been no deaths out of our company since I left, but the Boys is very funny, we are here at this place but it is uncertain how long we will stay.*

> *All the troops is moving East. We will go to that way when we leave but that is uncertain. I think we go to Corrinth when we leave this place. I think we will Draw Our Money Shortly probably before we leave this place. I have nothing of importance to write at this time. I wish you to answer this immediately. Give my Respects to all my Connection in that country and tell them to write me. JC*

> *I Rem your Husband until Death*

> > *J. W. Young*

Elizabeth Young.

Robert Hamilton's effusive letters to his darling Kate continued throughout the fall. In addition to sharing his unbridled emotions for his bride, he exhibits his romanticism as he speaks to a future where he will look back on this period with "cherished reminiscences". Also included, is a solid description of the Federal efforts to fortify the city as a major military base.

Camp on Walnut Hill
Near Vicksburg, Miss.
Thursday Sept 10, 1863

My Dearest,

My Devoted Wife:

With emotions too deep for utterance I take the pen to address you. I feel decidedly melancholy. An oppressing indescribable something weighs heavily on my usually buoyant spirits & fills me with feelings of sadness. What causes it? I don't know <u>certainly</u>, but I have a remote idea it is <u>Love Sickness.</u> I am subject to such feelings at regular intervals – semi-annually, say every spring and autumn. One thing certain I have a longing desire to see you & to enjoy your sweet <u>sweet</u> society. Well, I have the consolation of knowing we have only eleven short months to remain in the service at farthest or if it be Gods will I will then rejoin you. Be Cheerful, I may be home <u>before</u> then. At all events we will be in the enjoyment of each other's tender embraces <u>then</u> should our lives and health be spared & preserved. The time will soon glide away. "Remember in absence in sorrow and pain, There's <u>one</u> heart, unchanging, that beats but for thee. My eye has just glanced over the following sentence which is so applicable to my own case, in my present moody, gloomy condition that I have concluded to copy it. It is as follows: "There is but one way of fortifying the soul against all <u>gloomy presages & terrors</u> of <u>mind;</u> and that is by securing the friendship and protection of that Being, who disposes of events and governs futurity." What words of consolation! We are directed to secure the friendship and protection of God. And we are assured in Holy writ that if we trust in Him, we trust in a Being who never said "Seek ye my face in vain."

I have no news of consequence to write. There seems to be a lull in the Departments of the army. We anticipate stirring news from Charleston, Chattanooga and ___ Tennessee. The destruction of Lawrence another butchery of its inhabitants by the incarnate fiends. Quantrill & his bridal band of desperadoes elicit the bittered execrations from the soldiers. Many (seek) vengeance should they ever have an opportunity. It appears to be the beautiful wish of every one that the butchering banditti may be overtaken, captured and be subjected to the tender mercies of Jim Lane and his compassionate disciples. They will find "Jordan a hard road to travel," should they try any more such capers.

Col. Force is now a full-fledged Brigadier. He has already been appointed and the "lone star" graces his shoulder traps. We are all well pleased and think he merited his honors, for he is a brave & courteous officer – kind and affable to his men.

All the transports here have recently been pressed into the service to convey troops – somewhere and to take a large number of wagons & teams down the river for the purpose of hauling cotton to the river. Large quantities of the textile fabric have been discovered in the country bordering the lower Mississippi. Quimby's Division have been under marching orders & were waiting for transportation last night. It is said they will go the same route we did namely to Monroe. But it is not known generally when they are going.

Enclosed I send you a Confederate ten dollar bill and other Secesh money. I want you to keep them as souvenirs and preserve them as mementoes of Vicksburg & the "Louisiana Expedition". I desire you to take good care to preserve the Copy of the Daily Citizen printed on wall paper I sent you per last mail as a relic of the siege. Keep them all locked up in your little trunk. Many years hence "when this cruel war is over" they will awaken pleasing and cherished reminiscences of "The days when we went a soldiering."

Vicksburg is assigned to be an important military point. A circle of fortifications are in process of construction that will bid defiance to any force the enemy can bring against them. Forts are being built on all the prominent points around the city that are far superior to any the Confederates had to resist our army. The engineering skill excels anything displayed by the enemy. Many magnificent residences have been torn down that occupied the present sites of the new forts. One house, situated on a very prominent knoll beautifully terraced, built at a cost of $35,000 was totally demolished to make room for a fort. The rare gorgeous shrubbery, flowers and beautiful surroundings were all destroyed to make room for *hostile cannon. Moses Flory returned this morning. Adjutant Ryton also returned. He – the adjt – is lame yet, but otherwise in excellent health. Dunk and Bob Miller are both better. My own health is tolerably good except I am somewhat bilious, which may account for my lowness of spirits. I close reassuring you of my untiring love & unswerving fidelity to you Love. God bless you. I am thine <u>only</u> thine.*

Robert

Three days passed before Hamilton again took pen in hand to elaborate on his deep affection for his "Bonnie Blue-eyed Kate".

***Camp in Walnut Hills,
Near Vicksburg, Miss.
Sabbath, Sept. 13th 1863***

My Dearest,

   My Bonnie Blue-eyed Kate:

      It is wonderful how tenaciously the tendrils of genuine affection cling to their object. The rude winds of misfortune, the milden of popular censure, the corroding cares of life, the withering blight of poverty, the gnawing canker of slander, and even the fierce thunderbolts of Death alike fail to relax or loosen their firm twinnings. Time with its ever varying changes; and long continued absence, with all its weaning influences fail to alienate me from the ones we most love and cherish. Dearest Kate, it seems as though the whole powers of my soul are concentrated in the one passion of love for you. The love and regard I have for <u>others</u> sink into comparative insignificance when compared with the profound love and exacted regard I have for <u>you.</u>

      Oh may God give his angels charge over thee, to keep thee in all thy ways, and may they bear thee up in their hands, lest thou dash thy foot against a stone. God bless & protect you & the Good Spirit lead you in the ways of godliness & purity is my heartfelt prayer.

Your sweet lines of Aug 30ᵗʰ came to hand last Friday, but as we were in "fatigue" yesterday I did not reply till today. The assurances of your love and devotion cheer and revive me. My heart reposes all confidence in your love and fidelity to me. Were it not for that confidence I would of all creatures be most miserable.

From the contents of your note I presume little Jammie has passed that bound whence no traveler returns – that he "has gone to the land of light spirits above." May God sanctify the affliction of the bereaved parents to their eternal welfare, may they experience that these light afflictions, which are but for a moment work out a far more exceeding eternal weight of glory.

I am sorry to hear of the premature advent of his hoary majesty – Jack Frost. I trust however, he has not so rudely visited vegetation as you suppose, and that your fears as to the extent of his brief reign may not be realized.

I trust the deserter, whom Provost Marshall Moore captured will meet with his just deserts. I hope the redoubtable "Billy I." will succeed in finding out every deserter in his district & sending them to their posts forthwith. If he don't succeed in catching every one it will not be his fault. We wish him success. Two deserters from Co. "C" & one from "K" were brought to the Regt. Yesterday under guard. I have not yet learned the particulars of their desertions or captures. Two were taken prisoner at Britton's Lane & never returned when exchanged.

I trust the organization of returned soldiers into "home guard Co's." will have a wholesome effect upon the K. G. Co. & their coadjutors, the Copperheads.

I have but little news to write. It is rumored that Lieut. Jimmy Moore of Co "G" 9ᵗʰ La. Vol. African decent, has left the state of single blessedness & committed matrimony. It is said he married a young widow near Milliken's Bend, La. one day last week. May she not estrange his heart from true and patriotic sentiments as the wives of one celebrated for his wisdom estranged him from the true God is the sincere wish of his old fellow soldiers.

Quimby's Division embarked on transports and went up the river yesterday. It is thought they are going to Arkansas to reinforce Steels, who is reported to be in a "bad box" and in need of help. There is a rumor in circulation that Gen Blunt has been defeated with a loss of 800 by the Rebel Gen. Hughes (?) Hope there is no foundation for such a rumor. There is another painful report to the effect that Gen Grant was thrown from his horse or buggy in Natchez. New Orleans, Port Hudson or some other Port on the lower Miss. And seriously injured recently.

Captain David has recd. Twenty days leave of absence & is now waiting for the departure of a packet "upward bound." Lieut. Cheney of Co. "B" will have command of our Co. until Lt. McCreight returns.

You will have seen Mort Caunum & R.S. Finley ere this reaches you. They can give you all the news. My health is tolerably good. Dunk is some better. Bob Miller & Billy are both about well. The health of the troops is not so good as it has been Weather extremely warm & dry. Lately we have been pestered by mosquitoes. Myriads swarm around us at night constantly goading us and "presenting their bills" with a frequency quite annoying. Sleep is almost impossible, unless we make a little fire – smoke the tiny invaders out. Write soon. God bless you. Your loving, Faithful & Devoted husband. ROBERT

Hamilton's letter of September 24th shares his feelings regarding the "foul nest of treason," Charleston, and the fate it deserves. He also confirms news Kate had heard regarding the diminished respect for their colonel.

Camp at Walnut Hills
Near Vicksburg, Miss.
Thursday Sept 24, 1863

Dearest

Ever Beloved Kate:

I had just commenced to write you yesterday when I was detailed to go on fatigue. We went to the landing early in the morning were not relieved till five P.M., hence the postponed writing till today. When I returned to camp I found your kind sweet letter of the 13th inst. awaiting my perusal. I need not tell you that it was opened in a jiffy & the contents read with pleasure. I rejoice that you are in good health. But I am sorry you were disappointed in not receiving a letter from me when others had been received from the Co. I wrote you a <u>long</u> letter just after we returned from the La. Expedition and did not get it finished in time to send out by the first mail, so the letter had to lay over another day. But I think the letter you received will well repay you for the delay. Don't you think so?

The "<u>official dispatch</u>" you mentioned to the effect that Charleston had surrendered is rather premature, I opine. "Official Dispatches" the "Reliable gentleman" the "intelligent Contraband" are regarded to some extent as synonymous of "Humbug "with us.

We think Gilmore will be doing well if he has Charleston before Christmas. Beauregard may decide to surrender the city long before then to save it from destruction, but it is not probable. I predict the destruction of that foul nest of treason. The judgements of Heaven are about to come upon her. The more long delayed they will be the more terrible and the ruin more complete. She has been "Treasuring wrath against the day of wrath." The full possession of Morris Island by Gilmore, gives our troops a decided advantage of the leverage & their progress really be in arithmetical or geometrical ratio, cause it not only <u>decreases</u> the enemy's defenses but it <u>increases</u> our advantage for offensive operations like the old game of "prisoner's base", every <u>loss</u> on one side is also a <u>gain</u> on the other.

I regret to say your informant was correct in statements respecting Col. Shedd. He does not sustain the reputation he possessed a year ago. He has made himself quite unpopular with his men by his conduct since his promotion. It is not so much what he <u>does</u> that renders him so unpopular, as what he <u>fails to do.</u> He does not manifest that care or concern for the welfare of his men that becomes one in his position.

He appears to be too fearful of incurring responsibility. Every trivial order, he enforces to the very letter, without any regard to the conditions or convenience of his men. I have known him to make the men, when almost *ready to drop down in their tracks with the fatigue of marching, stand in line several minutes till all would close up, then make them dress in line & stack arms every time the troops halted. Often the columns began to move forward by the time the boys would be ready to sit down for rest. I do not think he does these things <u>designedly,</u> but through an unquestionable ignorance of the real suffering conditions of those under his command. I shall say nothing farther respecting him. What I have said is "sub rosa"; and is intended for <u>no one</u> but <u>yourself,</u> Love. It is merely an answer in part – to your question, and corroborating your informant's assertions.*

You spoke of hearing Geo. Norcop preach. He is an old classmate of mine. Give him my respects next time you see him. I think you are mistaken in his being inferior to John Brown as a preacher. Perhaps the sermons of each which you heard were no criterion by which to judge of their caliber. John, no doubt did his best and his production was the result of ….. (remainder illegible.)

Fatigue Duty and Fortifications

The process of building and improving forts around the city seems to be resting on Hamilton's division. His wit conveys to Kate the exhaustion he feels in a light hearted manner, but reveals the drudgery and fatigue of those garrisoned in Vicksburg. He dreams of her before the fire in their home as he suffers on the dirt in his tent on a drizzly fall afternoon. Further news of the war is also included.

Camp on Walnut Hills
Tuesday, Sept 29th 1863
Near Vicksburg, Miss.

My Dearest,

My Own Sweetest Wife:

As I am off duty today I cannot forbear to avail myself of the opportunity of writing you a <u>few lines,</u> if for no other purpose than to pass away the time. Indeed I find it the most agreeable & pleasant pastime, to in my <u>soldier life,</u> when occupied in conversing with you, Dearest, through the medium of letters. Yesterday I was on fatigue duty at the fort and trundled a wheelbarrow with the ease and dignity of a native of the "Emerald Isle." The consequence is I feel <u>older</u> by a year or two today, and a disposition hostile to what is normally called "Hard Work". The truth of the matter is, I am afraid the too frequent contact with it will ultimately produce <u>hardworkphobia</u> which has recently become an <u>epidemic</u> (or rather a contagion) in our Division. It appears we have the contract for constructing the defenses around the "Terraced City of the Hills" (Vicksburg). Herculean efforts are made to complete them soon as possible. Heavy details grow every night in the Div. and dayly is worked upon them. The details have to report at 4 ½ o'clock in the morning and are not relieved till five P.M. The conduct is about <u>"to sour"</u> on the boys. Consequently many see "the lion in the way" and many hide their hands in their bosoms, and it grieveth them to bring them, if not to their <u>mouths</u> at least to their <u>spades, picks</u> or <u>shovels.</u> Of course they are making haste slowly toward the completion of the forts.

Today has been cloudy & this afternoon is murky stormy and drizzly – and altogether, cheerless and uncomfortable. While you, perhaps, are sealed by a bright cozy fire, which diffuses a generous warmth and fills your heart with cheerfulness, - surrounded by all the delightful scenes of home, your <u>devoted</u> is sitting hunkered down on the floor of his cheerless tent, with no fire to dissipate the cold and gloom, writing with his paper on his knee, and in a strange land, surrounded with every element of gloom & discomfort. Yet I am so absorbed with contemplations of home, your sweet society and other domestic scenes that I am sometimes entirely oblivious of what is going on around me, and of the air of joylessness that surrounds me. What sacrifice would I not make, to be with you & be enjoying charming society this evening! Oh my loved, my honored, my cherished wife! God knows I deeply and ardently love you! God knows I love you more than all earthly objects!

A terrible catastrophe happened at or near Millikens Bend yesterday morning about daybreak. The Steamer "Albert Campbell" with a cargo of stores & a large number of furloughed soldiers enroute for this place, caught fire and was totally destroyed. Between thirty and forty soldiers were drowned or burned to death. The fire originated in the hold & had made considerable progress before it was discovered. Some one intentionally or unwittingly raised the aft hatch, when the flames leaped up and burned the rudder rope in twain in a twinkling. The boat was then at the mercy of the current and the flames. Although the boat was not more than thirty feet from shore, yet she could not be landed & many perished. We hear John Gilmore, Jim Riddell & Bill Adams were aboard as their leave of absence has run out.

The increasing list of steamboat disasters recently excites apprehensions of "foul play" somewhere. It is believed there is a conspiracy under the offices of Jeff. The First & Co. to destroy as far as possible our river transportation, by a regular system of incendiarism. Government should look into the matter. Guards should be placed on different parts of the boats, who should keep a vigilant look out for these hell-born scoundrels and should they be caught at their devilish work the utmost rigors of the law should be enforced.

Adjutant Bryton has resigned in consequence of the wound he received at Champion Hills. He is a little lame yet. Lieut. Poak of our Co. is acting Adjt. & will probably be commissioned as such.

The health of the troops is very good. Dunk is not over his diarrhea, but is better than he was a few days ago. Sherman's Corps is going up the river just as fast as transportation can be had. It is pretty well ascertained to be going to reinforce Rosecrans. News from Georgia is looked for with a great deal of interest and anxiety. I must close. With every wish for your health & happiness I remain as always your loving Devoted & Faithful Robert.

Barracks of the 124th Illinois Infantry at Vicksburg. The 124th Illinois were garrisoned at Vicksburg as part of McPherson's XVII corps, Logan's Division, 1st Brigade. Barracks like these would have been built by the troops as part of the fatigue duty described by Robert Hamilton. (Library of Congress)

In October, George Deal wrote home about a seven day scouting mission from which they had just returned. He mentions an encounter with Rebel troops who escaped their pursuit and the fine eating they had due to foraging.

Vicksburg. Mississippi
Oct 21st, 1863
Kind Friend,

I take this opportunity to answer your kind letter which I received yesterday. I am well at present and hope and trust that these few lines will reach and find you all well. In the first place, I will tell you that we have just got back to camp. We have been out on a 7 day scouting expedition. We did not do any fighting but I thought once we would get a fight out of them. The rebels showed themselves on the top of a hill about a mile in front of us. The(y) give us a few shot and shells which come pretty close but done us no harm. We formed in a line of battle and started for them through a field that had grew up with burrs about as high as a man's head but we did(n't) go far before they skedaddled away. We followed them some distance but it was no use. When those rebs gets to running it is a hard job to catch them.

I tell we had plenty to eat well on the march. Such as fresh pork, chickens and turkeys, sweet potatoes and other things too tedious to mention. We done some hard marching and a good many of the boys piped out and was hauled on the wagons and ambulances. I got to ride 12 miles. My leg is about the same as it has been for sometime past.

In November, James Riter, 29th Illinois, writes home from Vicksburg telling them that his regiment may be consolidated with another. This was common practice when regiments had been depleted by sickness and death to a level where they could no longer function as an independent unit.

Vicksburg Miss Nov the 4th 1863

Dear Mother and Father I take this kind pleasure of Wrighting you a few lines to let you know that I am Well at the Present Time and hoping when this comes to hand it may find you all the same. I am well and harty and has been since I left and if Reed was with me I would be satisfied and I think it would be best for him to come. I rote you a letter the other day but for fear that you did not get it I thought I would Rite a nother. I want you to Rite to me as soon as you get this and let me hear from you and let me know how things is going on. I want you to tell that young lady to inquire for letters at the office. We are not consolidated yet. I don't much believe we will be.

We are not paid of yet. I don't much think that we will be until next pay-day. I want you to get my trunk and clothes and too blankets and take care of them until I come. I cant tell when I will come if we are consolidated our time will be out next August. Do nothing more at ... (balance of letter missing)

On November 5th Robert Hamilton penned a letter to his wife, Kate. It is the last from him in this collection. It is a melancholy depiction of his pained love for her so far away exasperated by miserable November weather. He shares his observations and opinion regarding others blaming the war and their circumstances on the "Damn Niggers". It is quite poignant.

> **Camp on Walnut Hills**
> **Near Vicksburg, Miss**
> **Thursday Novem. 5, 1863**

Most Loved,

> *And Devoted Wife:*

> > *I am made thrice happy by the receipt of your sweet and loving missive of Oct 21 which came to hand the night before last – though brief and of older date than the one John Gilmore brought, yet it was read with eager zest.*

> > *Like an Angel of Mercy – which you are – you have been watching by the couch of a suffering – perhaps dieing fellow mortal. May you ultimately receive the welcome of those who visit the sick, clothe the naked, feed the hungry: Come, ye blessed of my Father, inherit the kingdom prepared for you from the foundation of the world! "In as much as ye have done it unto the one of the least of these my brothers, ye have done it unto me."*

> > *Be careful however, in your zeal in ministering to others, that you do not impair your <u>own</u> health. The <u>entire care</u> of one, who is so feeble, as your patient, is <u>too much</u> for even a hearty rugged nurse, let alone one of a weakly delicate constitution like yourself. I know however my advice will be like water thrown on wax, it will make no impression upon you, for I know your generosity and sympathy will be excited to such an extent by others'*

suffering, that your <u>own</u> health nor your own <u>life</u> even will ever once be consulted. I am glad there is yet no visible sign of your health giving way under the onerous and watchful duties to your charge. May God bless you, Dearest.

I feel decidedly Novermberish today – dull, gloomy, stupid. The day is just in the condition to inspire one with such feelings – gloomy, wet, drizzly. We cannot look out of our tent but what our eyes embrace a muddy, dreary landscape, with a squad of drenched, doleful looking pickets in the foreground. They look like a flock of domestic chickens during a rainstorm, or a herd of cattle humped up; their backs turned to the wind & rain enduring the storm in gloomy silence. I was just relieved from picket myself about nine o'clock this morning. I was on yesterday and last night, and my loss of sleep does not add any to my cheerfulness. While on my lonely beat during the dark hours of the night, <u>many, very many,</u> sweet thoughts of thee filled my mind, you accompanied me in imagination which made the hours pass on "angel wings". I stood on post from eight till eleven o'clock last night & my thoughts & prayers were lifted red hot, as it were, from my heart to a throne of grace in your behalf, and my own also. Dearest Kate, as I mused on you and thought of our grievous separation, my manhood gave away and I wept like a child. Often, as I think of you, Love, the big tear drops fill my eyes. I could give everything I have, for the pleasure of your society. When I lay down last night I dreamed of seeing you & behold you with speechless anguish of rapture, till the loud throbbing of my gladdened heart awoke me. Oh, you cannot conceive the agonizing disappointment I experienced on awaking! My throat filled up and for a long time I could not coax sleep in consequence. Oh My Most Sweet Kate! You are dear to me as "the ruddy drops that warm my breast." Heaven shield you from harm.

About two o'clock this morning it began to rain and from then till day light, "Nights Horrid car dragged very slow." We had to stand in the mud the remainder of the somber night.

Pess and Billy Adams both have jaundice. Pess's nose has bled considerably today. Billy Adams had hiccough yesterday & the day before so severe & incessant that it was feared he would not recover. He has got it checked, but is so reduced & so weak in consequence that he is not able to move himself.

He threw up last Tuesday from his stomach, a strange, intestinal looking substance that was a curiosity. It looked considerably like a common leech about five inches in length, covered with bloody mucous. I consider him in a very critical situation.

"Damn the Niggers!" They were the cause of all this war and bloodshed!" Such are the expressions I just overheard some wiseacre make respecting that benighted and much abused race – the "Everlasting Nigger." We often hear such remarks by some ignoramuses, who mistake the _innocent occasion_ of a thing for the primal or active cause. Did the Niggers go about the country inciting insurrection, or making inflammatory speeches or taking up arms to fight against _any one_ till compelled to do so? No! but we find a class of people who began a bloody war to uphold the institution of Slavery. But the nigger _himself_ had no more to do with the outbreak of this war or was no more the _cause_ of the war than the living _child_ which Solomon ordered to be divided was the cause of the strife between the true mother (and) the other harlot. So well say the _bone_ over which two dogs are contending is the cause of the contention. So well say the _apple_ Eve ate was the cause of sin in the world. But many persist in saddling the whole cause of the war upon the unfortunate African who really bears the same relation to the war that the bone does to the strife between the dogs.

I close. Don't call this a _letter_, but the miserable effusion of low spirits. Reassuring you of my measureless love & undeviating fidelity I remain wholly thine.

Robert.

Christmas 1863

Christmas in the field, separated from loved ones, is a source of longing for many soldiers. While many turn to celebratory liquor to enhance their spirits, others remain sober and look to home. Here are two letters written home on Christmas day.

> *Hede Qarters 75th Inf. Seconde Brigade*
> *17th Army Corps*
> *Vickesburg Miss.*
> *Decb 25 63'*

Dear Brother,

I recievd your very kinde letter this morninge (with a) right grate deal of satisfaction. It is the firste that I have herde from you cince laste April. I have written quite a number to you. I sente my likeness to Ida. you dide not say whether you had received it. please lete me no in your next letter. I am greatful to here that you are well. My health is good I feel truly thankful for it. The boys have good time to day as it is Christmas. I can not enjoy it myself. I feel very much disapointed in not here anny thinge from Adin. I thought you woulde here somthinge from him. I have not receive annye letter cince last June when (I worte) a number to him. it has wored (worried) me a good (bit). I can not express to you my feelings. I wished that I coulde ben with him. it seems to me that I coulde assisted him but (it) was not to be so. I feel very much caste down on his accounte. this ware (war) is a cruel thinge. I wished it was over, it lookes to me that it will be some time before it is brought to close. The guruilles (gorillas) is boated down here firing into boats almost every day. Weather here now ice has frozen about one inch thick it is quite healthy here now.

Elliot

George Deal writes on Christmas to Sarah telling her that he is remaining sober this day. He has two possible beaus for a friend and jokes about the children growing so quickly in his absence.

Vicksburg, Mississippi
Dec. the 25th, 1863

Kind Friend,

I take this opportunity to drop you a few lines to let you know that I am well at this time and hope that these few lines will find you all enjoying the same blessing. I just received a letter from you. I was glad to hear that you was all well and to hear that you had got a part of that money I sent but would a been beter pleased if you had got it all.

Well this is Christmas and a good many of the boys feels their whiskey but I am sober by chance and expect to keep sober. You wanted to know if Davenport was paid off when I was. He got his pay just when I did. Well I will give you a short description of Mr. David Barber. He is a stout heavy set fellow with black whiskers about twenty two. I think that he could do a woman justice in some respects if not in all but I think he ought to (have) a split put on his pants. As to George Blakely, he is a bully boy and so is Barber.

You mention about the children growing so fast. I expect we will have to buy a little boy when I come home for a pet. That is if I can. I think that I am as good as a man as I ever was. My weight is one hundred and ninety pounds. I will close for the present by asking you to write soon and often and I will do the same. I still remain your friend and husband till death. Do the best you can and hope for the better. And yes Jo Hames is in this company.

George Deal to Sarah

Deal, Farwell Deal

1864

By January of 1864 the 29th Illinois Volunteer Infantry was reassigned to Natchez, Mississippi just south of Vicksburg and still under the same overall command. In James Riter's letter of January 14th, 1864 he discusses the opportunity to reenlist in August and questions whether he should do so for the $411 bounty. Having lost his first wife to death he thinks he could "buy" a pretty young wife for that sum.

Natchez Miss Jan 14th 1864

Dear Father and Mother

    I take this kind pleasure of wrighting you a few lines in answer to your kind letter that came to hand a few days ago and found me and Reed both well and harty. I hope when this comes to hand it will find you all in good health doing well. I could have answered your letter sooner but I was mad and that I would not just for spite because I rote (wrote) and rote (wrote) to you and could not get answers. Not with standing I was glad to hear from you all. I want to see you all very bad but I can't tell when I will get to see you. I think we will get to come home soon as the Regiment is going to get a furlough for Joining again for three years more. They want the old 131st Reg to join again but we can't join until August. I have a notion of reenlisting and I want to know what you think about it. We will get 400 and 11 dollars bounty. I could buy a very pretty wife with that much. I am in better humer then I was when I commenced riting. I have just received a letter from you that was Rote the 30th of December. I was glad to hear from you but was sorry to hear that you was sick. We have not been in any battle yet. We went out about three weeks ago to fight a little but the Rebs did not stand. The 131st is all right yet. they have died some of them by sickness but none of them kild by bullets. I am glad to hear that you have got moved. I want you to get well fixt by the time I come home. I hope that me and Reed will both get home safe. I want to know what has become of that girl that I told you that I was going to mary and where Mr Ennis is living. I have rote about 17 lettters to you and I have received three from you. Give all the children my kind respects, tell Alford Baty howdy for me and Albert also. Reed says to tell Albert and Alford to prepare for getting there backs dirty for when he comes home he intends to wallar them both and I think he will get to come in the course of two or three weeks. Army has it the Regiment gets to come we will come with it. Henry Leary is well and harty. He sends his best respects to you all. He says he intends to rite to you all. I want to know whether John Henley and Ellen Goodman is married or not. If they have tell them I wish them much joys and a house full of children. We have not drawed any money yet. I cant tell when we will but as soon as we draw we well send you some. Try to do the best you can and we will try to help you. I had to stop riting to hear general Clark make a speech. He is from New Orleans. He made a very flowery speech. It was made to the volunteers. We have very fine weather here. A great deale of ice floting down the river know. We have had some very cold weather here. I believe I have said about all I have to say at present until you rite. Rite often and let me hear from you all. So no more at present, only I remain your affectionate son until death shall part us.

James A. Riter Co E 29th Reg
Ill Vols Natchez Miss

A Post Script to Riter's letter:

Supper is know Kracky Hard Tacks and sow belley that is good. You know I have a negro man that looks for us. I will give a list of my mess mates.

James A Riter , Reed Johnson, Daniel Songer, Henry Faust, Henry Strasick Maley Hunt William Walters William Songer. This is a list of my mess. We did have John Morse until he died. The poorest men in the Company E.

With little enemy activity and restless tedium in the camps like Natchez and Vicksburg, discipline was difficult to maintain. From time to time the troops took advantage of situations that arose for mischief, as Riter describes in his letter to his parents in February.

Natchez Miss Feburary the __ 1864

Dear Father and Mother I take this kind pleasure of answering your kind and affectionate letter which I thankfully received by here and found me and Bud both well and hardy and was glad to hear that you all was well and doing well. The letter that I got from you was the one that you rote in Columbia. You said you herd from me in Drew Morse letter I received your letter about one week ago but did not have the chance to rite until know. We got marching orders last Saturday and was gone four days. We got on a boat here and went down the river 60 miles and got off and march 20 miles Saturday knight. We got of the boat at 9 oclock that knight. We got in to Woodville at day breake Sunday Morning and surprise a little Reble camp and captured about 90 rebs. Theire was not much of a fight. Their was too Negro soldiers wounded was all the harm that was done. We got lots of tabaco and whiskey. It was at a little town called Woodville. It took us three days to march back to Natchez. We had a very hard time of it but got through safe. We went down there a boat and came back all mounted. Every fellow had a horse a peace. We stack Arms to rest a while and in one hour every man was so drunk that what was left sober had to take the drunk men and pile them in a wagon and hall them until they got sober. When we stack arms the boys scattered about to see what they could find. I commence looking for Bud and when I saw him he had a big glass bottle full of the best kind of Rum. We all took a big draw but me nor Bud. Neither one of us got drunk as we was expecting the Rebs every minunt. It was not a very good place to get drunk. Henry Leay got so drunk that we had to put him in the wagon. I never saw as many drunk men at one time in my life before. I think that we will get paid of in a few days and we will send you some money by Allen Biggs or by Express. One of the too. It is very cold here at this time. I cant rite much. Bud is stout and harty. He is hartyer know than you ever saw him and has been ever since he came here and is very well satisfied. Here is a silver ring that Bud found in a Reble maile that he send to you. He found severle song ballets and post stamps. This stamp that on this letter out of Reble maile. I will send you a ring and song ballet. The song ballet is to Navy Clay. I will send Albert one in the next letter. So no more at present only I remain your affectionate son until Death shall part us

James A Riter and
John Johnson

Campaigning in Mississippi

John Thornburn, a soldier in the 76th Illinois Volunteer Infantry was part of the 2nd brigade, 4th division of the XVI Army Corps. Late in 1863, part of the XVI and XVII Corps were detached and sent to Sherman in Chattanooga in order to break the siege being suffered at the hands of Confederate General Braxton Bragg. In the spring of 1864, these units would be part of Sherman's campaign to capture Atlanta. The remaining units, including Thornburn's, were left in place in Mississippi in order to protect the waterway and support the western theatre strategy as needed. This was accomplished through execution of short campaigns that kept Confederate troops occupied, thus unable to reinforce Johnston's Army of Tennessee, defending Atlanta. His letter of February 3 mentions one of those excursions as he informs his wife to let others know that they may not hear from their loved ones for a number of weeks.

Camp At clear creek Near Vicksburg Miss.
Feby 3 1864

My dear wife and son,

I take the present oppurtunity to right you a few lines hoping that they may find you all well as they leaves us at this time. Thank God for it. George received a letter on the second day of Feby. The one rought Jan. 24th and 26th. I understand by the letter Christopher sent to George that you sent me a letter the 26th of Jan,y. If you did it has not come to hand yet but I was glad to hear of you all being well. When brother Christopher rought and very glad that you had money enough to pay the tax with. Hannah I sent you two pen holders and 4 pipe stems for father with Capt. Ayers. If he do not bring them down to you, you will find him at Joseph Cunningham. ask him if he did not bring a little parcel for Mrs Hannah Thornburn. But he said that he would bring them down to you. I should have rought a few lines and sent with him but I rought the day before he started and put a silver ring in the letter. When you right you must tell me if you got the ring and like wise the penholders and what father said about his pipe steams.

We moved our camp on Sunday 31st of Jany. about 5 miles to clear creek on 3rd day Feby. We was ordered to move with twenty day rations. The 16th and 17th Army Corps was on the line of march before day light for twenty days.

I was left in camp to take care of CO. G and A things. George whent with the train guard. He has his napsack hald in the waggen and when he stops at night he can sleep in the wagen under the cover while the other boys sleep on the cold ground without cover.

Hannah Thos. Heldstone whants you to tell Mrs Heldstone that she need not feel disapointed if she do not get a letter for twenty days as the Regt .(h)as gone out on a expedition. Tell her that he said he would rought but he did not now what thime we should move.   we are glad to hear of mother getting well again.   give our best respec to sister Ursula and we hope that she will do well in her home. We are glad to hear of you having such a good time in both Churches. If they only do as they ought to do. Give our best respects to James Burnett, Christopher would like to have some of that plum pudding you talk about that mother is going to make when we come home. Could you if we have any and take apart yourself. I must bring my letter to a close by say no more at present.   From your affectionate husband and brother

John Thornburn and George Burnett

Co. G 76th Regt. Ill. Infty.

I will write again as soon as I get a letter right back by return mail

John Thornburn

Company G
76th Illinois Volunteer
Infantry

Later, Thornburn
served in the 17th Army
Corps Ambulance Corps
during the Atlanta
Campaign and March to
the sea with Sherman

February 10th finds Thornburn missing his regiment while it is out on its expedition, but he has been busy making souvenirs from the "Surrender Tree" where Grant and Pemberton met to finalize the surrender of Vicksburg. He believes the war should end after the spring campaign. The Union troops are squeezing the Confederates into a smaller and smaller area of operations, which bodes well for the north.

Clear Creek, near Vicksburg, Miss
Feby 10th, 1864

My Dear Wife and Son,

I take this morning to right you a few lines hoping that they may find you all well as it leaves me at present. Thank God for it. I received your kind letter on Monday the eight of Febry. The one you rought January 31st and mailed Febry 1st and was exceedingly glad to hear of you all being well at the time of you righting. But I am sorry to hear of mother feeling under the weather, but I hope before these few scribbling lines reach you that she will be enjoying good (health) again. Hannah Tho's Hill, a member of Co G started home to Urbana on Sunday Feby seventh on a sick furlough for thirty days. I sent with him a penholder for you made out of the tree that the rebel Gen Pemberton and the Union Gen Grant set or stood under at the time of surrender of Vicksburgy. He said that he would bring it to you if he should not bring to you can send Tho's down for it. He lives I think where Old Dr. Cunningham lived. Please tell me when you right if you have got them that I sent with Capt Ayer. If you got that I sent with Tho's Hill and them I sent with Capt Ayer you may give Christopher that large one and I will try to get a peace of wood and make one for William Burnett but the wood is very scarce. The tree was about two foot through and it is all gone and the boys as dug the most of the roots up.

My dear boy I shall enclose in this letter a ring for you. You may keep it as a token and remembrance of your Pap. I whant you to be a good boy and obey your mother in all she tells you to do, In which I think you do. Tho's if that ring do not fit your finger you may give it your ant Thomison Burnett. Tho's I am sorry to hear of Poor Old Magy not beening as fat as she was last winter. I am a fraid that you do not feed her will.

My dear Hannah you staited in your letter that you would like me to come home. I will the first opportunity to do so. I think that I shall get to come when my three years is up if not before. I think that this spring campaign will end this rebelion. I think the Rebels cannot stand it much longer. I am quiet loansome in camp since the boys has gone out on the expedition. I am left to take care of the company. Thing(s) I have me reliable new from the front up to this morning. it was in Camp that Our Boys marched nearly all the way to Jackson Miss in line of Battle but how true it is I cannot tell. They was in Jackson on Saturday Feby 6th and was going to leave the morning of the seventh to a place they call Meridian. Then they cut the railroad all to peaces so the rebs will only have a part of Georgia and North Carolina and South Carolina and I think a part of Florida to get they supplies in. I tell you that they bread in dinner is but very short. We are getting them in the small pen where they cannot dodge much more.

On the 21st of February Thornburn reminds his wife that others may not hear from their soldiers for some time yet. He goes on to tell her that he has been learning to bake bread since he was left behind by the regiment and what a fine occupation it may well be.

Clear Creek near Vicksburg, Miss
Sunday Night Feb. 21st 1864

My dear wife and son

I take these few moments to right you a few lines hoping that they may find you all well as they leave me a present. Thank God For it. I have not received any letter from you since the one you mailed Feb.1st. So by that I have not got very much to say to night I thought it would be best to try and right you a line just to tell you that I am well but perhaps you do not whant to now how I am. We have not heard from the Regt. since they left camp at Clear Creek. that is not correct.   some times we hear that they are on the way to Mobile so I Cannot tell you any thing about them this time but it might be that I may get some information before I right again. If you hear any of the women complain about not getting any letters from theire Dear Beloved Husband you can tell them that they are out on a twenty Days March if not more. Give my best respect to father and mother and brothers and sisters one and all

Hannah I am learning the Bread Baking Traide. We baked over one hundred Loaves of Bread and Forty Pies to day when the Regt. comes back it will take over six hundred loaves per day. I expect you will think that I am trying a great many things in the army. I find that a man can get along the best that can turn his hand to any thing. Specialy when he can fix any thing to eat. I think that bread baking is a good traide all over the world because people loves to eat and drink. Hannah I have not much to say to night. The weather hear for a few day back has been very could to be in the suny south, but today has been very plesent. You must make thease few words out as well as you can.   I will try to do better the next time. So I will bring my scibbling to a close for this time because it is getting to be late. Bed Time. So I must say no more at present from your affectionate and loving Husband until Death.

John Thornburn

Co. G 76th Ill Regt.
Ill. Vols. Infty.

Vicksburg Miss.
I will right again soon or scribble again soon so good night that I am going to bed.

George Deal was part of the expedition Thornburn wrote about in the previous letters. The force returned to Vicksburg on March 4th. On the 10th he writes home of the experience. He also mentions Sarah being forced from their home. Evidence, again, of the hardships and suffering experienced on the home front, in the absence of husbands from their families.

March 10th 1864
Camp near Vicksburg, Mississisppi
Dear Companion Sarah Deal,

Your kind letter came to hand yesterday and I am noticing that you was well at the time. You have written which I was glad to hear. As for myself at present, I am well and do sincerely hope when this note of reply reaches you, it may find you and the family all in good health.

Sarah, you must not think hard of me for not writing to you any sooner for we have had quite a long and wearisome march since I have written to you. We left Vicksburg on the 3rd day of February and marched on to Meradon (Meridian) which was 160 miles from here and arrived back on the 4th day of March which made it 31 days marching. The distance from (here) to Meradon and back is 320 miles. We had but little difficulty on the road with the rebs. Our loss was but small doing the expedition.

We expect to come home now in about 10 days if no preventing providence on a 30 day furlough. We are looking for transportation every day to start up the river. As I hain't much to write at present that is of any importance but I will announce to you the best of knowledge.

Sarah I am noticing from your letter that you have to give up the place which you now live on and I would just say to you that if you have to give it up before I get home try and get a house close about there as you possibly can until I get home and I will try and situate you as comfortable as possible before I leave again to come back to the army.

So I believe I have nothing more to relate to you at the present time so I will bring my few remarks to a close by wishing you good health until my return.

From your affectionate husband, George Deal

Deployments and Redeployments

Front line generals wanted as many veteran troops as they could collect. A more veteran force enabled them to pursue their campaigns with higher efficiency and confidence. Many new recruits to the Union army replaced veteran troops in garrison roles throughout captured territory. John Albright was a private in the 16th Wisconsin and as a replacement recruit had not seen combat when he wrote home to mother on March 26th. The original letter was chewed by rodents leaving numerous holes in the copy.

Direct to Vicksburg Miss
Co K 16th Reg Wis Vols

Camp Near B[ig Black] Bridge Miss March 26th 1864

Dear Mother.   I will try and write a few lines to you this lovely morning. this sun is shining brightly. the birds are singing their sweet praises. their are a great variety of songsters here. the prettyest bird here to my eye is the red bird. it is as large as a dove and as red as blood and their are a great many of them here. they look pretty I tell you.   hopping about on the shrubs and green covered earth. their songs being equel to ____ one would not think that their was war or blood shed here.   we may have an attack any day yet I hardly think we will. yet one dont know. if we do have an engagement it will try us greenhorns and see whether we will stand fire or no. Mother I did write to you about a week ago, but paper does not cost me any thing and I may as well write as not. yet I have a fashion of writing so fast and am afraid you will have quite a time to _____. I told you all about our march in _____ her letter so th[ere] is no use to say any _____ begins to go pretty_____ any yet myself as I have _____ [b]usy all the time writing we will ge_____ _____ugh in a week or so with most of it and then I will have more time. we draw beef twice in five days the rest of the time we have pickeled pork we get r_____(rice) peas, sugar, coffee, tea, vinegar salt and pepper [and] one loaf of bakers bread per day. Mother tomorrow will be Easter. oh how I would like to be home and then you could see whether I had any appetite for eggs. eggs are worth .75 cents per dozzen and then half of them be worthless. if I had any money at preasant I would get my picture taken and send it home for there is a picture galery close by here, but I guess I must wait till I get my next pay. I have got three letters from home since I was here an_____ any of the boys have got any yet. I hope Elmira will be well by the time this reaches you. good many soldiers have the measles and several out of our Co have had them. does Elly still go to the post office or does Samuel get them or who does go for them and how often do you expect letters from me. you need not look oftiner than once a week. this week I have written twice but I shall make it a practice to write once a week without _____ sick or something I have _____ now, most all_____ some. good by _____ me now methm_____ _____ld like it be _____ on getting this letter, but I would be _____ve as I should most-kill myself seating for a few days. good by write soon and direct as before from your son John A. Albright

Americans of African Descent

In March of 1863 the U.S. Congress passed act 323. This act allowed white regiments to enlist men of African Descent. Enlisted two per company as undercooks into white regiments, these men were paid ten dollars per month. Their jobs were to be cooking, tending horses and other tasks for the regiment. A group of freed slaves in the Vicksburg area after July 4, 1863 were enlisted into the Union Army.

On May 8, 1864, General Sherman gave orders that all noncombatants, cooks, undercooks and musicians would act as stretcher bearers when his army went into combat. During the Atlanta Campaign of that year these stretcher bearers crossed the battlefields saving the lives of man wounded white soldiers. Seventy two of the undercooks in Sherman's army were killed or mortally wounded during the campaign.

The 32nd Ohio Infantry enlisted thirty-two of these freed slaves while in Vicksburg. The regimental sergeant wrote "American of African Descent" on their enlistment forms. David Brooks mustered March 3, 1863 at Vicksburg, Mississippi as one of these men. A native of Mississippi, he was 27 when he enlisted. He was admitted into the hospital at Camp Chase in Columbus, Ohio on March 3, 1864. Upon recovering he returned to the regiment May 18, 1864 and served through the end of the war. Another American of African Descent, Jerry Andrews, enlisted September 1, 1863. He was taken prisoner on July 22, 1864 near Atlanta. He survived to be mustered out of the service on July 20, 1865 at Louisville, Kentucky. Yet, another example was Russell Watson. He enlisted September 1, 1863 and served throughout the Atlanta Campaign. His assignment for the months of July and August of that year was with the XVII Army Corps Hospital. Like Andrews, he mustered out of service July 20, 1865 at Louisville, Kentucky.

Other former slaves enlisted in black regiments with the understanding that their officers would be white. These regiments were enlisted as United States Colored Troops (USCT). Initially these regiments saw little action. As opportunities were presented to prove their metal, regiments like the 54th Massachusetts demonstrated remarkable fighting prowess. Soon, many of these regiments were engaged in combat with distinction for the Union and the cause of freedom.

In Mississippi some of these regiments were assigned to garrison duty as well as provost marshals.

James Riter, who had been reassigned to Natchez earlier in the year, writes home that he may be discharged in August if he doesn't reenlist. He is hopeful that he will be able to return home then and has apparently given up on the idea of receiving a $422 bounty by reenlisting. John Johnson, Bud, is his brother who also serves with him in the same company and contributes to these letters. Riter also mentions that there are Negro guards placed on the roads leading to town and that he must show them a pass if and when he wants to leave camp. This is something he never thought he'd see.

Natchez Miss April the 19th, 1864

Dear Father and Mother I take this most kind pleasure of answering your kind and Wellcom letter of the 9th Rote by Mr. E.J. Burk. It found I and Bud boath well and harty and was glad to hear from you all but very sory to hear that you have not got well yet. You must not get out of hart. There is som prospect of us getting out about the 1st of August Next. I have not fully believed it yet I am afraid to believe it for it is too good a thing for me. Our Major says we will be transferred out when the old 29th is if all those that don't joine again. I live in hopes that it may be so. I hope and trust to God it May be so. I would like very much to see you all. I hope I will get to see you all in too or three months. We will send you some more money as soon as we draw. You all must be saveing as you can. Bud says tell Albert that he need not brag of his weight. He says you would not have weighted that odd pound if you had taken your Big Boots off. He all so sends his best respects to Alferd Baty. Mother I want you to send Molley Trunk and her little notions and her fathers likeness to her. Mother she says she wants them and you must send them as soon as you can. I would rather she had them than to keep them myself. I got a letter from the old man Pullen the other day. They are all well. They want to see me very bad. The old lady wants me to send her my likeness. I'm going to have one taken and send it to her. We have a fine celibrated gard around us now all made of Negros. We cant go to town now with out showing our pass to a Negro gard. I have not went to town often since they have been put around us. I have all ways believed that I was fighting to fee Negros and now I now it. I never thought that White soldiers would have to present their pass to a Negro. So nothing more at present only we remain your affectionate sons until death

Jame A Riter

And John Johnson
Co. E 29th Regt. Ill
Natchez Miss

USCT (United States Colored Troops) serving as Provost Marshall in the Vicksburg area. Black Soldiers like these would have checked Riter's pass before he could enter or leave camp. (Library of Congress)

By May it is clear that Riter is becoming anxious for the war to end. His letter is fraught with fear that one of his parents has died because he hasn't heard from them and he's having dreams about it. His concern is palpable and he is encouraging those at home to do everything they can for George McClellan as the democratic presidential and peace candidate.

Natchez Miss May the 26th 1864

Dear Mother and father I take this kind and wellcom opportunity of addressing you with a few lines to inform you that I am will at the present time and all so Bud is well and hardy. I have not much to rite at the present time. Only I am very mad about not hearing from you. It has been about four weeks since I got a letter from you. I cant tell whether it is your fault or the Post Masters. I have rote this makes three letters that I have Rote to you since I received any from you. I am very uneasy about you. But has drempt twice that you was dead and I don't like the dream at all and not hearing from you in so long it makes me uneasy about you. I have been looking for to hear something back in the next letter I get though. I hope I will not. I would give fifty dollars to hear from you all now. There was a big maile yesterday come to the company but theire was not any for me. I don't think that you all have forgot me and but if you has – why just say so then. I will know what to do. Express $35 dollars to green McKee for you the 11th of this month. I want you to let me know whether you received it or not. I have sent so many letters to you that I have very near forgot all I have sent. We are still camp at Natchez yet. I don't now how long we will stay here. There is some talke of us coming in this month up the River but I don't much think we will come before July. Time are very quiet here. At this time the weather is very warm down here at this time and has been for about a month. Theire is plenty of garden vegitables here such as beans and pease onions cabage letice and other things too tedious to mension. I want you to let me know all about the times up theire and what they are all doing. Give the neighbors my best love and respects. Tell them to do all they can for old

George B. McCleman (McClellan) then tell them that I say three cheers for him for the next president. Mother I would like to see you very much and all the family. I feel in hopes that I will get to see you all before I die yet I am still in good hearts yet and you must be the same. It is getting nearly roll call. I will have to close hopeing I will hear from you soon. So no more at present. Only we remain your affectionate sons until Death.

James A Riter and Bud

Co E. 29th Ill Vols Natchez Miss

Bud says to tell Ell and Alf howdy. He says to tell them not to get out of heart. He will send them some money about pay day. He says to tell them to make a good crop an he will come home and help them gather it. He sends his best respects to them. He says to tell them to kiss his foot . Bud Johnson

James Struller, of the 58th Ohio Volunteer Infantry, arrived in Vicksburg the later part of July, 1864. His first letter home from there on July 21st shared his experience being transported down the Mississippi on a steamer. This included a tragic incident that took the life of a fellow soldier. He also mentions the defeat of Confederate Lt. General Stephen D. Lee and Major General Nathan Bedford Forrest by Major General Andrew Jackson Smith and Brigadier General Joseph Mower at the battle of Tupelo. While Smith did indeed inflict a severe defeat on the Confederates, Lee was the primary Rebel commander, not Forrest. Likewise, the rumor of 2,500 Confederate casualties was about double the actual loss.

July 21st A.D. 1864
Vicksburg Miss.

James Struller to father & mother, sisters & brothers,

I take my pen inI hand to let you know that we arrived here today. We all got here that started but one. That was Sol Stant he left us at Caro. We don't know where he was when He left there for it was in the night when we started & so we can't tell any thing about him. All our company is here & co. F that is all the co. that got all back. There is some twelve or fourteen back there yet. We don't expect they will come down under guard. Robert & me wrote one to you at Caro or rather to Emily Come. But was intended for you bothe. That was on the 15th of this month & took us ever since to come here. We came very slow it was of Big Boat & was very heavy loaded so that we had to go very slow. Our boat caught fire or was set of fire at Memphis. But we got it out before it done us any damage. We was not first at all coming down. A sad incident happened yesterday on the boat. We were shooting off our guns. The loads had been in there a day or two & one of Co. H was shooting his off & loading with his gun & putting on a cap. It went off. He was below on the second deck & the way he held his gun it went through the upper deck & shot one man in Co. C through the lungs, he died since we come to camp. It is a sertain fact that (more) men of our regiment was killed that way & by exposure then ever was killed by the Rebels. Our regiment & the one that is doing duty with them & some more was out on a scout after some rebel calvary. It did not amount to mutch as far as I can understand. We had a little spat with them but did not last long. Our men killed a few & took a few prisoners & we lost a few old men that fell out of ranks. They could not keep up & its supposed the gurilllas got them. They halve not heard from them yet they have not been on duty since they came back. They expected to go on another raid over in Lucianna (Louisiana) but it is about plaid out. They are going on duty 297cattere. So you may look for us to stay here all summer. The boys are all in good health & spirits & as far as I can learn the health of the place is good. We halve only two in the regiment that is in the hospital. I gave John several (of) his letter & he was glad to here from home. He said he had been writing study (steady) & got no answer. He is well & all the Co. I halve not much more to write this time but when we got to 297catter there was a 297cattere came from general Smith that he had met old Forrest & fought him & 297catter him 297catte. Forrest himself was wounded & general Faulkner was killed. The courier that fetched the dispatch said forrest loss was 2500 hundred & his army was anihalated & 297cattered all over. Write soon & direct as before from James Struller, and want John to stay at home.

58ᵗʰ Ohio Infantry

In September James Riter writes home that there is no chance of he and Bud coming home until the following August.

Natchez Miss Sept the 30ᵗʰ 1864

Dear Mother, I take this kind pleasure of answering your kind letter which come to hand today and found me and Bud boath well and hearty. I was very glad to hear from you all. The letter that I got today was Rote the 20ᵗʰ of this month. I was glad to hear that the old man was making something and doing as well as he is. I would like to see you all very much but I no hope till next August. I don't want you to come down here at all for I don't know how long we will stay here and we has not been paid of yet and I don't know when we will and I would not want you here and me (with) no money. I want you to bee there and not come. If you never see us we will bee home in next August Certain if we are alive. We will come home for good then. Try and do the best you can. I will send you some little money when we are paid off but don't depend on us. We will do the best we can and you must do the same. Rite and tell the old man I and Bud says Bulley for him. Tell Albert to go to worke and help him and between them they can make something. Tell Alferd Baty that me and Bud boath sends our repsects to him and was glad to hear from him. Give all the children my love and respects. I am in a very much of a hurry. I am on gard down town and I will have to go directly. I was very glad to hear from Aunt Nancy. I could not understand whos wife that was that was dead. You must rite and tell me in your next letter. I was very glad to hear that Mr. Stump was still living. Ellen is here. She is well and fat. She is looking at the wagon yard for the teamsters of this regt. So nothing more at the present. I will rite a gain soon and rite more to. No more at present. Only I remain your affectionate son until Death.

James A Riter and Bud Johnson

The End of the War

Chaplain W. L. Foster wrote his letter of Resignation to the Adjutant General of the Confederate Army on Feb 27, 1865. After three years at war he found it necessary to return home upon the death of his father-in-law.

Feb 27 1865
Head quarters 35. Mississippi

Gen. S. Cooper Adj. General

    Sir..

    As Chaplain of the 35th Mississippi I have the honor hereby to tender my unconditional Resignation for the following reasons.

    For nearly three years I have been engaged in the Confederate service, first as a private in the ranks then as Chaplain. During this time my family & property have been placed under the personal care & protection of my father in law, Col Simon Marxwell of Spere Co. Ala. By his recent death my own family & his together with some orphan children & a plantation containing more than seventy negroes, are now left without a male resident or superintendent, bringing to the station of man exemption from military duty & the latency of the name it will be entirely improbable to obtain a suitable person who can remain on the place – Under these circumstances I deem it my plain & indispensable duty to offer my unconditional resignation. Hoping that this application… (remainder missing)

An aspect of the final chapter of the conflict was that Vicksburg served as a transportation hub for Union prisoners released from Confederate Prisoner of War camps. Thousands of emaciated soldiers were funneled through Vicksburg on their way back home after months of horrific exposure and starvation in camps in Georgia and Alabama. Robert Cain wrote this letter for James Struller on April 16th, 1865.

Vicksburg Miss.

April 16 1865

My health is as well as it has been here in many months. I have not received any letters from home in many weeks. We are here in Vicksburg and I am helping the freed prisoners from Georgia and Alabama here. We have many transports that are to take these poor creatures home up the river to Illinois and more. I think we will not get many more here now as the rebs have cut some of the roads through miss. There are several thousand prisoners here and they are very sick and in poor clothes. I am glad to be here to help these prisoners to try and get home. There is not as many transports as we need here and we fill them as much as can be filled. Some boats are full to more then can (be held). I will come home when I can, but not until we have all the prisoners gone first as there will be not transports I can get until then.

Send no letters now. I will be home before a letter can get to me.

Eleven days after writing this letter, James Struller managed to board one of the transports headed north. It was a steamboat designed to accommodate 376 passengers. It was loaded to overflowing with 2,300 men, most being recently released prisoners of war from the infamous Andersonville camp in Georgia. The overloaded transport struggled to make way up the Mississippi. Just north of Memphis 3 of the Sultana's boilers exploded. Struller was one of nearly 1,700 men who died when the ship burned to the waterline and sank. Those who were not killed by the explosion or fire, drowned. To this day, the Sultana tragedy remains the greatest maritime disaster in United States history.

Last known image of the Sultana, loaded with recently released prisoners of war prior to the catastrophe. (Library of Congress)

Service Records and Known Biographies of Soldiers

The service records and any known information pertaining to the soldiers whose letters appear in this book are presented here in alphabetical order. In a number of cases they provide "the rest of the story" for that soldier. Brigade, Division and Corps affiliation are included in order to assist in locating soldier's positions on maps. There are some interesting and sometimes tragic endings here. There was no information located for William Carpenter or Elliott (75th Infantry).

John Albright Co. A   16th Wisconsin Volunteer Infantry

1st Brigade   Sixth Division (McArthur)   XVII Army Corps

United States

Albright was born in Bedford, Pennsylvania, moved to Wisconsin as a farmer and enlisted at Madison on February 2, 1862. He transferred to Co K in May of 1864 and was listed as a patient in the 17th Army Corps hospital at Marietta, Georgia on July 22, 1864. No further information.

George H Burns 34th Georgia Volunteers

2nd Brigade   Stevenson's Division   Army of Mississippi

Confederate States

G H Burns enlisted for three years at Dalton Georgia on May 15, 1862. He received a $50 bounty. He was captured at Vicksburg on July 4, 1863 and discharged from service May 15, 1865.

Ralph P. Buckland   72ⁿᵈ Ohio Volunteer Infantry

1ˢᵗ Brigade   Third Division (Tuttle)   XV Army Corps

United States

Buckland was commissioned as a colonel and instructed to raise a regiment by Governor William Dennison in the fall of 1861. That regiment, the 72ⁿᵈ Ohio, was mustered into service on January 10, 1682.

Buckland served as brigade commander twice during the next three years of the war. He was promoted to Brigadier General on November 29, 1862 and commanded the 1ˢᵗ brigade, third division of the XV Army Corps during the Vicksburg campaign.

He resigned his commission on January 6, 1865 after being elected to the United States Congress. On March 13, 1865 he was brevetted to Major General of Volunteers.

After the war Buckland served in congress and became the president of the BAR association for Sandusky County, Ohio after having served as Government Director of the Union Pacific Railroad from 1877 to 1880.

Andrew Bush Co. A   97ᵗʰ Indiana Volunteer Infantry

3ʳᵈ Brigade   First Division (Smith)   XVI Army Corps

United States

Bush enlisted at the age of 18 on August 26, 1862 and served for the balance of the war. His writings on Sherman's March to the Sea are fascinating reading. He mustered out of service as a sergeant on June 9, 1865.

Samuel H Byers   Co G   **26th Iowa Volunteer Infantry**

1st Brigade   Herron's Division   XVII Army Corps

United States

Byers enlisted at the age of 21 as 1st Corporal of his company. On July 15, 1862 he was promoted to Quartermaster Sergeant. He was promoted again to Adjutant on April 23, 1863 and was discharged March 19, 1865. Byers authored the book, Sherman's March to the Sea.

James Carlisle   Co D   37th Mississippi Volunteers

Hebert's Brigade   Forney's Division   Army of Mississippi

Confederate States

A Native American, Carlisle enlisted at the Choctaw Agency, May 5, 1862. He was promoted to Brigade Ordnance Sergeant on Sept. 1, 1862. After being captured at Vicksburg on July 4, 1863 he was exchanged on Dec 20, 1863 but never returned to service. He was listed as absent without leave from Jan 1 to August 31, 1864. No further information.

Frank Cassidy   Co G   26th Iowa Volunteer Infantry

1st Brigade   Herron's Division   XVII Army Corps

United States

Cassidy was a native of Canada who enlisted at the age of 18 on August 14, 1862 at Clinton County. He was promoted to 7th corporal on March 4, 1863, 4th corporal on November 30th, 1863 and 1st Corporal on January 5, 1864. Cassidy was killed August 9, 1864 near Atlanta.

Dallas Chapman Co B   34ᵗʰ Indiana Volunteer Infantry

1ˢᵗ Brigade   Twelfth Division (Hovey)   XIII Army Corps

United States

Chapman enlisted on Sept 30, 1861 at Portland, Indiana. He was promoted to Color Sergeant meaning he carried either the national or regimental colors in battle. In a letter to his mother he tells her that if anything should happen to him his name is recorded incorrectly in the company muster role. It has him as D. D. Chapman instead of A. D. Chapman. He was killed May 16, 1863 during the battle of Champion Hill.

William Christy   1ˢᵗ Independent Minnesota Artillery

Sixth Division (McArthur)   XVII Army Corps

United States

Christy enlisted in August of 1861 and survived the war. (His letter reproduced here is courtesy of the Minnesota Historical Society)

George Davis Co E   30ᵗʰ Massachusetts Volunteer Infantry

1ˢᵗ Brigade First Division Dept of the Gulf   XIX Army Corps

United States

Davis enlisted on November 7, 1861 at Camp Chase, Massachusetts. He was 18 at the time. He died December 4, 1862 at the regimental hospital, U.S. barracks of Dysentery. He is buried in Vicksburg.

George Deal   Co K   30th Ohio Volunteer Infantry

3rd Brigade   Second Division (Blair)   XV Army Corps

United States

Deal was 38 when he enlisted October 1, 1862 at Sidney, Ohio. He received a $400 bounty. He was married and had two children. As evidenced in his letters there was great strain on his wife in his absence. This was greatly disturbing to him but there was nothing he could do about it. He was never to return to her and ease her struggles. Deal was killed at the Battle of Atlanta, July 22, 1864. He is buried in Marietta National Cemetery under grave marker 5816. Brad Quinlin has proven his identity and a new marker bearing his name will be erected.

John M Douthit   Co K   52nd Georgia Volunteers

1st Brigade   Stevenson's Division   Army of Mississippi

Confederate States

On April 13, 1862 Douthit enlisted at Montgomery, Georgia for three years. He received a $50 bounty for doing so. He was one of the surrendered troops captured at Vicksburg and died July 23, 1863 of chronic diarrhea in a Federal hospital in New Orleans. He is buried there. His letters often referred to digestive issues he suffered due to the army fare. Four months after his death, his wife was still trying to find out what had happened to him. No one could tell her.

Henry A. Ellsworth   Co A   4th Illinois Volunteer Cavalry

Attached XV Army Corps

United States

Ellsworth enlisted at Ottawa, Illinois on September 26, 1861. He died on June 26, 1863 from a wound inflicted on the 25th of that month while in front of Vicksburg. His comrades must have thought very highly of him as they all contributed funds to buy a coffin and have his body returned to his parents.

W. L. Foster   Co C   35th Mississippi Volunteers

Moore's Brigade   Forney's Division   Army of Mississippi

Confederate States

Reverend Foster enlisted to fight as a private at Starkville, Mississippi on March 1, 1862. The regiment was mustered into Confederate service for three years May 1, 1862. Foster was promoted to chaplain on February 1, 1863. His epic letter to his wife, describing his experience during the siege, is a significant contribution to this book. Upon the death of his father-in-law, Foster resigned from Confederate service on February 23, 1865 in order to return home to fend for his family. April 11, 1865 he was admitted to Yandel Hospital at Meridian, Mississippi. No further information.

Judson Gill   Co B   33rd Illinois Volunteer Infantry

1st Brigade   Fourteenth Division (Carr)   XIII Army Corps

United States

Gill enlisted on September 2, 1861 at Toulon, Illinois. He was promoted to 2nd Lieutenant on January 23, 1863 and 1st Lieutenant on May 1, 1863. He resigned his commission on September 23, 1863 due to illness.

Seth E. Hall   Co F   8th Iowa Volunteer Infantry

1st Brigade   Fourteenth Division (Carr)   XIII Army Corps

United States

Hall was 30 years of age when he enlisted at the 2nd sergeant for Co F on August 10, 1861. He was promoted to 1st Sergeant on July 1, 1863 and reenlisted as a veteran volunteer on January 11, 1864. Hall was promoted again to 1st Lieutenant on February 24, 1865. He was discharged that same day due to disability.

Robert Hamilton   Co A   30th Illinois Volunteer Infantry

2nd Brigade   3rd Division (Logan)   XVII Army Corps

United States

Hamilton enlisted at Ohio Grove, Illinois on August 29, 1861 as a private. He remained a private throughout the war. He survived the war, moving to Keota, Iowa sometime after his discharge where he became a farmer. He bought 40 acres and put up his own house. In 1870, Hamilton married Josephine Cabeon. We can only assume from his endearing letters to his first wife Kate that she had died sometime after the last of his Vicksburg letters were written.

John McIntyre Lemmon   72nd Ohio Volunteer Infantry

1st Brigade   Third Division (Tuttle)   XV Army Corps

United States

Lemmon enlisted as a private in Co. B, 72nd Ohio in October 1861. He was promoted to 2nd Lieutenant in May of 1862 after showing leadership skills during the battle of Shiloh where he was wounded three times. Later promoted to Captain of Co. I he served in this role for the remainder of the war.

Lemmon also served as a correspondent for the *Fremont Journal,* under the pseudonym "Seventy Six", sending letters to the editor of that paper throughout the war.

Following the war he settled in Clyde, Ohio and practiced law where he was elected as the city's first mayor. In 1886 he was appointed judge of the Common Pleas Court for the 1st "Subdivision of the 4th Judicial District of Ohio. After ten months he was again elected mayor of Clyde where he served until his death in August of 1895.

William L. McMillen 95th Ohio Volunteer Infantry

1st Brigade   Third Division (Tuttle)   XV Army Corps

United States

McMillen volunteered as surgeon of the 1st Ohio Volunteer Infantry in 1861 and served as Surgeon General of Ohio in 1861 and 1862.

In 1863 he was commissioned Colonel of the 95th OVI and commanded the regiment with Sherman's Corps during the Vicksburg campaign. When his brigade commander was temporarily removed for illness, McMillen commanded the 1st brigade for a period.

Ultimately promoted to Brigadier General of the 4th brigade he fought at the battle of Nashville in that capacity. After the battle, he reportedly assaulted Confederate General Thomas Benton Smith with Smith's own sword, striking him in the head with the hilt several times.

On March 13th 1865 he was brevetted to Major General of Volunteers.

After the war he moved to Louisiana and planted cotton for a time. He served as Post Master and Surveyor of the Port of New Orleans toward the end of his life.

Upon retirement he moved back to Ohio where he died in 1902.

C. W. "Charlie" Moore Co A   9th Texas Volunteers

Ector's Texas Brigade McCown's Division   Army of Tennessee

Confederate States

Moore enlisted at the age of 19 for a period of 12 months at Camp Rusk, Lamar County, Texas. He became Sergeant Major of the regiment about the time of Vicksburg. The 9th Texas was part of the relief forces Joseph Johnston had assembled in a feeble effort to break the siege on Vicksburg. He was wounded at the battle of Chickamauga on Sept 19, 1863. He was still with the regiment on November 27, 1863 when he was issued clothing; a jacket pants and drawers. The last record of service listed him as absent in September 1864. No further information.

Osborn Oldroyd   Co E   20th Ohio Volunteer Infantry

2nd Brigade   Third Division (Logan)   XVII Army Corps

United States

At the age of 19, Oldroyd enlisted on October 15, 1861. He mustered out of service on July 16, 1865. After the war, Oldroyd became a very significant collector of President Lincoln memorabilia. His collection was displayed at the Lincoln home in Springfield, Illinois. Eventually the collection was moved to the Patterson House where Lincoln died. Near the end of his life, Oldroyd sold the collection to the Federal Government for $50,000. It is now housed in Ford's Theater. Oldroyd died in 1930.

William Porter   Co E   55th Illinois Volunteer Infantry

2nd Brigade   Second Division (Blair)   XV Army Corps

United States

Porter's enlistment began on October 31, 1861 at Naperville, Illinois. He was promoted to sergeant before becoming 2nd Lieutenant on September 17, 1862. He was promoted again to Captain on September 26, 1863. Porter was killed on June 27th 1864 at the battle of Kennesaw Mountain.

John O Pullen   Co C   20th Illinois Volunteer Infantry

1st Brigade   Third Division (Logan)   XVII Army Crops

United States

Pullen enlisted at Bloomington, Ill, June 13, 1861. He resigned June 2nd 1864.

James Ritter   29th   Illinois Volunteer Infantry

3rd Brigade   Reserve Corps   Military Division of West Mississippi

United States

Ritter enlisted at Metropolis, Illinois on November 13, 1862. The regiment participated in the Corinth Campaign, captured at Holly Springs by Van Dorn and paroled at Benton Barracks until July, 1863. Upon being exchanged they were detailed as garrison troops around Natchez. He died in Natchez, Mississippi on Oct 8, 1864 from disease.

Jared Sanders   Co. B   26th Louisiana Volunteers

Shoup's Brigade   Smith's Division   Army of Mississippi

Confederate States

Sanders enlisted on March 27, 1862. He served as a lieutenant in Co. B and was captured and paroled on July 4th, 1863 at Vicksburg. No further information.

James W Shafer   Co K   60th Tennessee Mounted Infantry

Vaughn's Brigade   Smith's Division   Army of Mississippi

Confederate States

Shafer enlisted September 27, 1862. He was captured at the surrender of Vicksburg on July 4th 1863. He subsequently reported to parole camp in Jonesboro Tennessee April 1, 1864 and returned to his regiment in October of that year. Surviving the war he signed an oath of allegiance to the United States on May 21, 1865.

Ashbel Smith   2nd Texas

Waul's Texas Legion   Stevenson's Division Army of Mississippi

Confederate States

Smith enlisted August 13, 1861 at Galveston, Texas. He was wounded severely in the arm at Shiloh then promoted to Lt. Colonel on June 5, 1862. He served as acting Inspector General of the 1st Brigade, 3rd Division, Army of the West from June 5th to October 25, 1862. He was captured at Vicksburg and paroled on August 8, 1864. He served as President of the Examining Board from October 30, 1864 to April 5, 1865. He was appointed as a commissioner by the Texas governor to negotiate peace terms with Union officials.

A successful physician before the war, Smith was very accomplished after the war. He served as president of the Texas History Society, of the University of Texas Board of Regents, of the Texas State Medial Association, honorary commissioner to the Paris International Exposition and served two terms in the Texas House of Representatives.

He died on January 21, 1886 and is considered the "Father of the University of Texas".

David Spigener Co. A&B   46th Alabama Volunteers

3rd Brigade (Lee)   Stevenson's Division   Army of Mississippi

Confederate States

Spigener enlisted at Montgomery, Alabama on March 1, 1863 for a three year term. He received a $50 bounty. He was first captured on June 27, 1863 at Bakers Creek near Vicksburg. After being exchanged he was captured during the Atlanta campaign at Jonesboro, Georgia on September 1, 1864. He was listed as present at Ladies Hospital in

Montgomery, Alabama on November 15, 1864. No further information.

James Struller   Co. K   58th Ohio Volunteer Infantry

1st Brigade 1st Div (Mississippi River Squadron) XVII Army Corps

United States

Struller enlisted November 4, 1861 at Camp Chase near Columbus, Ohio. He transferred from company K to company A upon his reenlistment as a veteran volunteer on January 2, 1864. He died 11 days after writing his final letter to his wife as a result of the Sultana tragedy on April 27, 1865.

George Thomas   Quarter Master 53rd Indiana Volunteer Infantry

2nd Brigade   Fourth Division (Lauman) XVI Army Corps

United States

Thomas enlisted on Oct 28, 1861 and served as Quarter Master for the 53rd Indiana as a lieutenant. In October of 1862 he was detached to convey wounded troops to Cairo, Ill then on to Indianapolis to provision rubber blankets for the regiment. In July and August of 1863 he served as acting Quarter Master for the brigade. He recruited at home from November of 1863 to March of 1864 before returning to the regiment. He was mustered out of service July 21, 1865.

John Thornton   Co. G   76th Illinois Volunteer Infantry

2Nd Brigade   Fourth Division (Lauman)   XVI Army Corps

United States

Thornton Enlisted at Urbana, Illinois on August 22, 1862. He became a member of the United States Ambulance Corps and served in that role through the Atlanta Campaign and Sherman's march to the sea. He mustered out of service on July 22, 1865.

Thomas Tunnell   Co. B   43rd Mississippi Volunteers

Hebert's Brigade   Forney's Division   Army of Mississippi

Confederate States

Tunnelll enlisted at Columbus, Mississippi on May 17, 1862. He was captured as a result of the Vicksburg surrender on July 4, 1863. Upon rejoining his unit after being exchanged, he was captured again on December 17th at Franklin Tennessee. Being determined as unfit for duty he was serving as a teamster at the time of his capture during the Confederate retreat after the Battle of Nashville. He was initially sent to Louisville, Kentucky as a prisoner, then on to Camp Chase at Columbus, Ohio in January of 1865. No further information.

Joseph Young   97th Indiana Volunteer Infantry

3rd Brigade   First Division (Smith)   XVI Army Corps

United States

Young enlisted at Bloomington, Indiana on September 30, 1861. He was promoted to Captain on January 1, 1864. On march 20, 1864 he reenlisted as a captain of veteran volunteers. He was killed on June 27, 1864 at the battle of Kennesaw Mountain. He is buried in unknown grave in Marietta National Cemetery. His great-great granddaughter, Lori Perkins, granted permission to have his letters published in this book.

Vicksburg National Cemetery and Soldiers Rest Confederate Cemetery at Cedar Hill.

Ten of our thirty-two soldiers whose letters appear in this book, did not survive the war. Three of those ten are interred in Vicksburg.

Vicksburg National Cemetery was established by an act of Congress in 1866. It includes 116 acres of land north of the city that was the extreme right of the Federal lines during the siege.

After the war, the War Department made every effort to find, exhume and reinter soldiers from the region in the National Cemetery. Burial sites in Mississippi, Arkansas and Louisiana were located and the remains of as many soldiers as possible were relocated here.

Vicksburg National Cemetery is the final resting place for more Union soldiers than any other national cemetery. Unfortunately, over 13,000 of the approximately 17,000 Union troops buried here lay in unknown graves, identified by just a number.

The first two letters recorded in this book were written by George Davis of the 30th Massachusetts describing his preparation for and occupation of New Orleans. The Surgeon General's Office, in response to a pension request, reported on May 23, 1882 that Private Davis died on December 4, 1862 in the Regimental Hospital of chronic diarrhea. He is buried at the Vicksburg National Cemetery.

This book contained just one letter from Dallas Chapman while bivouacked in Memphis in June of 1862. He prophetically made a point that his name was incorrectly listed on the company roster at that time, if anything was to happen to him. He was killed on May 16th from the effects of "gun shot or shell" at the Battle of Champion Hill, according to the Mother's Pension Declaration of 1890. He is buried here.

James Riter died in the hospital of "disease" on October 8, 1864. After the war, he was one of the thousands of bodies reinterred Vicksburg National Cemetery.

While letters home were not recorded in this book from Brad's great, great grandfather, John J. James, found his final resting place here as well.

Soldiers Rest is an area in Cedar Hill cemetery that was allocated for the burial of Confederate dead during the siege of Vicksburg. Those within the lines who were killed outright or died from wounds or disease were buried there. The total Confederate dead here number approximately 5,000. The records of these men's deaths were lost after the occupation of the city.

In the early 1960s a portion of the list was found an 1,600 graves were able to be identified. Nearly 3,500 are marked as unknown as of today.

None of our Confederate letter writers are buried here.

Bibliography

Narrative:

1. *War on the Mississippi – Grant's Vicksburg Campaign*, Jerry Korn, Time Life Books 1985
2. Siege of Vicksburg - Wikipedia
   https://en.wikipedia.org/wiki/Siege_of_Vicksburg
3. Sultana (Steamboat) – Wikipedia
   https://en.wikipedia.org/wiki/Sultana_(steamboat)
4. Battle Summary – Vicksburg MS – National Park Service
   https://www.nps.gov/abpp/battles/ms011.htm

Soldiers Letters:

1. <u>Vicksburg National Battlefield Park Library provided</u>:

Andrew Bush	Robert Hamilton
James Carlisle	Charlie Moore
John M. Douthit	Jared Sanders
W. L. Foster	David Spigener
Judson Gill	Thomas Tunell

2. <u>Mother's Pension Records National Archives – United States</u> provided:

John Albright	William Porter
Samuel H Byers	John Pullen
Frank Cassidy	James Ritter
Dallas Chapman	James Struller
George Davis	George Thomas
Henry Ellsworth	Joseph Young
Osborn Oldroyd	

3. Old City Hall and Museum of Vicksburg provided:
    George H Burns   James K Shafer
    Seth Hall

4. *Sherman's Praetorian Guard: Civil War Letters of John McIntyre Lemmon 72nd Ohio Volunteer Infantry.* Daniel A. Masters Columbian Arsenal Press Perrysburg, OH 2017
    John M. Lemmon   William L. McMillen
    Ralph P Buckland

5. Minnesota Historical Society provided:
    William Christy

6. Steve and Becky Deal Provided:
    George Deal

7. Barbara Grace Wilson –great, great granddaughter provided:
    John Thornburn

8. Briscoe American History Museum University of Texas Austin-Ashbel Smith Papaers 1823-1926 Box 2G224
    Ashbel Smith

Soldiers Service Records/Bios

1. Vicksburg Union Order of Battle
    https://en.wikipedia.org/wiki/Vicksburg_Union_Order_of_Battle
2. Vicksburg Confederate Order of Battle
3. https://en.wikipedia.org/wiki/Vicksburg_Confederate_Order_of_Battle
4. 29th Ill. Infantry Regiment History Adjutant General's Report
    https://civilwar.illinoisgenweb.org/history/029.html
5. 4th Ill. Cavalry Regiment History
    https://civilwar.illinoisgenwarorg/history/c04cav.html

6. National Archives – United States of America
7. Wikipidia – Ashbel Smith
   https://en.wikipedia.org/wiki/Ashbel_Smith

Cemeteries

1. Vicksburg National Cemetery - Vicksburg National Military Park
   https://www.nps.gov/vick/learn/historyculture/cemhistory.html

About the Authors

Brad Quinlin noted Historian & Genealogist, is Author of *"Duty Well Performed: The Twenty-first Ohio Infantry in the Civil War"*, *"Borne in Battle: Regimental Book and Eyewitness Accounts of the 123rd New York Volunteer Infantry"* and multiple other books and is currently working on the new United States Colored Troop exhibit for the Atlanta History Center/Cyclorama. Through in-depth research he has identified over 365 US and CSA soldiers buried in Unknown graves, is Historical Advisor and Lead Researcher for the Kennesaw Mountain National Battlefield Park Visitors Center movie: *"Kennesaw: One Last Mountain"* & the PBS 5-part Mini-Series *"Civil War: The Untold Story"*.

Dick Ransom recently completed a successful career as a business owner, proficient in sales and leadership development, training, operations and business writing. For twenty-eight years his avocation has been the study and living history portrayal of the American Civil War.

This is his first book.